Palgrave Macmillan Studies in Banking and Financial Institutions

Series Editor: **Professor Philip Molyneux**

The Palgrave Macmillan Studies in Banking and Financial Institutions are international in orientation and include studies of banking within particular countries or regions, and studies of particular themes such as Corporate Banking, Risk Management, Mergers and Acquisitions, etc. The books' focus is on research and practice, and they include up-to-date and innovative studies on contemporary topics in banking that will have global impact and influence.

Titles include:

Yener Altunbaş, Blaise Gadanecz and Alper Kara
SYNDICATED LOANS
A Hybrid of Relationship Lending and Publicly Traded Debt

Yener Altunbaş, Alper Kara and Öslem Olgu
TURKISH BANKING
Banking under Political Instability and Chronic High Inflation

Steffen E. Andersen
THE EVOLUTION OF NORDIC FINANCE

Seth Apati
THE NIGERIAN BANKING SECTOR REFORMS
Power and Politics

Elena Beccalli
IT AND EUROPEAN BANK PERFORMANCE

Paola Bongini, Stefano Chiarlone and Giovanni Ferri (*editors*)
EMERGING BANKING SYSTEMS

Vittorio Boscia, Alessandro Carretta and Paola Schwizer
COOPERATIVE BANKING: INNOVATIONS AND DEVELOPMENTS

COOPERATIVE BANKING IN EUROPE: CASE STUDIES

Roberto Bottiglia, Elisabetta Gualandri and Gian Nereo Mazzocco (*editors*)
CONSOLIDATION IN THE EUROPEAN FINANCIAL INDUSTRY

Alessandro Carretta, Franco Fiordelisi and Gianluca Mattarocci (*editors*)
NEW DRIVERS OF PERFORMANCE IN A CHANGING FINANCIAL WORLD

Dimitris N. Chorafas
CAPITALISM WITHOUT CAPITAL

Dimitris N. Chorafas
FINANCIAL BOOM AND GLOOM
The Credit and Banking Crisis of 2007–2009 and Beyond

Violaine Cousin
BANKING IN CHINA

Vincenzo D'Apice and Giovanni Ferri
FINANCIAL INSTABILITY
Toolkit for Interpreting Boom and Bust Cycles

Peter Falush and Robert L. Carter OBE
THE BRITISH INSURANCE INDUSTRY SINCE 1900
The Era of Transformation

Franco Fiordelisi
MERGERS AND ACQUISITIONS IN EUROPEAN BANKING

Franco Fiordelisi, Philip Molyneux and Daniele Previati (*editors*)
NEW ISSUES IN FINANCIAL AND CREDIT MARKETS

Franco Fiordelisi, Philip Molyneux and Daniele Previati (*editors*)
NEW ISSUES IN FINANCIAL INSTITUTIONS MANAGEMENT

Franco Fiordelisi and Philip Molyneux
SHAREHOLDER VALUE IN BANKING

Hans Genberg and Cho-Hoi Hui
THE BANKING SECTOR IN HONG KONG
Competition, Efficiency, Performance and Risk

Carlo Gola and Alessandro Roselli
THE UK BANKING SYSTEM AND ITS REGULATORY AND SUPERVISORY FRAMEWORK

Elisabetta Gualandri and Valeria Venturelli (*editors*)
BRIDGING THE EQUITY GAP FOR INNOVATIVE SMEs

Kim Hawtrey
AFFORDABLE HOUSING FINANCE

The full list of titles available is on the website:
www.palgrave.com/finance/sbfi.asp

Palgrave Macmillan Studies in Banking and Financial Institutions
Series Standing Order ISBN 978–1–4039–4872–4

You can receive future titles in this series as they are published by placing a standing order. Please contact your bookseller or, in case of difficulty, write to us at the address below with your name and address, the title of the series and the ISBN quoted above. Customer Services Department, Macmillan Distribution Ltd, Houndmills, Basingstoke, Hampshire RG21 6XS, England

---

Banking in China

Second edition

Violaine Cousin

ISBN 978-1-349-32344-9   ISBN 978-0-230-30696-7 (eBook)
DOI 10.1057/9780230306967

First edition published 2007
Second edition published 2011 by
PALGRAVE MACMILLAN

Palgrave Macmillan in the UK is an imprint of Macmillan Publishers Limited,
registered in England, company number 785998, of Houndmills, Basingstoke,
Hampshire RG21 6XS.

Palgrave Macmillan in the US is a division of St Martin's Press LLC,
175 Fifth Avenue, New York, NY 10010.

Palgrave Macmillan is the global academic imprint of the above companies
and has companies and representatives throughout the world.

Palgrave® and Macmillan® are registered trademarks in the United States,
the United Kingdom, Europe and other countries

This book is printed on paper suitable for recycling and made from fully
managed and sustained forest sources. Logging, pulping and manufacturing
processes are expected to conform to the environmental regulations of the
country of origin.

A catalogue record for this book is available from the British Library.

Library of Congress Cataloging-in-Publication Data
Cousin, Violaine, 1975–
Banking in China / Violaine Cousin. — 2nd ed.
p. cm. — (Palgrave Macmillan studies in banking and financial
institutions)
Includes bibliographical references and index.

1. Banks and banking—China. I. Title.
HG3334.C68 2011
332.10951—dc22   2011001475

10 9 8 7 6 5 4 3 2 1
20 19 18 17 16 15 14 13 12 11

To Ewald and Oryane

Contents

List of Tables

List of Figures

List of Abbreviations

A-IRB	Advanced internal rating-based (approach)
ABC	Agricultural Bank of China
ABS	Asset-backed securities
ADBC	Agriculture Development Bank of China
AMC	Asset Management Company
art.	Article
Avg.	Average
Basel I	Basel Capital Accord of 1988
Basel II	New Basel Capital Accord (2004)
BCBS	Basel Committee on Banking Supervision
BCG	Boston Consulting Group
BCP	Basel Core Principles
BIS	Bank for International Settlements
bln	billion (1,000,000,000)
bp	basis point(s)
BOC	Bank of China
BoD	Board of directors
CAR	Capital adequacy ratio
CBRC	China Banking Regulatory Commission
CCB	China Construction Bank
CCBs	City commercial banks (preceded by a place name, it is written in the singular and refers to the city commercial bank in that locality)
CDB	China Development Bank
CDIC	Central Discipline Inspection Commission
CEQ	China Economic Quarterly
C/I ratio	Cost income ratio
CIRC	China Insurance Regulatory Commission

CNY	Chinese Yuan; also Renminbi (RMB) or Yuan
CPC	Communist Party of China
CPI	Consumer price index
CSRC	China Securities Regulatory Commission
E&Y	Ernst & Young
EAD	Exposure at default
EU	European Union
EUR	euro
EVA	Economic value added®
Exim Bank	Export–Import Bank of China
FDIC	Federal Deposit Insurance Corporation
FC	Finance company
FI	Financial institution
F-IRB	Foundation Internal ratings-based (approach)
GDP	Gross domestic product
HK	Hong Kong
HKD	Hong Kong Dollar
HR	Human resources
ICBC	Industrial and Commercial Bank of China
IIF	International Institute of Finance
IMF	International Monetary Fund
IPO	Initial public offering
IRB	Internal ratings-based (approach)
ITIC	International trust and investment corporation
JSCB	Joint-stock commercial bank
LC	Loan companies
LGD	Loss given default
LLP	Loan loss provisions
LP	Loan portfolio
M	Maturity
MAFG	Mutual aid financial group

MFI	Microfinance institutions
MIS	Management information system
mln	million (1,000,000)
NBFI	Non-bank financial institution
NDRC	National Development and Reform Commission
NPA	Non-performing assets
NPC	National People's Congress
NPL	Non-performing loan
OD	Organisation department
OECD	Organisation for Economic Co-operation and Development
OTC	Over the counter
p.a.	per annum
PBOC	People's Bank of China
PD	Probability of default
PPP	Power purchasing parity
PRC	People's Republic of China
PSBC	Postal Savings Bank of China
PwC	PricewaterhouseCoopers
QDII	Qualified domestic institutional investor
QFII	Qualified foreign institutional investor
QIS	Quantitative impact studies
RAROC	Risk-adjusted return on capital
RBC	Risk-based capital
RCB	Rural commercial bank
RcoB	Rural cooperative bank
RCC	Rural credit cooperative
RCF	Rural credit fund
RCU	Rural credit union
RMB	Renminbi (Chinese currency, also CNY or Yuan)
ROA	Return on assets
ROE	Return on equity

RWA	Risk-weighted assets
S&P	Standard and Poor's
SA	Standardised approach
SAFE	State Administration of Foreign Exchange
SASAC	State-owned Assets Supervision and Administration Commission
SB	Supervisory Board
SM	Special mention (loan)
SME	Small and medium enterprises
SOE	State-owned enterprises
SOCB	State-owned commercial bank
TIC	Trust and investment corporation
trn	trillion (1,000,000,000,000)
TVE	Township and village enterprise
UCCs	Urban credit cooperatives
VTB	Village and township bank
WTO	World Trade Organization

Introduction

Is it the financial crisis driving further reforms or the crisis closing reforms? China remains a host to low interest rates and high liquidity – good ingredients for a crisis. At the same time – viewed through a Chinese lens – the crisis has put a question mark against the western model of banking. Nevertheless the interdependence between the different banking industries across the world means that the actions of others have an influence on our own lives, so that we should be considering them more closely. Therefore given its growing importance, we should take the time to better understand the Chinese banking system.

Chinese banks play a central role in financial intermediation in China and possess such global weight that their development has implications for everybody outside China. The global economic powerhouse that is China cannot run without its banks and they need to be reliable enough to ensure no crisis which would be too costly for the country. Are Chinese banks on a path of sustainable development?

Just as China has taken steps to introduce some elements of western banking practices, we might justifiably ask why and to what effect. At the same time China is taking an increased degree of international responsibility, so that the question marks over the Chinese banking industry might also lead to answers that can offer lessons for banking operations elsewhere in the world. This is particularly the case in relation to the role of the state and its interference. For the time being China is illustrating that the role of the state can be much greater and much more positive than has previously been argued. What is the best kind of balance between the private and the state sector?

Have Chinese banks emerged as winners of the financial crisis? Significant reforms and clean up have emerged at just the right time, now that the gap with best practices is growing smaller although still existent. Chinese banks were less exposed to the international financial markets. Moreover, Chinese banks tend to serve as 'shock absorbers' – as noted by the economic consultancy Dragonomics – through sacrificing profits in the interest of economic growth under the 'leadership of the state'.

In a period of just over thirty years, Chinese banks have changed from socialist money tellers to modern financial institutions with a healthy and market-oriented outlook. But is this more a case of what the Chinese term 形似神不似 ("appears to be a saint but is not")? What lies beneath the surface? Is the inner core as robust as the outer shell? In 1979, Deng Xiaoping said that banks need to be transformed into real ones. In the past ten years outsiders have had the opportunity to take a glimpse at what lies beneath. But they were able to see very little because the veil is thick and opaque.

At least the current round of reforms has been completed successfully – but was this perhaps the last supper? The government has chosen an approach to get the banks to be banks that exploits a win–win situation for all stakeholders. The banks are restructured and listed so that the main shareholder – the central government – has an opportunity to realise its holdings. The (foreign) investors also get a share of the cake – albeit a much smaller one. The narrative told is very market-oriented and presents reforms and opening as the sole and unavoidable alternatives towards a world which westerners recognise as their own. However, the words reserved for Chinese ears strike a different note.

With all these themes rising before our eyes, we need to adopt a progressive approach to our analysis of the Chinese banking sector. In an attempt to answer the questions that come to mind, the present book will first give an overview of the Chinese banking sector. In Part II, the reader will be introduced to the financial infrastructure – that is, the regulators, the banking safety net and the role of the state. The state has such a pervasive influence that it is important to consider it in some detail. Understanding the rationale that lies behind its actions will also provide answers about its future direction. Part III will concentrate on some aspects of the demand side of the banking sector. It will consider financial intermediation with enterprises and individuals and also look at new areas such as microfinance, rural finance and retail finance. The fourth part will examine the other side of the balance sheet: the supply of financial services by banks. These include large commercial banks – some of them already very familiar to stock markets, smaller local banks and foreign banks as well as rural financial institutions – both old and new ones. In rounding off the discussion of the banking industry, the book will conclude with an examination of the risks that China will face in future: asset quality, capital adequacy, corporate governance, foreign competition and the banks' ability to withstand crises.

Note: This book reflects the events and knowledge of the author up to 11 August 2010. The opinions presented in the book are solely those of the author.

Part I
Overview

1
Banking System Features and History

With the unfolding of the financial crisis in 2007–2009 many turned to China in the hope of finding a solution to the western world's problems. This was something that might have been considered completely unthinkable just five years earlier. Chinese banks have clearly made rapid advances in recent years. The positive stance that western eyes ascribe to the Chinese banking system say as much about the observers as about those being observed. For this reason it is worth examining the system in some detail.

This chapter will set the stage by outlining the broad features of the Chinese banking system and the different institutions that operate in the system.

For reference, Table 1.1 presents a range of economic and financial indicators for China.

The Chinese banking system has been transformed from a mono-banking system (with a single bank) into a multitude of banking institutions managing CNY52 trn loans (by the end of 2009). As many other things in China, the banks are for most huge, as are the issues they carry with them.

1.1 Historical developments

To understand the evolution of the banking system, it is necessary to have an insight into the historic legacies of the Chinese banking system. Deng Xiaoping is often quoted in this context as having said that 'banks should be changed into real banks', because in the past 'our banks were money printing enterprises, cash vaults, but not real banks' (Jing X., 2005).

Table 1.1   Macroeconomic indicators for China, 2008

Real GDP (bln CNY)	30,686
Real GDP % change	9.6
Share of world GDP in %	7.47
Goods & services export: volume (CNY bln)	10,980
Goods & services imports: volume (CNY bln)	8,567
Trade balance (USD bln)	360.7
Total external debt (USD bln)	399.4*
External debt as % GDP	9.0
Reserves excl. gold (USD bln)	1,949
Equity market capitalisation (CNY bln)	12,136.6
Gross fixed investment (% of GDP)	41.1
Gross private consumption (% of GDP)	35.3
Population (mln)	1,328
Per capita GDP (USD at PPP)	6,180
Exchange rate (year-end, CNY:USD)	6.84

Source: Economist Intelligence Unit (*estimates).

For a long time the Chinese banking system was organised around the People's Bank of China (PBOC), which was established in 1948 and for some 30 years assumed the functions of commercial bank, supervisor and government treasury. From 1979, under the opening and reform policy introduced by Deng Xiaoping, the PBOC was given the function of a supervisory body and of a central bank, while commercial activities and treasury functions were transferred to other newly (re-)established entities. This process was finalised with the establishment of the PBOC as a central bank and of the Industrial and Commercial Bank of China (ICBC) as an independent entity in 1984.

The reform efforts can be subdivided into three phases:

In a first reform wave, spanning from 1978 to 1993, the banking system moved from a mono-bank system, with the PBOC at its core, to a two-tier system when the four state-owned commercial banks (SOCBs) were formerly established as independent entities (then under the trust of the Ministry of Finance and the State Council[1]). This phase prepared the environment setting for future reforms.

A second series of reforms, between 1994 and 2000, entailed a progressive move towards less administrative and more independent banking operations. The banking system thus reflected budgetary constraints less. In 1995, the *Commercial Banking Law* and the *Law of the People's Bank of China* (References for laws 1 and 3[2]) were issued to establish the legal underpinning for banking in China. Policy banks were established to take over the policy lending business of SOCBs and asset management companies (AMCs) were further established to orchestrate the transfer of non-performing loans of the SOCBs.

The twenty-first century saw the beginning of a new phase in banking sector reforms with the progressive move towards the WTO agreement on which most of the motivation for reform was based (Griffiths, 2005). In this last phase only, observers are able to distinguish reform efforts that run deeper into the banking system and even in banking practices. Evidence of this can be found, for example, in newly promulgated laws and regulations, in the introduction of foreign entities as new stakeholders and in the management of banks. Reforms, however, never went as far as to close down a large bank or as to open fully the banking market.

Since the banks in their current form and with the new practices have yet to experience a full economic cycle, it remains to be seen how they will deal with more challenging times.

1.2 Organisation and structure of the banking landscape

Financial institutions

As of December 2009, the Chinese banking system was made up of some 3,857 financial institutions (CBRC, 2010) (see Table 1.2). The main institutions in terms of size and weight in the banking system are (Figure 1.1):

- the four state-owned commercial banks (SOCBs),
- the three policy banks,

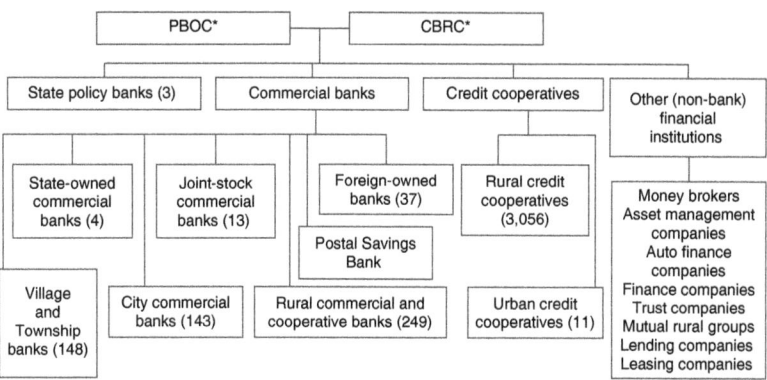

Figure 1.1 The structure of the Chinese banking system
Note: *PBOC People's Bank of China, CBRC China Banking Regulatory Commission. Both regulatory agencies are described in detail below.
Source: CBRC (2010).

Table 1.2 Banking industry in China

Year	2009				2008			
Bank type	Total assets CNY bln	Number of institutions	Market share	Avg. assets by institution CNY bln	Total assets CNY bln	Number of institutions	Market share	Avg. assets by institution CNY bln
SOCBs	36,780	4	46.7%	9,195.0	29,158	4	46.7%	7,289.5
JSCBs	15,094	13	19.2%	1,161.1	11,491	13	18.4%	883.9
CCBs	5,680	143	7.2%	39.7	4,132	136	6.6%	30.4
Others*	21,215	3,697	26.9%	5.7	17,610	5,481	28.2%	3.2
Total	78,769	3,857	100%	20.4	62,391	5,634	100%	11.1

Note: *Others include state-owned policy banks, rural commercial banks, rural commercial and cooperative banks, urban and rural credit cooperatives, foreign banks, postal savings bank as well as non-bank financial institutions.
Source: based on figures from www.cbrc.org.cn and banks' annual reports.

- the 13 joint-stock commercial banks[3] (JSCBs),
- the 143 city commercial banks (CCBs),
- the recently re-established Postal Savings Bank of China,
- the 3056 rural banks and cooperatives, among which the most numerous: rural credit cooperatives (RCCs).

Within the banking system, the 37 foreign banks as well as the much larger number of foreign banks' branches and finally the remaining 11 urban credit cooperatives (UCCs) have only a small weight. Further to the banking institutions, one should also mention non-bank financial institutions, such as the five state-owned asset management companies, 58 re-registered trust companies, 91 finance companies, 12 financial leasing companies,[4] three money brokers, ten auto financing companies, and finally eight loan companies, 16 rural mutual groups and 148 village and township banks which are limited to rural areas. There exist further financial institutions that do not fall within the regulatory responsibility of the China Banking Regulatory Commission such as pawn shops, loan guarantee companies or microfinance NGOs.

The state-owned commercial banks (SOCBs), joint-stock commercial banks (JSCBs) and city commercial banks (CCBs) accounted for 73.1% of all banking assets at the end of 2009 (their respective market shares are 46.7%, 19.2% and 7.2%). Details of the banks can be found in Part IV.

1.3 Growth of the Chinese banking system

China is one of the largest countries in the world, something which is reflected in the scale of its banking sector. Banking assets made up 240% of GDP at the end of 2005, and at the same time loans outstanding made up 125% of GDP (see Table 1.3). These percentages are among the highest in the world and highlight the importance of banks for the country.

Between 2005 and 2010 the Chinese banking system witnessed a 17% average growth – not an exceptional level of growth (see Figure 1.2).

Growth in the Chinese banking industry is not spread evenly: smaller banks grew more strongly in the past (Table 1.4) – even if we do not take into account the crisis effect.

McKinsey estimates that bank lending needs to grow by 15% a year to ensure a 7–8% GDP annual growth as targeted by the central government (Bekier, Huang and Wilson, 2005). However the analysts suggest that the banking system can only sustain a loan growth rate of 7–8% annually (Table 1.5).

Table 1.3 Relation between GDP, M2 and banking assets in China

CNY bln, %	2006	2007	2008
Real GDP	22,165	26,309	30,686
M2	34,609	40,711	47,517
Total assets	43,950	52,598	62,391
Total loans	23,828	27,775	32,004
M2 as % of GDP	156.1	154.7	154.8
Assets as % of GDP	198.3	199.9	203.3
Loans as % of GDP	107.5	105.6	104.3

Source: Based on data from www.cbrc.org.cn, www.pbc.org.cn and EIU.

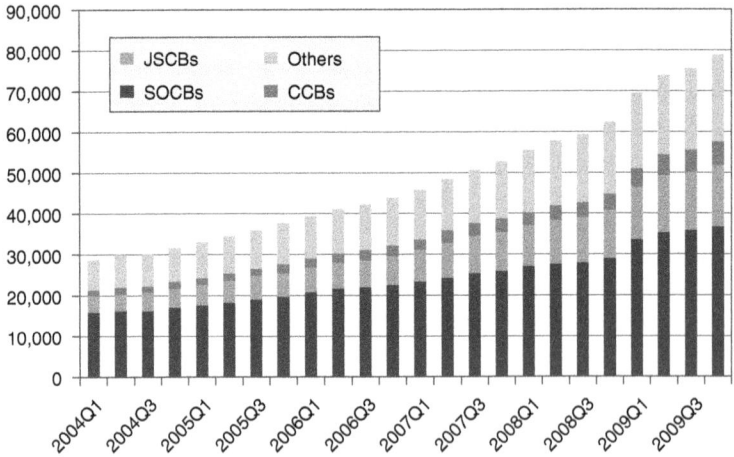

Figure 1.2 Banking asset growth in China (CNY bln)
Note: The Bank of Communications asserts have been counted under JSCBs to ensure conti-
nuity in the data (from 2007 onwards).
Source: based on data from www.cbrc.org.cn.

Within the past few years, there has been a change in the maturity structure of lending. Short-term loans have made space for more
medium- to long-term lending (Figure 1.3). The growth rates for short-
term loans are much lower than for longer-term loans (Table 1.6).

The stronger growth for long-term loans can be explained (Liu L.,
2004), despite the higher risks and the lower actual returns achieved on
these, by the strong correlation between loan growth and the growth
of infrastructure projects, by the strong bias towards larger enterprises
which are still felt to be safer borrowers than smaller ones (their borrowing requirements are likelier to entail larger longer-term loans), and

Table 1.4 Banking asset growth in China (half-yearly growth rates, %)

	Jan.–Jun. 2007	Jul.–Dec. 2007	Jan.–Jun. 2008	Jul.–Dec. 2008	Jan.–Jun. 2009	Jul.–Dec. 2009
SOCBs	7.9	6.5	6.9	5.3	20.7	4.5
JSCBs	19.8	9.3	12.3	9.4	23.1	6.7
CCBs	12.5	14.5	7.5	15.0	19.9	14.6
Others	9.0	10.0	13.9	10.4	10.5	9.0
Total assets	10.4	8.4	9.8	8.1	18.2	6.8

Source: Based on CBRC data.

Table 1.5 Lending yearly growth rates

Year	2000	2001	2002	2003	2004	2005	2006	2007	2008
Total loans (%)	6.0	13.0	16.9	21.1	11.6	9.8	15.7	16.2	15.9
for comparison Real GDP % growth	8.4	8.3	9.1	10.0	10.1	9.9	10.4	11.2	6.8

Source: Based on data from IIF, EIU and from www.pbc.org.cn.

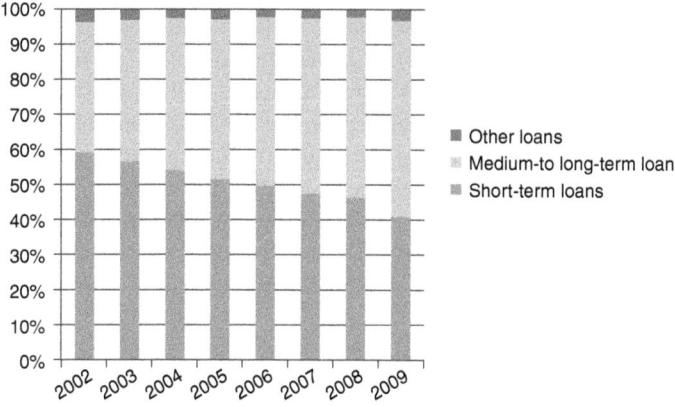

Figure 1.3 Loans by maturity
Note: Short-term loans also include bills financing.
Source: Based on data from www.pbc.org.cn.

Table 1.6   Growth rates based on loan maturities (year on year growth, in %)

	2003	2004	2005	2006	2007	2008	2009
Short-term loans	16.95	6.00	4.93	10.75	10.71	12.22	18.49
Medium- to long-term loans	30.00	20.46	14.73	21.59	22.63	18.46	43.51
Other loans	8.16	−12.89	25.20	−2.85	18.35	8.39	84.77

Source: Based on data from www.pbc.gov.cn.

finally by the strong growth in consumer mortgage loan growth (with maturities ranging from 10 to 30 years).

1.4   Reform of the Chinese banking sector

The aim of the financial sector reforms is to increase the efficiency of the financial system while preserving the financial and economic stability and improving the development of the economy (Jing X., 2005).

> The fragile banking system is the long-term secret worry of the already tattered Chinese economy and poses the largest potential threat to the Chinese macro-economy, the financial stability and the long-term economic growth. (Hu Z., 2005)

For many observers, China's economic reforms have been remarkable by any standards. However, reforms have not been equally deep and broad in all sectors of the economy. This has resulted in China's financial sector lagging behind other economic sectors. One reason for this late start may be found in the centrality of banking to the Chinese economy, meaning that the Chinese leadership did not dare introduce major banking sector reforms as they wished to preserve the status quo. Another reason for the slow rate of reform of the banking industry compared to other sectors was that the state does not wish to lose control over financial flows and resource allocation (for both central and local authorities). A third reason for the slow pace of reform relates to the challenge posed by the large unprofitable state-owned enterprises (SOEs), which are also seen as of paramount importance to the state. Reform of the banking system could not go ahead without a concurrent reform of SOEs. Finally, as in many cases where reforms are required, there was reluctance by politicians to recognise that reform was necessary and a general reluctance to abandon established practices.

Systemic risk

The banking system is the source of financing for enterprises but also the source of systemic risk to the economy as a whole (Longueville and Ngo, 2004). The central role played by the banking sector (Table 1.7) highlights the vulnerability of the country to banking crises.[5]

Each of the larger banks weight heavily on the banking system and also on the consideration of authorities for systemic risk (that is, ensuring financial stability and avoiding bank runs or bankruptcies).

The Herfindahl Index (Table 1.8) indicates a highly competitive industry for the banks as a whole. However, it appears misleading as different banks are active in different markets – both regionally and in terms of financial offerings. Thus when comparing SOCBs and JSCBs which tend to be present in the same areas and all offer universal banking products – and finally they all face the same restrictions in their expansion – the Herfindahl Index shows a much higher concentration. Nevertheless the competition is improving and concentration is lower with the decreasing index.[6]

Allocation of resources and banking sector reform

As mentioned above, the choice of reform of the banking system is clearly linked to the reform of the whole economy. Before the beginning

Table 1.7 Origin of financing for Chinese companies (in %)

	2006	2007	2008	2009
Loans	82.0	78.9	82.4	80.5
Equity	5.6	13.1	5.8	3.8
Bonds	13.4	8	11.8	15.7

Source: PBOC (2006, 2007, 2008b, 2009d).

Table 1.8 Herfindahl Index for the Chinese banking industry

	For the whole industry	For the SOCBs and JSCBs
2004	0.074	0.260
2005	0.071	0.253
2006	0.068	0.242
2007	0.058	0.398
2008	0.057	0.205

Note: The index is calculated based on average assets per institution as derived from total assets and number of institutions data from CBRC.
Source: Based on CBRC data.

of the reforms, the government was the sole creator of wealth and investment, and there was no differentiation among legal, economic and administrative activities. All were integrated into one entity. As such, it made no difference if loans were repaid, because they represented only a money transfer from one state pocket to another. Now, however, the question of resources allocation (land, labour and capital) has become crucial. The government still has the final say in many issues relevant to the allocation of resources. The market has not yet had the chance to allocate resources efficiently.

This also applies to the banking sector. The allocation of important resources is still not separated from state affairs: loans are directed at infrastructure investments and loan portfolios are geared towards state enterprises; important positions in banks are filled with government officials, bonds of state entities are sold to banks, and so on. Private or foreign shareholders and depositors are left with little choice and say in governing financial institutions.

Impetus for banking sector reform

In an interview (Ling H., 2005a), Zhou Xiaochuan, PBOC's director, underlined the importance of internal and external (from the point of view of the banks) factors which made reforms possible and which heightened the pace of reforms. After the Asian Financial Crisis, Chinese banks (mainly the state-owned ones) faced a strong decline in asset quality on their portfolios and became increasingly aware of the necessity and urgency to take steps to improve internal controls. He wrote later 'that China's financial system was a large time-bomb that could go off at any time [...] and that China's financial system would be a drag on its economic growth, making it impossible for the system to service the economy and support development' (Zhou X., 2009). Zhou Xiaochuan identifies three further factors: the introduction of much more efficient accounting standards, the introduction of the internationally prevalent loan classification standards and finally the setting of clear reform goals for SOCBs at the central level.

In order to make the reforms work at all levels and in all places, the central government and the regulators put pressure on local governments to push through reforms and make the banking system leaner. Banks suffered for ills similar to those experienced by large state-owned enterprises (such as government interference, weak management incentives, and poor corporate governance) which made the reforms of the banking system a corollary to reforms in SOEs. Other factors that have helped start the reform process include such factors as exchanges with foreign experts, the better education that new leaders have enjoyed, and so on.

Reform focus

In the mid-2000s, the basic methods for reforming the state-owned commercial banking system were (Hu Z., 2005 as well as Zhang J., Yu N. and Guo Q., 2006):

- Financial restructuring (财务重组) to resolve as soon as possible the historical burdens through recapitalisation and stripping of bad loans (with the help of the authorities);
- Fundamental reform of the traditional bank ownership structure (银行结构重组) and operational mechanisms to achieve a sound corporate governance through the transformation of the capital into shareholding capital (including the introduction of international strategic investors, introduction of Central Huijin (Box 5) as representing the Chinese state, and so on); and
- Strengthening market controls for banks, ensuring that banks are committed to continued reforms, strengthen and consolidate the reforms' latest results, through the public offering of shares (上市冲刺, while this is not an aim in itself).

But, as recently highlighted by Liu Mingkang (Zhang M., 2010d), 'restructuring is the "root" exercise, listing is only the basis of restructuring and the ultimate goal is to increase the establishment of a sustained competitive advantage of the Chinese banking industry compared to international first-class banks'.

Superficial and cosmetic changes alone cannot guarantee sustainable improvements in state-owned entities. Two bailouts at the SOCBs did not decrease the number of scandals and thus reforms must run much deeper within the system. And this is not a question of whether sufficient money is available to support such expensive actions. Rather it points to the long-term pointlessness and inefficiency of short-term superficial actions on a standalone basis. Short-term bailouts are needed to give banks the chance to have a fresh start and to get the authorities to take responsibility for years of policy lending. What would be more important, however, is to ensure that a precondition for a bailout is the implementation of high governance and risk management standards, of less government interference, and so on. All efforts of the regulatory authorities have focused on these issues.

Before the financial crisis the clear requirement for good regulation was laid down by western regulators and accepted more or less willingly by Chinese authorities. The financial crisis has changed that power balance. Without negating previous efforts or changing regulatory course, the authorities in China have been able to shed increased external pressure to realise their reform agenda which had previously been relegated to the background. Convergence towards best practices as well as further support to Basel II regulations remains forthcoming, but globalisation in the form of greater openness of the financial sector to foreign funds has been put on the sidelines. While Chinese regulatory bodies continue to converge thematically on the international scene, no such case can be made in terms of processes and institutional arrangements.[7]

In a recent speech, Liu Mingkang, the chairman of the bank regulator, stated the following focus for 2010 (Liu M., 2010): the focus will be on basic regulations (that is, simple measures and restrictions but which are effective – such as LLP ratios and so on), corporate governance and risk management improvements. To do so, the banks will first have to get rid of any toxic assets, reduce leverage and to reduce overreliance on free market mechanisms (in addition, concentration risks will be watched carefully). There are still some areas to be reformed: the standardisation of reporting and accounting, the establishment of a derivatives trading system, and the extension of the regulatory scope to off-balance sheet instruments and to finalise the exit mechanisms for banks. He foresees three challenges: establishing a social safety network, restructuring the industry structure in China and improving the quality of economic development. Finally, the PBOC is also working on improving the ability of the domestic finance industry to withstand systemic risk. Taken as a whole, the focus is on controlling risks (Qiao X., Dong Y. and Yuan M., 2010). In parallel with international developments, CBRC is focusing on all types of risks: from reputational to liquidity risks and concentration risks.

To summarise, the Chinese banking system is characterised by the following:[8]

- It is highly concentrated, but remains competitive in most areas.
- It is crucial for the economy and for the development of the country as bond and equity markets each play a very small role.
- Business lines are increasingly blurred as banks can progressively enter leasing or insurance.
- The banking sector is as the financial sector as a whole the focus of the intervention – both explicit and implicit – of central and local authorities.

- The banks are regulated through a very hands-on approach to regulation.
- The bankruptcy regime is not favourable to banks' exposures and neither is there any resolution mechanism for banks.
- Deposit insurance has been discussed on a number of occasions but remains implicit for now.
- Financial liberalisation remains low for now as the band within which lending and deposit rates can vary remains narrow.
- Market orientation of banks and introduction of banking best practices appeared only in recent years – thus there is a lack of experience.
- Reforms have also brought restructuring for the ownership structure, nevertheless the state remains – directly or indirectly – fully in charge of most the banking assets.

Part II
Infrastructure and the State

The second part of this book presents the financial infrastructure surrounding Chinese banks. Their environment is in principle determined solely by the current legal and regulatory framework which is heavily influenced by the state.

For a better understanding of the structure of the following chapters, the reader might get acquainted with Figure 2.0. The issues ascertained there are discussed in details in the coming chapters.

The bank, with its internal stakeholders, is painted in the central quadrant. Below it are its customers – depositors and borrowers. Above it are a first layer of closer stakeholders: regulators foremost, but also direct competitors (thus mainly local ones), as well as auditors and other lenders to the bank or investors in its debt papers.

The second layer comprises stakeholders that are even further away: apart from society as a whole, this layer consists of legislators and credit agencies and also international rules, regulators and other banks.

Those stakeholders where the Chinese state[1] is dominant have a white background. Most of the capital of Chinese banks is held directly

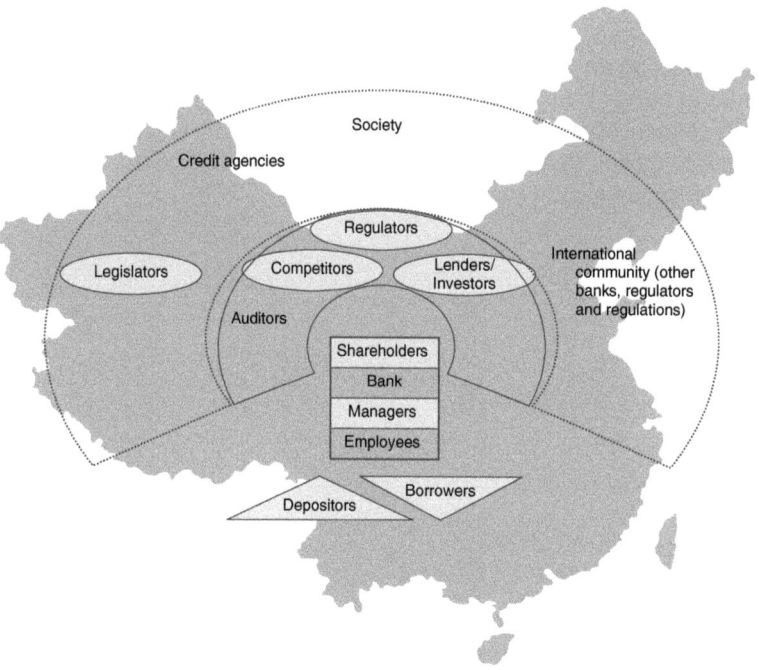

Figure 2.0 Stakeholders of a Chinese bank

and indirectly by the state (and also of its bank competitors) which also nominates the most senior managers. Since borrowers are mostly state-owned enterprises, the loan volume is to those with a state background. In terms of volumes, the deposits are from similar sources.

Regulators, for example the central bank, the bank regulator, the Ministry of Finance, are fully under the leadership of the State Council – the state's highest executive organ – as are legislators which possess little independence. Lenders and the sources of bank debts can be assumed to be either local financial institutions or, albeit to a much smaller extent, international ones. The only institutions that can be assumed to be fully outside the realm and power capacity of the Chinese state are international credit agencies, the international community and large international auditing firms.

The goal of the state is to ensure its own long-term survival, meaning that it requires sufficient resources and reputation to remain in power. Resources include, for example, the financial, economic or natural resources at its disposal. Reputation is driven by the need to avoid any actions that may reduce the standing of the state in the view of Chinese people.

The banks are the main liquidity warehouses and as such are the main focus and target of regulation. Banking regulation ensures that the banking system remains under the control of the state and that deviations from this pattern are kept to a minimum (to balance out the power of banks as quasi-monopolies of funds and to ensure that they do not keep these to themselves, which would seriously distort the current allocation of resources) and that the costs of keeping the banking system afloat and solvent do not exceed the costs of failure.

2
The State as Regulator

This chapter will first present the players in the regulatory environment, it will then outline the instruments they use for regulation and, finally, it will consider the overall impact and influence of these two in light of the activities and actions taken in the past few years.

2.1 Regulatory authorities

The financial sector is regulated by one bank [the central bank or PBOC] and three commissions [regulatory commissions for banking, securities and insurance], 一行三会. The banking sector is principally under the supervision of the People's Bank of China (PBOC) and the China Banking Regulatory Commission (CBRC).

The People's Bank of China

The People's Bank of China (PBOC) was established in December 1948. For a long time it served three main functions: commercial bank, government treasury and supervisor of the financial system. Until 1978 it also extended short-term working capital loans to state-owned enterprises to fulfil the annually set credit quota.[1] Gradually, the introduction of reforms has reduced its role solely to that of a central bank, controlling the currency and money supply.

PBOC is an administration with ministerial rank which works under the leadership of the State Council. This means that the power over final decisions and approval lies with the State Council, rather than with the central bank itself. PBOC reports to the State Council in order to secure its approval on all important issues – for example, setting interest rates, money supply targets and exchange rates.[2] PBOC's capital is held by the Chinese state. Its governors are nominated, appointed and removed by the Premier and approved (that is, rubber-stamped) by China's legislative body, the National People's Congress (NPC). Zhou Xiaochuan was reappointed in 2008 for another five-year term after Zhu Rongji and Dai Xianglong. The terms of the governors are not limited officially (in terms of recurrence and overall length), but in practice renewable terms of four to five years seem to be the norm.

The PBOC is responsible for the formulation and implementation of monetary policy and its goal is to ensure the stability of the financial system. It has a number of major functions: issuing local currency, administering its circulation, implementing monetary policy through administrative and market-driven mechanisms, managing China's foreign exchanges and gold reserves (through the State Administration for Foreign Exchange, SAFE), regulating the interbank market, fighting money laundering and managing the credit registry and the payment system. From the mid-1990s to the mid-2000s, the PBOC has progressively delegated its previous supervisory functions for parts of the financial system to other bodies: the China Securities Regulatory Commission (CSRC) and the China Insurance Regulatory Commission (CIRC).

Since the establishment of a specialised regulator for banks, PBOC has not interfered in the daily supervision of financial institutions. However, it often discusses general issues, such as the strategic direction of reforms and their goals, and retains the role of lender of last resort (Xiao Z., 2005). Because it has responsibility for the stability of the financial system, it also needs to evaluate the riskiness of the financial system to prevent and solve financial crises (Xiao Z., 2005 and PBOC, 2005d). For that reason it also collects information from the banks. Its responsibilities are closely linked to the management of those risks that are inherent to the system. This is sometimes the source of conflicts over responsibilities with the CBRC – especially with the growing importance of macroprudential regulation.

The China Banking Regulatory Commission

With the aim of increasing the independence of the central bank and the efficiency of the regulatory function, in March 2003 the central government established the China Banking Regulatory Commission (CBRC). The CBRC is the supervisor of financial institutions[3] under the leadership of the State Council.

Its goals are stated in the *Law on Banking Supervision and Administration* (References for laws 2) and these include making sure financial institutions keep to the law, and ensuring the stability of their operations and the trust of the public in such institutions. Furthermore the Law aims to ensure fair competition among institutions and to raise their level of competitiveness (Art. 3). Its responsibilities include the defining of relevant rules and regulations[4] for supervising financial institutions in China, licensing financial institutions, conducting the off-site and on-site supervision of all financial institutions, approving the adequacy and qualifications of senior management in these institutions, and making proposals for resolving banking crises or high-risk situations in the banking system. The CBRC can fire top senior managers and issue fines when an institution or an individual violates rules.

With the promulgation of the revised *Law on Banking Supervision and Administration* in 2006, the supervisor acquired more teeth: loans foreclosures and, in cases of suspected frauds, it can also investigate any third parties that are involved (chapters IV and V). Overall, CBRC remains focused on shortening the current gap between Chinese and international banking practices. This involves resolving issues related to non-performing loans, credit risk management, capital adequacy, corporate governance and, in general, effective financial intermediation. Liberalising and gradually opening up the banking system is seen as an effective way of enhancing its capacity.

To establish a differentiated and more focused supervision (分类监管), CBRC is divided into six operational departments (as opposed to research and administrative departments) supervising the following individual areas: state-owned commercial banks, joint-stock commercial banks and urban local lenders, foreign banks, rural financial institutions, non-bank financial institutions, and the remaining asset management companies, policy banks and the postal savings bank.

The creation of a specialised regulatory agency for financial institutions in China is believed to have had a positive effect on reforms of the Chinese banking system (Shih, 2005). It has reduced conflicts of interests arising from multiple goals in supervision and monetary policy. It has also eliminated further conflicts of interest that had arisen because PBOC – through its foreign exchange reserves manager, SAFE – was acting as a shareholder in some institutions. Finally, the separation increased the focus on asset quality and risk management and on more technical matters. This could be witnessed clearly in recent years and has been underlined by the healthy financial indicators in the overall banking system.

Other regulatory agencies

In addition to being under the regulatory authority of the PBOC and the CBRC, banks also fall under the China Securities Regulatory Commission (CSRC), which is in charge of regulating the securities markets.

Furthermore, they also have to follow the regulations of the State Administration of Foreign Exchange (SAFE) which manages currency reserves and the exchange rate (under the umbrella of the PBOC). Other departments or ministries also have an influence on the banks' operating environments: the Ministry of Finance is responsible, among other things, for promulgating accounting and tax rules and the NDRC (National Development and Reform Commission) is responsible for enterprises finance issues and industry policies. These two institutions are very powerful and have an overarching role in terms of defining future policies.

Multiplicity of regulators

The multiplicity of regulation adds a layer of costs and risks to the banking system. Various commentators, including Xiao Z. (2006), note the lack of established communication and coordination among the different regulators and authorities. This often leads to contradictory situations and adds to the workload of the regulated entities. The differentiated supervision increases focus and specialisation but at the same time acts – in some instances – as a barrier to development and innovation.

Since the separation between PBOC and CRBC, China's banks have grown increasingly complex. They have also been able to enter new business lines such as leasing, trust and the acquisition of other banks. While financial conglomerates existed well before this time, no regulation mitigates the negative effects of complex shareholding structures, of intra-group transfers and transactions, and cross-guarantees. The only aspect that has been dealt with is related-parties transactions (EIU, 2010a). The efforts of the CBRC to deal with these issues led in early 2008 to the *Directive on banks consolidated supervision* in early 2008 (References for laws 37).[5]

In 2008 cross-industry supervision has already been discussed, but the outcome was only a superficial compromise to work at two regulatory levels: the first one comprising the Ministry of Finance, PBOC and NDRC, the second one made up of the three commissions. The anchor coordinator is the PBOC. The agreed loose coordinating mechanisms (with no systematic format or defined responsibilities) and exchange of information cannot, however, close the loopholes in financial regulation (*Caijing Magazine*, 2009b).

The potential for regulatory arbitrage to be used by banking institutions in China is even higher since the additional costs incurred by the banks due to multiple regulators and because of the lack of coordination between them must be – from a bank point of view – recapped somewhere.

Regulatory competition

A further concern and source of risk at the regulatory level remains the competition between regulators: something that could become a real challenge when a crisis needs to be resolved rapidly. One example of such competition appeared over the issue of macro-prudential regulation. The PBOC still views itself as the guardian of financial stability in China, and the CBRC considers that its counter-cyclical policies (such as higher capital buffers and provisioning) will be sufficient to avert any future crisis.[6]

The issue of macro-prudential regulation first came to the fore with the unfolding of the financial crisis in 2008. From a legal point of view, both of the supervisors – the PBOC and the CBRC – have a responsibility and a role to play in times of financial or banking crisis. Recently, the CRBC has started to require predefined stress tests at financial institutions. In mid-2009 the CBRC – with a view to managing contagion risk – has also required to calculate capital adequacy without taking into account the subordinated debts that are held by other domestic banks (for those issued after July 2009). Since 2006, it has also established an early warning system (art. 27 of the amended law on Banking Regulation) and shall design action plans for dealing with crisis situations in the banking system – together with the PBOC and the Ministry of Finance. Meanwhile it has the power to take actions (for example suspensions, prohibiting the payment of dividends, restricting the power of shareholders, and replacing directors) against those institutions that fail to comply with its prudential requirements (art. 37 of the amended law). The CRBC even has the power to take over a failed institution (art. 38 of the amended law).

It appears that the sphere of action of the CBRC is focused on individual institutions while that of the PBOC has been focused more on the financial system as a whole. Nevertheless, past experience has shown that the devil often lies in the details.

The competition between regulators and between different layers of government (central and local) might induce changes in regulatory practices. The different regulators and governments produce different and powerful constituencies within the existing framework. They are not always able to enforce their own views and there are frequent shifts in the balance of power.

Regulators' independence

To ensure the institutional, personal and functional independence of supervisors, regulatory authorities should be free from the influence of local and central authorities and other government departments. The independence of the regulatory authorities depends largely upon their role and position and also scope for action.

The de jure independence which is written down in the relevant regulations and laws (References for laws 2, art. 5) does not guarantee a de facto independence. While the promulgation of the *Law of the People's Bank of China* and the *Law on Banking Supervision and Administration* has enhanced the regulators' scope for action, both remain under the pervasive influence of the State Council. Parts of these founding laws do point to some degree of independence, while other parts refer to the strong position of the State Council or other ministerial agencies and their instructions (in any case, the laws always use the words 'banking regulatory authority under the State Council'). For some important decisions, regulators are required to secure the prior approval of the State Council.

Both of the regulators, PBOC and CBRC, are established under the State Council and are subordinated to it. Committees in both PBOC and CBRC are staffed mostly with personnel from the Communist Party chosen by the State Council. Furthermore, the capital of the PBOC is fully in the hands of the state, under the State Council. The regulations do not give any details about the duration of a chairman's or governor's term; the person can be removed or transferred whenever it is deemed necessary – the same is true for CBRC. Through the committee for monetary issues, the National People's Congress also gets an opportunity to oversee the work of the PBOC (Grimm, 2005 and Wei W., 2005) – but it cannot control the issues it deals with nor ask for investigations over its role. The same holds for CBRC.

Political influence is also facilitated by the fact that the organisational structure of the PBOC runs almost in parallel with that of other administrations (although now regional offices do not report to provincial governments any more). Theoretically, any type of political influence at local level is forbidden (for example, amended law for CBRC, art. 5). However, the cooperation of local authorities is required in resolving and investigating problem institutions.

The independence is dented further by the lack of independent financial resources, even though CBRC collects supervisory fees.[7] The fees are then forwarded as part of the central budget and the Ministry of Finance then allocates the annual budget required by the CBRC in return. Over the years since 2003, the CBRC has been able to increase its human resources to more than 23,000 staff. The level of professionalism has certainly increased and regulations have provided more power, but the daily regulatory work will show how independent these are.

As a result of the strong influence exerted by the State Council, PBOC and CBRC cannot be made fully accountable for their policies and actions – although their staff face fines and penalties for misconduct. Their subordination to the State Council reduces the degree of achievable functional, institutional, personal and financial independence.

One final comment is necessary for the role of the Communist Party in the banking sector. All of the important and strategic decisions affecting it are ultimately reviewed and taken by the Leading Group for Finance and Economics[8] – a group under the guidance of the party and staffed by high-level government bureaucrats. The Financial Work Conference, which meets every four years to decide upon the reforms of the financial system, is run under its aegis. The group is also working together with the Communist Party's Organisation Department[9] to oversee senior appointments at both authorities and financial institutions. The blurred dividing line between Party and state leads to yearly rounds of 'musical chairs' in which senior managers rotate from one financial institution to another.[10]

Table 2.1 Summary of the supervisory function in China

Structure of the banking market	Concentrated and homogenous with regard to ownership types (all in majority state-owned and most as shareholding types now)
Authority structure	Fragmented and competitive
Regulatory goals	Not unified
Work manner	Highly politicised in the sense that politicians have a full role to play, but not in the sense that regulatory questions are discussed openly
Style of regulation	Non-confrontative, discussions behind closed doors, with closely defined hierarchies and power structures
Diversity of supervisory players	Vertically and horizontally
Legislation	Weak parliament and control is exercised solely through Party and State Council
Need for codification	Low
Tendency	Towards higher convergence but still at a very low and limited level
Bank crises experience	Yes but under a fully different regulatory arrangement
Experience	State known as 'saviour', hands-on approach to regulation, strong state

Source: Author's own research, based on Busch, 2003.

The influence even reaches into the furthest corners of the banking system – for public and private institutions, and for those at the national or the local level. The political sphere is actively integrated into the financial system. The years of reforms have not dented its influence – even though this is now exercised in a more subtle manner. Financial regulatory bodies are a good example thereof – their influence channels remain even though they are less obvious.

2.2   Regulatory instruments

The regulators have in their hands a number of instruments to ensure that their own goals are met. Overall, China is moving away progressively from decree-based towards rules-based regulation. In their daily work PBOC and CBRC issue administrative rules that should help to implement and regulate the laws issued at a higher level. These rules define the business scope of financial institutions and the permissible activities as well as basic licensing requirements.

Licensing of banks

The most important laws and regulations of the PRC include the *Law of the People's Bank of China*, the *Commercial Banking Law* and the *Law on Banking Supervision and Administration*. These all represent the foundation of banking sector supervision.

The *People's Bank of China Law* (References for laws 3) regulates the status of the PBOC as well as the sharing of responsibilities with CBRC. The law also details the instruments that can be used by the PBOC to take up its responsibilities. PBOC shall not give any guarantees to outside entities and should not lend funds to other entities other than banks. When suspecting problems in one bank which might endanger the financial stability, PBOC can inspect the bank, with the authorisation of the State Council (art. 34).

The *Commercial Banking Law* (References for laws 1) provides details of the requirements for the operation of commercial banks and includes general provisions for depositors' protection, licensing, prudential supervision, and so on. The law gives commercial banks the needed operational independence and protects them from any outside interference. The law stipulates that banks have to bear the risks they incur and notes that they should make independent lending decisions based on the borrower's creditworthiness.

Commercial banks are defined as receiving deposits and lending to the public, and providing settlement services as well as other financial services (arts 2 and 3). Banks are required to analyse their borrowers before extending loans (art. 6).[11] Requirements for establishing a commercial bank include having a professional senior management team, as well as having adequate registered capital, shareholders and a complete organisation. Changes in name, business scope, important shareholders and capital have to be approved by CBRC. As art. 34 states: 'A commercial bank shall conduct its loan business in accordance with the need for the development of the national economy and social progress and under the guidance of the state industrial policy' – it therefore, however, remains unclear how freely a bank can operate. The situation of state-owned commercial banks is clearer: 'A commercial bank owned solely by the state should provide loans for special projects approved by the State Council. Losses resulting from such loans shall be compensated with appropriate measures taken by the State Council' (art. 41).

The earlier limitation to traditional banking businesses has been removed progressively. On a case-by-case basis, the CBRC grants authorisations to commercial banks to conduct insurance and leasing businesses. For trust and securities business as well as asset management they play the role of marketers. Banks can also, in a limited fashion, invest in other banks' capital. Financial holdings have always existed in China but they are now becoming increasingly common.

To establish a bank, a branch thereof or a new business line, the applicant has to apply for a licence for which sufficient capital is needed and other prudential requirements must be met.

Apart from the above minimum capital required, banks also have to fulfil general prudential requirements before submitting a banking application. They need to show professional directors and senior managers, a sound organisational structure and management system, business premises and a security system, sound corporate governance, appropriate risk management and internal controls, and a good HR management system. Shareholders also need to show their sound credentials: if they are a commercial bank CAR 8% (otherwise 10% risk-based capital ratio), equity investments not exceeding 50% of own capital, to have achieved a profit in the past three years, to have a good level of corporate governance and internal controls, and to be in compliance with the prudential indicators of supervisors. If the financial institution is a foreign investor, they have to meet the following additional requirements: total assets at least USD10 bln, a good international credit rating and profitability in the past two years, and a sound supervisory and economic environment at home.

To be able to open domestic branches, sound corporate governance, risk management and internal controls, appropriate capital adequacy

Table 2.2   Summary of capital requirements for commercial banks licences

Institution type	Min. registered capital	Min. operating capital for branches*
JSCBs	CNY1 bln	CNY100 mln
CCBs	CNY100 mln	
UCCs	CNY50 mln	
RCCs	CNY1 mln	CNY0.3 mln
RCCs unions	CNY1 mln	
Combination of RCCs and unions	CNY10 mln***	CNY1 mln***
Rural credit unions	CNY5 mln	
Rural cooperative banks	CNY20 mln	CNY1 mln (outlet:
Rural commercial banks	CNY50 mln	CNY0.5 mln)
Foreign invested bank incorporated in China	CNY1 bln	CNY100 mln**
Foreign domiciled banks' branches****	CNY200 mln	–

Notes:
*Making up no more than 60% of the HQ's capital.
**Further outlets in one city where a branch is already established can be opened with an operating capital of CNY10 mln.
***May be adjusted by CBRC but cannot be less than half that amount.
****Such banks are not allowed to take deposits less than CNY1 mln. These are mainly the banks as regulated under the pre-2006 arrangement.
SOCBs branches require the same operational capital as JSCBs. Further capital for new business lines or expansion of business lines is not required.
Source: References for laws 14.

and asset quality, full profitability, no unlawful activities in the past two years, a good CAMELS (Annex table A.1) rating needs to be displayed. To open a foreign branch, the following further requirements are listed: CAR of at least 8%, equity investments less than 50% of own capital, profitability in the past three years, be in possession of CNY100 bln in total assets, have access to foreign currency funds, exhibit sound corporate governance and internal controls, and comply with prudential indicators.

In general, as further approval is required for new types of services – for example, foreign exchange business or the issuing of subordinated debt – the CBRC also applies prudential preconditions to such applications. Most conditions refer to sound financial ratios (Table 2.3).

The following changes need to be approved by CBRC: changes in shareholders or shareholding (above 10%), operational capital, statutes of the institution, business premises, and bank name.

Table 2.3 Prudential indicators for banks

Capital adequacy ratio	>8% (core capital > 4%)[12]
Loans to deposit ratio	<75%
Loans over a year to deposits over a year	<120%
Current assets/current liabilities	>25%
PBOC reserves and cash held/deposits	>5–7%
Single client exposure	<10% of bank capital
Single group exposure	<15% of bank capital
Ten largest clients exposures	<50% of bank capital
Interbank loans/ interbank deposits	<8%
Shareholder loan	<100% of paid-in capital
NPL ratio	<5%
NPA ratio	<4%
Core liabilities to total liabilities	>60%
Percentage of liquidity maturing in 90 days to liquidity gap for 90 days.	>10% (on- and off-balance sheet)
Aggregated forex exposure	<20% of bank capital
Operational costs and depreciation	<35% of operational income
Return on average assets after tax	>0.6%
Return on average equity after tax	>11%
For loans and assets the loss provisions	>100% of the required provisions
Credit exposure to all related parties	<50% of the bank's net worth
Common shares & retained earnings/tier one capital	>75%
Dividend payout ratio	*<45% (in discussion)*

Source: References for laws 5 and 17.

In general, requirements for establishing a rural financial institution follow a similar pattern. However, due to the need for a restructuring of their shareholdings the requirements are stricter in terms of the number and quality or origin of shareholders. The requirements differ for each type of institution. Shareholdings by employees, managers and local governments are limited (see Annex tables A.3 to A.5).

Prudential indicators

Prudential indicators were published in 1995 by PBOC and in early 2006 by CBRC. Until just recently, prudential indicators were not really enforced. Only the re-publication of prudential rules by the newly established CBRC has improved prospects for thorough enforcement.

All of the banks were also progressively required to report their financial position according to the new Chinese Accounting Standards – which are similar to the internationally recognised International Financial Reporting Standards (IFRS). The implementation process began in 2007 for listed companies. In 2008 it was extended most remaining financial institutions and in 2009 to all rural financial institutions.

Further prudential regulations also require a bank's senior managers to pass a fit and proper test and that the bank shows a proper and functioning risk management system. Newly established financial institutions – such as foreign-funded banks and rural financial institutions – are also required to have certain types of shareholders and these again are required to have a certain standing (credit rating, minimum capital, minimum time of profitability).

Monitoring of banks' riskiness

In February 2004, CBRC published its rating system for assessing commercial banks (amended in 2005, References for laws 29). It is similar to the CAMELS system employed in other developed countries. Scores are attributed depending on quantitative and qualitative assessment of the banks' capital adequacy, asset quality, liquidity management, profitability, market risk, and overall management. Each area has a weighting ranging from 15% to 25%.

Since 2007, this new CAMELS system is supported by a set of newly published risk-based supervisory indicators that will apply to all Chinese

Table 2.4 Bank assessment system CAMELS

Weights	Capital adequacy situation 20%
	Asset safety situation 20%
	Management situation 25%
	Earnings situation 10%
	Liquidity 15%
	Sensitivity to market 10%
	No overriding factor
Overall and single factor assessment	Level 1 over 85 Excellent
	Level 2 75 to 85 Good
	Level 3 60 to 75 Special Mention
	Level 4 50 to 60 Substandard
	Level 5 below 50 Bad
Period of the assessment	One year
Disclosure	Assessment results will be announced to related sectors and after inspections

Note: Details of the grading for each single factor can be found in the annex (Table A.1).
Source: References for laws 29.

Table 2.5 Risk supervision in banks

Risk aspects	Measurement/Definition
Risk level 风险水平	Liquidity (ratio, gap), credit (asset quality, largest client group and related parties exposure), market (forex gap, interest rate sensitivity) and operational risk indicators (loss rate)
Risk migration 风险迁徙	Measured through the migration rate of loans between performing and all other categories of the loan classification
Risk prevention/offsetting 风险抵补	measured by the ability of the bank to make profits to cover losses (C/I Ratio, ROE, ROA, CAR and LLP)

Source: References for laws 5.

commercial banks (References for laws 5). In a similar fashion, a rating tool for rural financial institutions and for branches of larger banks has been designed and progressively implemented since then (CBRC, 2008).

In the case of most of the indicators, the CBRC has published the calculation method as well as the definition of the components. It has also finally indicated the minimum or maximum level allowed for each.

In addition, the CBRC has developed an early warning system for the banking sector in 2007 and 2008 (CBRC, 2009c). It is not fully clear what exactly is being monitored by the system. CBRC will also start categorising the banks according to their CAR levels (Reuters News, 2009b).

To date no information has been publicly available about banks that did not comply with the above indicators or at least showed very poor results. This does not mean that there are no such cases in China. However, it is not possible to judge on the implementation of such indicators as they are used in China by the CBRC.

Lending and deposit rates

Instruments used by PBOC have evolved, but it still uses a mix of administrative and market-driven instruments for policy purposes. Market-driven instruments and mechanisms used to influence financial flows emerged in the mid-1980s. A first step was made with the introduction of minimum deposits and reserves requirements as well as discounting activities. These mechanisms became necessary with the end of the strict allocation of loans until 1995 and the increased opening and diversification of the banking sector.

PBOC can intervene in financial markets through a number of instruments (to which certain interest rates are attached):

- interest rates for loans and deposits (until recently also through interest rates controls), and window guidance (a softer version of the credit quotas),
- minimum reserve requirements,
- rediscounting,
- central bank re-lending,[13] and
- open market interventions.

Administrative measures are used whenever required to support SOEs' reforms, to support the state sector in general or to direct funds to specific economic sectors or regions. During 2008–09, the PBOC used its injunctions to first induce the banks into lending more to support the fiscal stimulus and then to calm the loan growth that appeared too strong and could potentially carry large risks. Higher deposit requirements were used only at the end of that period (Table 2.6). Further administrative controls were introduced as well to reduce lending in overheated sectors such as real estate and construction. Finally the impact of market instruments is reduced by the fact that the Chinese economy still depends to a large extent upon administrative steering.

Reserve requirements have fluctuated over the years. Usually the PBOC uses steps of 0.5% to 1% points. In 2009, the reserve requirements remained almost unchanged. Additionally, they do not appear to influence much of the new loans generation (Figure 2.1).

Until 2004, to ensure an inexpensive financial support to enterprises and to retain some power over terms and uses of loans (Girardin, 1997),

Table 2.6 Monetary policy and loan growth (at year end, %)

	2009	2008	2007	2006	2005	2004	2003	2002
PBOC lending rate (20 days)	2.79	2.79	3.33	3.33	3.33	3.33	2.7	2.7
Bank lending rate (1 year)	5.31	5.31	7.47	6.12	5.58	5.58	5.31	5.31
Bank deposit rate (1 year)	2.25	2.25	4.14	2.52	2.25	2.25	2.25	1.98
Large bank reserve requirements	15.5	15.0	14.5	9.0	7.5	7.5	7.0	6.0

Source: PBOC.

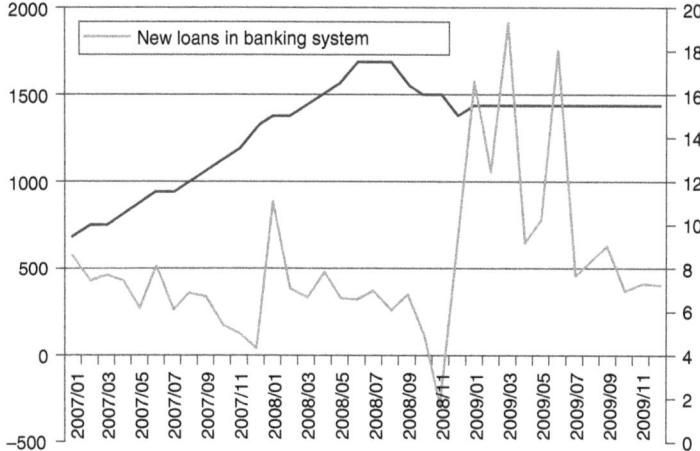

Figure 2.1 New loans volumes (CNY bln) vs reserve requirements (%)
Source: Data collected on PBOC website.

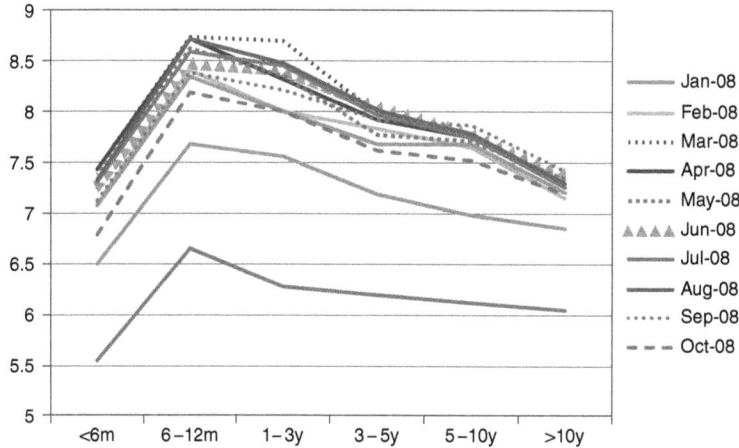

Figure 2.2 Lending rates by maturity bands for 2008
Source: PBOC quarterly monetary reports 2008.

PBOC authorised only a small band within which interest rates could move compared to the base rate (Figure 2.2).

Since 29 October 2004, commercial banks in urban areas have been free to set their own level of interest rates.[14] However, a ruling by the Chinese Supreme Court a few years ago set the definition of a usury rate

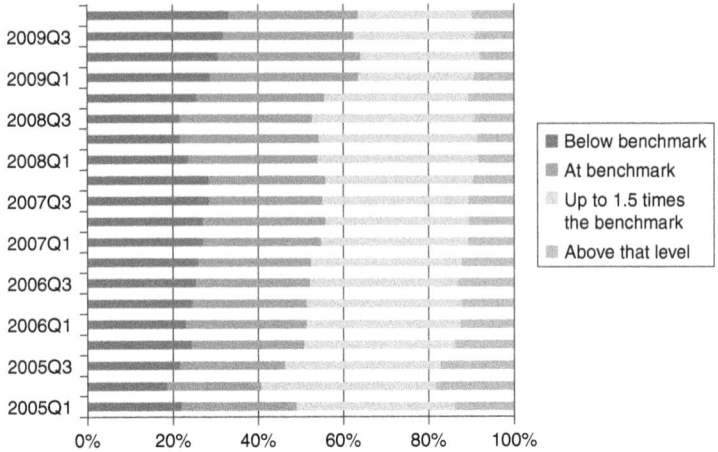

Figure 2.3 Departure from the benchmark rate
Note: Expressed in % of the loan portfolio, all banks, for CNY one-year loans.
Source: PBOC quarterly monetary reports between 2005 and 2009.

as being equivalent to four times the base rate set by PBOC (Jiang X. and Ding C., 2004).

Lending interest rates at banks have changed only slightly since the removal of the ceiling. Since 2005, the institutions that price the furthest away from the benchmark are rural financial institutions (Figure 2.3). Overall, banks still lack the tools to price their loans according to the risks incurred, and therefore the effect of the interest rate liberalisation has not yet been felt in full. Loan demand is also becoming slightly more dependent on changes in market interest rates (Koivu, 2008). Market mechanisms are being introduced, but have not yet taken root.

Open market operations

To support its use of interest rates and reserve requirements, the central bank also makes frequent use of open market operations to reinforce its stance.

Figure 2.4 shows clearly that at the onset of the worldwide financial crisis, the PBOC was still working to combat the overheating of the Chinese economy. In mid-2008 it then had to change course completely and open market operations came almost to a halt. Later as the fiscal stimulus appeared to be working almost too well, the PBOC intervened again strongly to prevent a renewed overheating.

When looking at the volume of new loans in the system on a monthly basis for the same period of time, it appears that there is no strong correlation between the two factors (see also *Caijing Magazine*, 2010a).

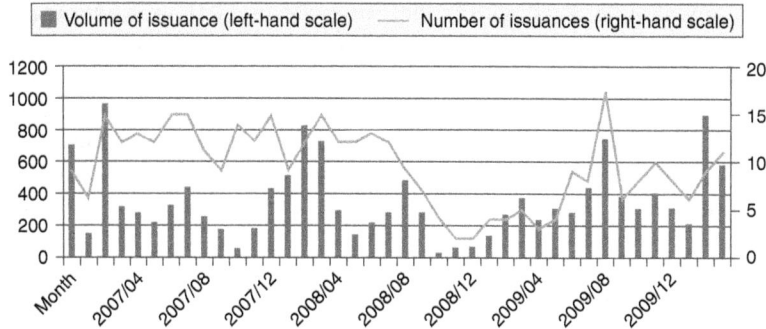

Figure 2.4 Issuance of PBOC bills between January 2007 and April 2010 (CNY bln)
Source: Based on chinabond.com.cn.

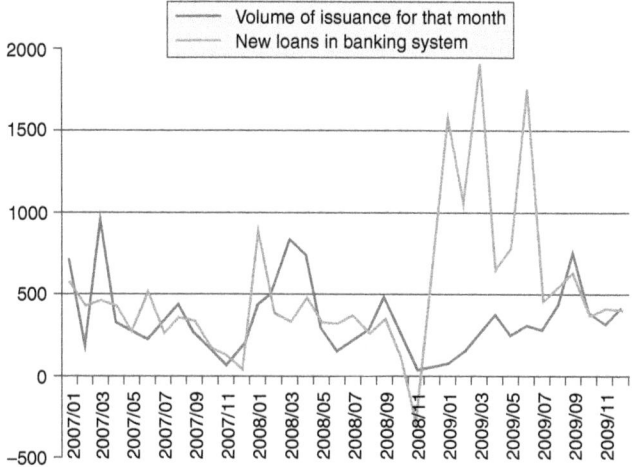

Figure 2.5 Monthly issuance of PBOC bills and new loans volume (CNY bln)
Source: Data collected from chinabond.com.cn and PBOC website.

While the monthly data appear to suggest a close relationship during 2007 and 2008 (Figure 2.5), this is no longer the case in the first half of 2009. During that period of time the actual measures and market operations by the PBOC were actually almost driven to a halt before resuming in the second half of that year – which reflected the much stronger and more restrictive approach chosen by both CBRC and PBOC in controlling (euphemistically called 'guiding' in bureaucrats' interviews) the pace of loan growth.

In the first half of 2009, the regulators essentially sat on the sidelines watching the industry growing their loan portfolios and giving sporadic warnings about increasing risks. Only in the second half were both regulators able to make full use of their own instruments (PBOC with bills issuance and later on reserve requirements, although these work to a much lesser extent; CBRC with stricter capital adequacy calculations rules, stricter loan loss provisions requirements up to 150%, capital adequacy ratios raised to 11% for larger banks, investigations into loan uses together with the CNAO; and in both cases private calls and meetings with bank officials to require a slower loan growth).

Instruments for enforcement

Because of its limited resources, CBRC is not in a position to investigate all of China's financial institutions. In fact, the China National Audit Office (CNAO) also conducts on-site investigations into the banks' activities. The nature of the investigation is not dictated: it can target illegal lending, wrongful loan purposes, fraud payments or other matters.

For example, during 2009 CNAO investigated ABC (CNAO, 2009). The results show that the auditors found CNY4.8 bln in illegally disbursed loans (that is, loans that did not comply with policies of the bank among others), CNY4.8 bln in commercial bills without a trade purpose (that is, they were used fraudulently), and CNY0.5 bln in illegal fund transfers. In addition, they found that CNY2.5 bln of the CNY23 bln of loans to local government platforms investigated were for financial purposes (that is, without any projects generating revenues to repay the loans). This example should not imply that only ABC is prone to fraud – all other banks face the same problems. CNAO investigations are routine ones whose focus is defined on a yearly basis by CNAO.

CBRC also has to rely on local authorities to ensure that some of its guidelines and requirements are followed. When it comes to lending prudently, however, one can cast doubts over the quality of local governments' oversight on their own projects that should boost local economic development.

Administrative measures

2009 was exemplary in terms of administrative measures to interfere in lending. The fiscal stimulus was to be carried out by the country's banks as well (banks had to proceed in line with the phrase '保增长、扩内需、调结构': 'keep growth, widen domestic demand and adjust the structure [of the economy]'). The banks did their utmost to lend as much as possible and loan growth was over 30% year on year. But the central government's stimulus was not the sole source of administrative measures or euphemistically called 'window guidance'.

The lending surge in 2009 was initially a reality at the largest banks but during the second half of that year the main lenders were smaller local banks and also rural credit cooperatives. The pressure exerted came not from central authorities but rather from local governments. They used both carrots and sticks to ensure a steady flow of funds: giving the banks preferential treatments where needed as long as they put forward more loans to their finance platforms (Li T., Wen X. and Zhang M., 2009b).

In a more official tone, several authorities and ministries issued a notice in 2009 requiring the banks not to lend to specific industries and enterprises – specifically those crunching much energy and environmentally doubtful (References for laws 38). Industry policies are a strong worry for Chinese bankers – an indicator to which they constantly need to pay attention because they change quickly (PwC, 2009c).

Since the regulators sounded a word of caution over blind growth and lending, the banks knew that they should act cautiously so as to remain compliant with all prudential requirements (especially in capital and lending). CBRC issued a notice which was not made public (*Notice on further strengthening loan management*), which reportedly required the banks to lend only for sound economic purposes (Xinhua Net Comprehensive, 2009). Banks often take active steps even ahead of attempts to impose concrete restrictions to curb their activities (Li T., Wen X. and Zhang M., 2009a) or even to simply close their approval systems for a few days (Wen X., Zhang M. and Fang H., 2009 and McMahon, 2010a).

Risk warnings (风险指引) can be viewed as among the soft instruments which do not always result in prompt corrective action by the banks. Strong figures at regulatory agencies – such as Liu Mingkang and Zhou Xiaochuan – are listened to widely in order to understand and estimate the direction of future policies and probable changes of regulations.[15]

In addition, the banks define their own lending limits or quotas and these are discussed, possibly in collaboration with the regulator (Wall Street Journal, 2010a). 'Window guidance' meetings take place both ways: to increase or to curb loans at large commercial banks in order either to support growth or to keep credit risks in check (Li T. and Wen X., 2009). For larger loans, the system works the other way round: banks become simple utilities at the hand of the authorities (such as ministries overseeing a whole industry) (The Economist, 2010a).

Another instrument was used to curb the level of lending. This was a hybrid between market and administrative measures: the forced sales of PBOC bills to large lenders (Zhang M., 2009 and Huo, K., Wang J., Yu H. and Wang L., 2009). In contrast to the past, the PBOC did not issue loan quotas – this marked the only difference to the past interference. On the contrary, CBRC loosened its stance on the loan to deposit ratio by allowing some of the smaller commercial banks to breach the 75% limit (Chu C., Wen C., Chen F., 2009).

All of these administrative measures – while being legacies of a socialist economy – also have advantages: they still can be useful when authorities do not wish to raise interest rates which would hurt certain economic entities with higher interest costs.

2.3   Chinese regulations and BCP – A comparison

The Basel Committee for Banking Supervision (BCBS) has issued a set of principles for the sound supervision of banks. It is worthwhile considering the compliance of CBRC with the *Core Principles for Effective Banking Supervision* (BCBS, 1997).

With regard to BCP compliance, we can conclude the following:

- the requirements of the first principle (BCP 1) are met albeit for one central issue: the potentially strong interference that state agencies can have in the bank's management, on the regulatory function and on its resources and enforcement work (it makes however its ability to contact and oversee the management of banks much easier);
- requirements for licensing and structures (BCP 2–5) are met in full;
- prudential regulations and requirements on minimum capital and risk management (BCP 6–15) are met in full, the level of details in the regulations has become much higher since the 2008–09 regulations were issued which do reflect most of the Basel II content (for example country and transfer risks are now treated in greater detail, see references for laws 39);
- ongoing supervision methods (BCP 16–20) are complied with strongly;
- information requirements as stated under BCP 21 have been increasingly implemented, and in combination with CSRC requirements on listed banks is a reality for all largest banks at least (it is noteworthy as well that requirements and pressure to comply are higher than maybe elsewhere because of the intrusiveness of supervision and the ramifications of the state-cum-party); and
- requirements (BCP 22–25) concerning remedial measures and cross-border banking are fully complied with, but details of the off-site supervision and remedial actions as well as consolidated supervision are not known or developed sufficiently.

There is little evidence about the effect of compliance with *Basel Core Principles* on the stability of the banking system. Few studies have been conducted and most deal with a small number of countries and of indicators of bank health (NPLs or CAR). The latest study (Demirgüc-Kunt and Detragiache, 2009) finds that bank soundness (as measured with z-scores) does not increase with higher compliance – when considering compliance as a whole or compliance with single principles and criteria.

3
The State and the Banking Safety Net

With the banking institutions playing such a central role in the financial system in China, a safety net[1] is crucial to ensuring the prompt resolution of any crisis touching on the central nerve of the economy. As mentioned by Wu Xiaoling in an interview (Ye W. and Hu J., 2006), the banking industry in China needs a functioning and efficient exit mechanism: 'In a market economy, only if there is a pressure to exit a market, is there a good incentive for operations; [the pressure] improves the healthiness of operations of financial institutions, optimises the allocation of financial resources, and protects the system from financial instability.'

The PBOC acts as described above as a lender of last resort and the CBRC has the power to take over failed institutions. So the exit mechanisms for banks is part of the legal infrastructure and come mainly in two forms: through bankruptcy proceedings and through deposit insurance.

3.1 Deposit insurance

As a second line of defence behind the lender of last resort – but before a government bailout, deposit insurance could have a role to play – however, in China it is still not a reality. While the financial crisis has highlighted the need to have a functioning deposit insurance mechanism and not to dismantle the financial safety net completely (that is, to leave the oversight to depositors), disagreements over the mechanism's structure in China have kept any compromise from becoming reality.

In 1993 the State Council outlined for the first time its intention to build a deposit insurance scheme in order to preserve the financial stability of the system in times of crisis. In 1997 a working group was established with the aim of reviewing the possibility of establishing such a scheme. After the large increases in non-performing assets following the Asian crisis the state stepped in to support bankrupt entities.

Preliminary conditions and regulations that deal with the guarantee of bank deposits have been promulgated. CBRC, CSRC, PBOC and the Ministry of Finance jointly issued in November 2004 an *Opinion on purchasing personal creditor's rights and client securities transaction liquidation funds* (References for laws 20). It aims to protect the interests of small depositors and investors, the stability and continuous operations of securities markets, the stability of society, to raise the risk awareness and market discipline and decrease moral hazard. The *Opinion* stipulates that full compensation would be required for deposits in commercial banks and rural credit cooperatives (RCCs) and related interest. Eligible deposits eligible are those of individuals (including also trust transactions and securities). For all deposits before 30 September 2004, the deposits and securities transactions of customers amounting to less than CNY100,000 are covered in full by the insurance scheme. Above that amount, 90% will be repaid. The responsibility is now not the sole responsibility of local governments, but with both central and local government who share costs (for securities and savings deposits the central government carries the costs, for all other deposit types the costs are covered 10% by the local government and 90% by central authorities). However, there are no provisions for deposits after that date and 90% is a large portion (Ye W. and Hu J., 2006).

The idea of a deposit insurance scheme resurfaced in 2004: a scheme was said to be awaiting approval at the highest level (Chen Y., 2004). A compulsory system, which would be similar to that of the USA, was envisaged. It was also expected that different premium rates would apply, depending upon the bank's CAR (Yue G., 2005). The fund to be created would be under the control of the State Council.

Experts have warned that such a scheme offers a market exit mechanism but also increases the risk of moral hazard and of using people's money to save bankrupt banks (Wang C., 2005 and EIU, 2006b). The scope of the deposit insurance scheme determines the amount by which moral hazard will be influenced. In establishing such a scheme the authorities will first need to clarify its funding mechanism (probably with a mix of banks' and government contributions to price the cost of being rescued) and the scope of participation (size of the banks but also their riskiness). In addition, the relation between the deposit insurer and state-owned banks would need to be clarified (as they would both have similar owners, OECD, 2005). Various commentators suggested that the new scheme should be independent from authorities (Deloitte and Touche, 2004).

The current implicit arrangement is that banks are rescued by the state – either through forced mergers, outright closures, restructurings, name changes or re-lending facilities. It has already shown its willingness and capacity to do so in various cases with urban and rural credit cooperatives, with large and smaller commercial banks. The financial crisis in 2007–09 might have further confirmed their expectation. Prior to it, the central and local governments had mentioned that they do not want to bankroll the industry from time to time.

Finally, in November 2008, the influential finance magazine *Caijing* wrote that a deposit insurance scheme was in the final stages of preparation (EIU, 2010a). However, the structure is nothing to rejoice about: first, the institution would not be independent but rather part of the PBOC; secondly, that department would have weak rights to investigate and thus poor incentives to act quickly; and third, the full deposit amount would be guaranteed. The only consolation was that the planned deposit insurance scheme would give a level playing field to all banks incorporated in China.

One might rightly ask, however, what would be the difference between being taken over by the state or by a deposit insurance institution that was positioned directly below the state. In either case bank managers would be relieved of their responsibilities. Under both implicit and explicit arrangements, Chinese depositors do not need to be vigilant of reckless risk-taking in banks – safety is assured at all times. Although a deposit insurance institution would add a pair of supervisory eyes to increase systemic stability but this might not prove cost-effective. Speed of resolution could possibly be hampered if three rather than two regulatory agencies compete for the taking over of the failed bank. In 2009 the 2008 proposal was quickly shelved again (EIU, 2010a).

Actually in China there is at present no need for a deposit insurance scheme: the state will always bail out the banks or the system. The state takes the form of being either a lender of last resort (PBOC) or the main or sole shareholder (through SAFE or Huijin or MOF). If bad loans are such that recapitalisation is required, then the shareholder – in other words the state – steps in with fresh capital (that is, a government bailout is also a bailout by shareholders). If banks experience a run, the state implicitly guarantees the repayment of almost all deposits (any bank would count as too big to fail) – so that the risk of a social crisis is eliminated (as long as the state has the resources to fulfil its promises).

Since there are no costs to the banks for being bailed out and neither is there a cost to depositors because they know that the state is willing and capable of rescuing them in *all* cases, incentives for bank risk management are flawed. Some argue that the issuance of subordinated debt can act to restore the incentivisation (Mandanis Schooner and Taylor, 2009), but in China, since subordinated debts are held by other financial institutions (mainly banks) which are themselves mostly controlled by the state, there is no independent function of the investor.

With such credible and tested implicit deposit insurance, there is no need to establish an explicit mechanism. Banks would forego earnings when paying for the deposit insurance scheme which they now distribute to their shareholders among which are individual investors (but to a greater extent to the state as shareholder). As a majority shareholder the state can set the level of required dividends and taxes the banks should pay – funds that can be used by the same state when in the role of a saviour.

Instead of adding a regulatory layer with a deposit insurance mechanism, the bankruptcy of banks could also help. The new Bankruptcy Law was promulgated in 2006 but does not deal with banks and the CBRC is said to be working on one specifically for banks.

3.2 Bankruptcy

Bankruptcy is a double issue for banks, in terms of both the impact of the failure of enterprises as well as banking institutions themselves. According to the *Doing Business Report 2010* of the World Bank (WB, 2010), it takes 34 procedures and 406 days in China (compared with 31 procedures and 462 days in OECD countries) to enforce a commercial contract and the average cost amounts to 11% of the debt to be enforced (since 2005, the costs of decreased but the procedures and time spent has increased). In China bankruptcy proceedings take on average 1.7 years to complete and cost 22% of the value of the underlying assets (compared with an average of 1.7 years and a cost of 8.4% in OECD countries). The recovery rates achieved by investors are around 35.3% (compared to 68.6% in OECD countries).

Bankruptcy of enterprises

After years of bickering the new *Bankruptcy Law* was promulgated in 2007 (passed in August 2006, References for laws 41) and this finally closed a number of shortcomings of the previous trial law. Consequently, the rights of creditors have found higher protection – even though in practice the courts have been proceeding carefully with implementation.

The new law enhanced the banks' prospects in recovering their funds and thus they might find more incentives to lend to private enterprises.

Together with the secured interests law (References for laws 40), the secured creditors now have priority over workers' wages, social insurance claims and other unsecured creditors. But in policy-led restructurings, the banks might be pushed towards the end of the priority spectrum.

Nevertheless, the law now covers all types of enterprises – foreign and domestic as well as private and public. The conditions for applying for bankruptcy are based on either a cash flow test (that is, unable to pay its debts when they fall due) or a balance sheet test (that is, insufficient assets to cover liabilities). A debtor but also a creditor can file for bankruptcy. Once the application is accepted, the court names an administrator instead of the previously used liquidation committees. An administrator can be an individual or a firm with relevant experience and is supervised by the creditors.

The role of the administrator encloses the following tasks: taking over the property, investigating financial states, managing the current affairs, determining the scope of business to be carried out during the proceedings, disposing of the property where necessary, acting on behalf of the debtor and meeting with creditors. Resolution has to take place within a limited time frame.

Alternatively, the parties can apply to the court for a reorganisation – with the consent of a majority of creditors. Before the debtor is declared bankrupt, it can apply for a debt compromise which should cover the majority of all debts due (PwC, 2007a, Tomasic, 2010 and Hong S., 2009).

In reality, the prospects of resolution have been hampered by the lack of understanding of the new law and experience on the ground has shown that many prefer informal resolution and restructuring to going to court (The Economist, 2008). Furthermore, uncertainties remain for foreign lenders and investors. Their treatment is far from clear and the ultimate decisions remain with the courts – the issue is especially thorny when bankruptcy covers assets deemed to be of importance to the state. Clarification over debtor-in-possession financing (based on the debtor's pledged assets with a super-seniority of that lender) needs to be given by courts because the law remains too vague. Finally, courts and administrators still have to build up experience with that new law (PwC, 2009a).

Proceedings for banks

The new *Bankruptcy Law* also deals succinctly with financial institutions. Only their respective supervisor is allowed to apply for bankruptcy for them. Further details are to be worked out by the supervisors themselves and the CBRC is said to be working on bankruptcy proceedings for banks.

For commercial banks insolvency proceedings can only be opened once insolvency has been declared and once PBOC has approved of the proceedings (*Commercial Banking Law*). In those cases, seniority is as follows: first come salaries and social insurance, then deposits of private persons and interest payments to lenders (Art. 71). In addition to the rules above, China has issued the *Rules on dissolution of banks*. Dissolution can be ordered for a number of reasons including unlawful activities, mismanagement, and not only the inability to repay debts. The rules describe the process of dissolution and management of the dissolved entity, but do not actually regulate debts issues.

However, these regulations are not frequently used in the case of banks. More often the authorities use an administrative decree rather than legal means to resolve the problems faced by individual banks, in complete disregard of economic and market principles. The reason for preferring such methods is the stated goal of social stability.

Often in the past, sound financial institutions were ordered by regulators to merge or take over failed banks in their geographical area (Table 3.1). This was the case in 1997 when Hainan Development Bank was asked to take over urban credit cooperatives which had suffered a run, or in Chengdu where Chengdu City Commercial Bank was asked to take over the failed Huitong Urban Credit Cooperative in 2000 after a liquidity crisis. In the first case, Hainan Development Bank was driven into bankruptcy by the takeover and was finally closed down in 1998 (Zhao S., 2004). It was the first official closure, but not a true bankruptcy. Chengdu City Commercial Bank was still digesting the failed Huitong cooperative five years later.

By way of removal, dissolution, closure or bankruptcy, between 1997 and 2001, the central bank has dealt with 427 smaller financial institutions which were conducting illegal or irregular operations or which were unable to repay their debts. It also closed some 28,588 informal rural (rotating) funds or credit associations. In 2001, through name changes, forced mergers, acquisitions, and restructurings, it disposed of 766 urban credit cooperatives (Yu N., 2005). Only trust and investment corporations, such as Guangdong ITIC,[2] were allowed to go bankrupt in the past (as it did not hold any public deposits).

In China, as in many other emerging or developing countries, adherence to the 'too big to fail' doctrine, however, creates moral hazard problems and reduces incentives for introducing best practices in banking. Thus recently, Chinese regulators have made calls for increasing market discipline and reducing the likelihood of administrative state bailouts.

Table 3.1   Selected rescue activities of bad banks in recent years in China

Bank name	Year	Rescue method
Qingzhen Hongfeng RCC	1996	Payment crisis. Merged to Guiyang CCB in 1999
Haikou UCCs (33)	1997	Closed. Takeover by Hainan Development Bank.
Hainan Development Bank	1998	Closed. Relending by PBOC of CNY 4 bln.
Zhengzhou Rural Cooperative Bank	1998	Run in 1998. Fully taken over by PBOC in 1999
Various FIs in Enping City	1998	CCB branch removed, ABC branch cleaned, 20 UCCs closed. Total loss to PBOC CNY 6.8 bln.
Guangxi Beihai City Cooperative	1998	12 closed, 2 had their licenses withdrawn
Hunan Changge UCC	1998	Operating without license, closed down.
Guangzhou Shantou Commercial Bank	1999	Payment difficulties. Restructuring
China Investment Bank	1999	Bought by China Everbright Bank (CEB). Provisions at CEB increased by CNY 7.3 bln and it struggled with it for the following eight years.
Huitong UCC	1999	Payment difficulties. Merged into Chengdu CCB

Note: The list does not include rescue activities for securities firms, insurance companies, trust and investment companies.
Source: Based on information from Zhang H. and Cheng M., 2003, as well as author's own research.

In a speech in December 2005, the Chinese regulators somewhat changed their stance towards failed smaller banks. They warned those high-risk banks[3] that they may be closed altogether (CBRC, 2005a). In these cases, the resolution will involve the repayment of debts (according to the percentage of debts to assets) to natural persons by local authorities (using central government special loans as well as using re-discounting by the central bank). The closures may however also include the mergers or restructuring or rescuing in some form or another for some of the urban credit cooperatives.

In 2005, Tang Shuangning, then CBRC's vice-chairman in charge of CCBs supervision, clearly outlined measures to support the worst-performing CCBs[4] (Liu Y., 2006): 'Seek support, Add strength, Grasp the focal point and Reduce risks (求支持、加力度、抓重点、解风险)'.

'Seek support' means looking for the support of local authorities. 'Add strength' means increasing NPLs disposal and the reduction of other inherited risks. 'Grasp the focal point' means focusing attention on the reduction of high risks. 'Reduce risks' is self-explanatory. Closure is only the last option when nothing else has worked and all other ideas and measures have been exhausted.

Such an approach has been relatively credible in the past but also discourages sound banking practices. First, these impact negatively on the incentives for banks to learn and to avoid bankruptcy. Second, the costs of bankruptcy proceedings for enterprises are often higher than those of keeping credit lines open.

Despite a few improvements that have taken place in the financial infrastructure of the Chinese banking system, banks appear to have few incentives to introduce best practice – and yet they still do. While rules and regulations have become more detailed and target risk management practices and enhance prudential benchmarks, serious moral hazard problems still remain within the system.

4
Further Roles of the State

While it may be surprising to western eyes that the state and the Communist Party are to be considered as one in the present book, in the context of China it makes sense as the structures of the Party and of the state run in parallel from top to bottom and the Party permeates *all* state activities, even though it is not always mentioned as such.

Qin Xiao wrote in a guest article in *Caijing*:

> The solidification and strengthening of the role of the authorities has not only been influenced on the notional level (that is there is no real 'Beijing model' of economic development), but also has become the driver of a special interest group with a form uniting power and capital. (Qin X., 2010)

4.1 The financier

In each of the state-owned commercial banks the state has a direct hold over two-thirds of their capital (either through Central Huiin or through the Ministry of Finance; Table 8.3). Their listings did not fundamentally alter the majority holdings – all they did was to clarify the holding entity. In all other banks, the state also holds banking assets indirectly through local governments and state-owned enterprises. While it is now almost impossible to measure the actual holdings of local state-owned enterprises in the capital of each bank, researchers assumed in 2004 that the Chinese state held between 95 and 99% of all banking assets (Bekier, Huang and Wilson, 2005 and OECD, 2005). Even though listings have increased the number of shares held widely and state shares reform has also transformed the listed shares into liquid ones, the total percentage might have dropped by only a few percentage points and the state-related shares are not likely to be sold in any case as it is the state's stated goal to keep them under its control. The only bank for which a majority of the capital is held is in private hands is China Minsheng Bank.

Through controlling equity stakes, central and local authorities exercise a so-called *lishu* (隶属) relationship: the entity's owner is entitled to direct control over that entity. Such a relationship is not based solely on ownership rights. Where necessary control can be exercised administratively (Tan et al., 2007). Depending on the nature of such a relationship, environments might be more lenient or more supportive of a firm's development – depending on the local government exercising the power (incentives can take the form of tax holidays, subsidies, loan applications, licences and so on to facilitate transactions). Closeness to varying levels of government enhances performance and the firm's prospects (this is especially true at township level or below, and also at the central level).

Apart from having a controlling equity stake in the banking sector, the Chinese state has also provided generous financial support to financial institutions. Overall, up to 2006, the state has spent around CNY2.3 trn to support the main commercial banks – through fresh capital injections in 1998 and, in the mid-2000s, transfers of NPLs to the four asset management companies (AMCs). The SOCBs were certainly not the only ones being supported. PBOC issued special bank bills in June 2008 amounting to CNY165.6 bln in exchange for NPLs totalling CNY135.3 bln to help the restructuring of rural credit cooperatives. Between 2005 and 2008, Central Huijin injected fresh capital to replenish the SOCBs (see chapters on the respective bank types).

Local governments have also had to rescue their local financial institutions both because they were required to do so by the central authorities and also because they held most of the capital in these institutions. No data are available on the total amount of financial support provided, but experience has showed that the local authorities could not avoid rescue operations.

The influence of the authorities is in some cases welcomed by the banks themselves (Luo J., 2002a). Banks have a number of reasons for supporting state involvement as this can help with restructuring efforts and the local authorities as shareholders put little pressure on managers to address NPL problems. Since local authorities' ownership rights are not always defined explicitly (most local banks were only incorporated recently and before that they were part of local government budgets), these still have strong administrative power in decision-making but they place less stringent disclosure and governance requirements on the banks. Finally, banks require local government participation to resolve non-performing loan issues that they have helped to create (Luo J., 2002b).

While central and local governments may be viewed as 'saviours' in terms of their financial support for the system they can also be viewed as 'wrongdoers' in terms of interference, destroying incentives to introduce best practice and establishing an environment where moral hazard predominates.

4.2   The businessman

Before the start of the reforms in 1978, the banking system was just one of many parts of a huge state administration. Financial flows were organised around the planning exercises for the whole economy and flows were directed to specific industries and regions based on political decisions. Since this time the authorities have remained influential in the decision-making process of banks, especially the larger ones. While credit quotas have been removed, practices remain, especially for large government projects and SOEs (in disregard of creditworthiness and repayment ability and willingness). This is the case not only with central authorities, but also with local ones.

The Chinese state has business interests. As illustrated by Shih (2004), the Chinese authorities can obtain private gains and advancement through bank loans. He showed that more loans were likely to flow to a specific province when that province was headed by a party official with ties to the central leadership. Another way of increasing the flow of loans is to generate more revenues for the central government (Shih, 2004). For many local governments a tight grip on bank lending decisions can help the development of the local economy by securing financing for infrastructure projects and real estate development (local governments have a monopoly on land, and therefore on land prices and land transfers; The Economist, 2006; Box 8).

In addition, the reforms of the state banking sectors are a means of realising the state's assets rather than a true privatisation. The restructurings never changed the balance of power at the banks; rather they enabled the Party to strengthen its leadership and to broaden its power based on written rules (corporate governance rules and laws for example). The first step to a consolidation of power on the part of the Party and the central authorities came in the banking sector with the first reforms after the Asian Financial Crisis in 1998. At this time Zhu Rongji took the opportunity to put the whole banking system under two leading groups (McGregor 2010, Heilmann 2005b and 2008).

In order to achieve the highest gains on its assets, the Party has required bank executives to run the companies and banks it ultimately owns in a commercial and market-oriented way. The structures ensure in the end that the revenues thereby generated flow to the Party itself. It is therefore unlikely to relinquish any of its current powers.

In some cases, the state appears to use bank lending to compensate for lower levels of government spending and government-financed projects. Thus local authorities needed to exert more influence on the lending decisions and processes – that is, essentially, to politicise lending (Heilmann, 2005a). At the same time this weakens the power and pressure that regulators can place on local financial institutions. While corporate governance mechanisms have limited the influence channels of party and local governments, these have not been removed completely (Heilmann, 2005a).

Part of the stimulus of 2008 was orchestrated through banks. Some executives have underlined the fact that the lending binge in 2009 was based on market pressures rather than on authorities' iron hands (Asia Pulse, 2009b). There is, however, little credibility to such claims.

4.3 The employer

The Chinese state also has personnel interests in the banks. '[...] the most significant feature of the Chinese banking system was the pervasive influence of the Chinese communist party, which induced a high sensitivity among bankers to political signals from the top' (Shih, 2009: 31). Party members answer to the Party first. In the case of state-owned banks, as the majority or sole shareholder, the authorities have the right to choose senior managers. The Party permeates every level of the state – but it remains on the sidelines – without being a simple watcher: it has the strings in its hands. For example, all senior managers and board members of the four SOCBs are appointed by the Communist Party[1] and the regulator (CBRC and PBOC). This ensures the alignment of interests between the Party or the state and the individual banks.

Foreign observers should not be misled by the fact that personnel changes are announced by relevant ministries or regulators or by the fact that no official and publicly available bank documents mention the Party. Banks are instruments of national economic policy and will have to act along the Party lines where necessary (the rules and regulations are nonetheless issued by the relevant ministries and departments). The same applies to senior appointments. To ensure social stability and successful macroeconomic policies, the Party – through the bank's individual Party Committees – is in charge of personnel and strategic issues.

This is in line with the government's policy of choosing senior managers and board members reflecting political credentials rather than business acumen.[2] This activity is euphemistically called 'leadership' rather than 'interference' (McGregor, 2010: 23). The authorities also have the power to remove or transfer the managers as it sees fit, in *all* banks in China: some 80% of CEOs and 56% of senior executives in SOEs are appointed by the party (Pei M., 2006b).

Such policies are now centralised at highest level, reducing the influence of local and regional offices and authorities (Heilmann, 2005a) by establishing the since then defunct Central Finance Work Commission.[3] This enabled the management of the banks with higher efficiency and more consistency (through higher party discipline, less loopholes allowing rent-seeking, and so on).

Under such conditions, managers are given the incentive to reach a higher position in their (political) career rather than profit maximisation (Goodhart and Zeng, 2005). In Victor Shih's interviews, he found that 'the single clearest message that emerges [...] is that, above all else, Chinese leaders care about political survival and actively formulate strategies to expand or maintain power' (Shih, 2009: 16). The high level of decentralised management in Chinese banks makes it even easier for these authorities to intervene efficiently at the branch level. Since 1993 the influence of local authorities over the choice of bank managers has been forbidden, but unofficially influence channels remain lively (Grimm, 2005).

The supervision of the bank managers after their appointment is twofold: political acumen or party discipline is the responsibility of the Central Discipline Inspection Commission (CDIC) which deals with issues such as corruption, compliance with party policies, and so on. The second one is based on professional standards encompassing compliance with lending ratios and quotas as well as quality indicators (McGregor, 2009). Bank performance is linked to compliance with regulatory prudential ratios and market shares (Wen X., Zhang M. and Fang H., 2009). These are only tested by PBOC and/or CBRC (Shih, 2009).

Finally, the influence of the Communist Party at the local level should not be underestimated. Formally, it operates at the local level through 'financial services offices' which are set up to provide administrative services to financial institutions (such as encouraging their establishment in certain geographic areas). Its work in local-level financial supervision can be influential (Heilmann, 2005a) and is often orchestrated through local governments' finance bureaux and diverse work commissions. However, since 1998, local governments have lost their influence in appointing bank managers at their administrative level (for nationwide banks but not for local banks). The approval of appointments has been centralised in the headquarters thus making interference more difficult.

In financial institutions, party committees do influence the appointment and removal of senior bank managers and branch directors in local banks by proposing managers and reviewing preliminary applications (which are then submitted to CBRC for final approval).[4] Party committees can also influence strategic lending decisions if necessary. These committees have the same role at regulators: at PBOC a recent innovative move entails open and competitive applications[5] within the organisation for all posts above a certain hierarchical level (Hu J., 2010). This does not preclude, however, investigations of the candidates to reveal their political acumen. Candidates also need to sit exams and go through interviews. This is in contrast to the previous scheme of being proposed by their senior manager to the vice-president whose office then take the decision. Such experimentation will be extended and broaden where successful.

Throughout the history of the banking system, the loyalty of state staff is to the Party and not to the specific institution or entity to which they belong.[6]

5
State Interference

5.1 Pervasiveness of the state

As shown above, the state permeates every area of the financial system:

- As the regulator: all regulators with a say in the financial sector – CBRC, CSRC, CIRC, PBOC, MOF, SAFE, NDRC – are under the leadership of the State Council.
- As the provider of emergency funds to rescue any beleaguered financial company. The PBOC, Central Huijin Investment Co., the securities, the futures and the insurance protection funds are de facto lenders of last resort. Even in times of crisis, the availability of financial resources does not appear to present a challenge, with huge foreign exchange reserves ensuring a buffered supply.
- As the provider of indirect and implicit guarantees to all larger SOEs and commercial banks. This ensures that funds can flow easily between the two groups, often without any regard to accountability or risk.
- As the dominant shareholder in banks, securities companies, fund management companies, insurers and most of the companies listed on domestic stock markets. Control is direct and indirect (through local governments and SOEs).
- As an employer: the powerful Organisation Department chooses and proposes candidates deemed acceptable for all senior posts, these are then approved and nominated by the relevant regulatory commission. The choice of a candidate is more than likely to reflect his own political acumen rather than any professional qualifications or relevant experience. Further to this, the rotation habit within the industry reduces the effectiveness of monitoring. Experience has shown that private entities are no exception to this.

The regulator, the shareholder, the financier, the businessman, the guarantor and the employer are not independent from one another; they are all part of the same entity: the party-cum-state. The interference of the state or the party is pervasive and permeates all decision areas, all economic sectors and all institutional levels. At least the state lends to these institutions its good international credit ratings. It also ensures support to an investment-led GDP growth.

The state or even the party is not one but many: the state includes the central government, a wide range of local governments, regulatory agencies, ministries and other administrative units. These often have conflicting and contradictory views or compete for power and prestige.

All entities fear a loss of power and control over the activities in the financial industry, over the allocation of funds and resources, over decisions and over ownership. This high number of actors in the financial industry can have a strong influence on decisions and on compromising arrangements, but also points to a strong potential for conflicts of interest.

Victor Shih has found a powerful explanation behind the seemingly shifts of power between the many entities within the state (Shih, 2009). He finds that power changes hands between two types of factions: the generalist faction running vertically from central to local governments and the technocratic faction which runs horizontally at central level.[1] The first sort of faction is mostly interested in the unhindered flow of financial resources to their own projects – mostly in their provinces. The second faction type is focused on the contrary on financial centralisation because their ability to solve financial challenges is the basis for promotion. The two types of factions succeed to one another around an equilibrium state that ensures that lending and inflation are sufficient without being too high to ensure the creation of financial resources of the state.[2]

To underline the pervasiveness of the state's two main factions, analogously to Shih, we can look at the movements between inflation and quarterly loan growth (Figure 5.1).

Not only does such a model explain recurrent episodes of low and high inflation as well as economic development but it also supports the idea that the banking reform agenda is fully in the hands of the political elite. The seemingly pro-market reforms introduced in China in the last 10–15 years are the result of the technocratic faction being successful at erecting mechanisms to mitigate the effects of the expansionary and decentralising stance of the generalist faction (for example through risk management ratios[3] (capital, lending, asset quality limits), through the centralisation of senior bank appointments, the timid introduction of

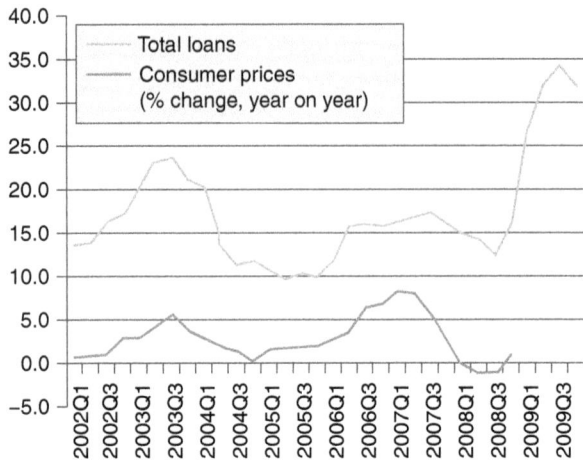

Figure 5.1 Loan growth and CPI in China (2002–2009, %)
Note: The data between lending and inflation are lagged to reflect the fact that loans first
have to feed into the lending system to produce inflation about four quarters later.
Source: Based on Economist Intelligence data.

private monitoring mechanisms – see below). The mitigating mechanisms
are not a kow-tow to private markets and players or reflections of an
intrinsic interest in pro-market reforms: they are much more instruments
of power to stabilise around the equilibrium state (between the two factions) and avoid too large deviations which would be costly to the state.

Recent success with large-scale IPOs have allowed the state to collect the
fruits, that is, capital which does not need to be repaid together with dividends. Partial listings are the rage – just as joint-ventures were the answer
to the early years of reform and opening policy – because on one side they
provide much needed technical knowledge and capital (and additional
layers of independent oversight) without using state resources (even creating additional revenues from investments) and on the other side few
strings are attached and neither power nor influence are relinquished.

McKinsey Global Institute analysts estimate that foregone GDP growth
at 13% a year by reforms that could have been handled better by the
higher efficiency of the finance industry (MGI, 2006). This might appear
like a hefty price. But the risks with speedier growth would have been
higher and the technocratic faction would not have allowed it to go
that far. Instead the two factions settled for a compromise: a slightly
lower rate of growth but more stability which do not put the financial
resources unnecessarily at risk.

To ensure keeping the status quo, reforms need to focus on truly reliable control mechanisms and structures – private ownership and market forces would unfortunately mean a loss of power for the ruling elites. Thus, Zhou Xiaochuan argued in an article in the *People's Daily* in 2000 that 'to preserve sufficient state control and defence capacity against external shocks during a period of economic system transformation and of further opening to the outside world, the state can preserve an absolute right of control over some large commercial banks, for example 75%' (republished in Zhou 2005).

History in Taiwan and in China has shown that, with clear objectives, professional bureaucrats who can differentiate between administration and business and are monitored externally, and are given the right financial and social incentives can foster independent and specialised institutions that achieve set performance standards (Peng, 2007). But can the equilibrium between the two factions be changed to enforce an arm's-length relationship with financial institutions at all administrative levels based on a mix of carefully staged legal rules and administrative mechanisms?

5.2 Rationale for state interference

Chinese regulators follow a very hands-on approach to regulation as they represent extensions of the state. Their role is to ensure that fruits of the banking system do indeed flow to the state itself (being in the form of state-owned enterprises with lower costs of funding or state coffers refilled with dividends and taxes paid by the financial institutions).

Nevertheless, the basis for regulatory intervention follows the same pattern as Mandanis, Schooner and Taylor (2009) assert: intervention is the result of three market failures namely existence of monopoly power (banks as a group form a strong monopoly in finance intermediation with enterprises and individuals), the existence of negative externalities (failure is then fully covered by the state) and to reduce information asymmetries (regulators concentrate a high level of information and of data from banks, either reported or inspected – the regulators play that role for the state).

The regulators interact between state and banks and not as usually between bank customers and banks themselves. The objectives of financial supervision are still to promote systemic stability, efficiency and competition, to ensure market confidence and protect depositors. These goals are points on the overarching goal of keeping the political elite in power – by allowing it to reign in a stable and predictable environment and by providing it the necessary financial resources for further development.

Interestingly, public perceptions and credibility of regulators are not an issue here. This is mainly due to the fact that most issues of regulation are not put up for discussion in the public at large. Issues are discussed at best behind closed doors and with those directly involved. The public has fully delegated the discussion and the decision-taking to regulators.

5.3   Private monitoring functions

In a seminal book, Barth, Caprio and Levine (2006) study what affects bank regulation and how banking regulation works. Their findings show that strong regulators and capital adequacy standards 'do not boost bank development, improve bank efficiency, reduce corruption in lending, or lower banking system fragility' (p. 12). They conclude that the sole working mechanism is a private monitoring[4] of banks – thus supporting the case for the Basel II third pillar on information disclosure and transparency. In addition to the aforementioned two aspects, the rights of private investors and creditors also ensure strong banks.

From Table 5.1, it is clear that the regulators in China retain a restrictive stance over the banking sector and that they are powerful. Their handling of licences for new institutions, new branches and new lines of business is highly restrictive and works on a case-by-case basis. For foreign institutions, acquisitions and capital participation in Chinese entities is limited to 20% control. Supervisory action is fully controlled by the CBRC. If not, it is done so by the PBOC. Involvement of the judicial or legislative powers is highly unlikely or even impossible. Meanwhile, regulators lack independence and there is no explicit deposit insurance mechanism as mentioned above (thus the values of the indicators in the above table might give a misleading impression because it does not account for an implicit and credible mechanism).

The most interesting factors here are the private monitoring variable and the external governance variable. The first describes whether certified auditing is required, whether the largest ten banks are rated nationally and internationally, and which accounting standards are in use. The second indicator relates to the quality of external auditing, the transparency of financial information as well as accounting practices and use of credit ratings. While both cover similar issues, it is striking how strong external governance and private monitoring are – bearing in mind such a pervasive state.

Reconciling the two above remarks is the fact that officials and regulators act in the interests of the state and not of the public. They are

Table 5.1 Summary of banking regulation indicators according to Barth, Caprio & Levine

	Indicators	Actual (2008)	Max. achievable points	Comment	Lower Middle Income Avg. (2003)	East Asia Pacific Avg. (2003)
1	Bank activity regulatory variable	11	12	highly restrictive	7.6	7.5
2	Financial conglomerate variable	9	12	highly restrictive	7.1	7
3	Competition regulatory variable					
	Limitations on bank ownership	2	3	low stringency	2.7	2.8
	Entry into banking requirements	7	7	high stringency	7.6	7.5
	Fraction of entry applications denied	unknown	–	–	38.2	37.4
4	Capital regulatory variable	5	10	mildly stringent	6.1	5.8
5	Official supervisory action variable					
	Official supervisory power	9	16	high power	10.4	11.3
	Prompt corrective power	2	6	low power	2.9	2.1
	Restructuring power	3	3	high power	2.6	2.4
	Declaring insolvency power	2	2	high power	1.5	1.4
	Supervisory forbearance discretion	2	4	middle power	1.1	1.6
	Court involvement	0	3	high discretion	1.6	1.6
	Provisioning stringency	175			165.5	170
	Diversification index	1	2	Low diversification required	1.1	1.3

(Continued)

Table 5.1 Continued

Indicators		Actual (2008)	Max. achievable points	Comment	Lower Middle Income Avg. (2003)	East Asia Pacific Avg. (2003)
6 Official supervisory structural variable	Supervisory tenure	No limit	2		7.5	6.4
	Independence of supervisory authority	0	3	poor independence	1.6	1.5
7 Private monitoring variable	(certified auditing, international ratings available, no explicit deposit insurance, international accounting standards)	9	9	high private monitoring	7.3	8.7
8 Deposit insurance scheme	Deposit insurer power	0	4	No explicit mechanism	1	1.2
	Deposit insured funds	0%	100%		37.9	87
	Factors mitigating moral hazard	0	3		1.2	0.5
9 External governance variable	Strength of external audit	5	7	High power of audit	5.6	5.8
	Financial statement transparency	5	6	high transparency	4.5	5.1
	Accounting practices	1	1	good practices	0.8	0.9
	External ratings and creditors monitoring	2	5	poor monitoring	1.6	2.1
	External governance index	13	19		12.4	14.1

Source: Author's own research, framework based on Barth, Caprio and Levine (2006). Details can be found in the annex.

all supposed to work to ensure that the state keeps sufficient capacity of action and power. As a result there is an independent private sector oversight (see Box 1) to ensure information transparency – but which serves the interests the state in the end.

Furthermore, the regulators still exercise control over the provision of information and the transparency of the institutions they are supposed to control with the goal of reducing risks to the state (risk of its power being withdrawn). Market discipline or information transparency is advocated but not to fulfil the interests of private investors or of the public at large, but the internal stakeholders and the state in the end. The dissemination of information is promoted within the state and its structures and 'accidentally' to the outside.

At the same time this provides the argument for a strong regulator (in front of the banks but not the executive). To ensure the right flows of information and of financial resources and that these do not reach outside the framework, it is required that banks remain sheltered from too much competition or outside interests. A small dose of competition and outside influences is sufficient to provide a counter-balance to the potentially damaging misallocation or even dilapidation of resources (either through bad lending decisions or through corruption).

The goal of social stability is a peripheral goal which is 'accidentally' fulfilled when the state remains in power and does so in a stable and expected manner. The same can be said of the prevention of crises. A crisis would almost certainly lead to social instability and put a question mark over the state's capacity – thus the state also has an interest in not spending on a crisis resolution but rather take pre-emptive measures through regulation. Failure of the banking system is defined as the loss of power over allocation of financial resources. Thus all regulatory actions and decisions tend to guarantee the continuity of the present arrangement.

The private market and private players have only an instrumented role to play and are intended to delegate their oversight duties to the state. The state remains powerful in that it delegates its own oversight only one step below: to the regulatory agencies and which remain fully dependent of it.

5.4 State interest view

Compared to the opposing views or approaches to bank regulation (Barth, Caprio and Levine, 2006), China follows a 'state interest view', being neither public nor private – but rather using a closed circuit of state interests where public and private constituencies are satisfied as a by-product (for the public – the state interests also mean that economic development should be boosted and that consumers should be protected) and by chance (for the private investors: they may take their gains and dividends home but remain in distinctively disadvantaged position in terms of influence and information channels). The state interest view fully excludes any interested potential entrant (being a private enterprise and borrower or a private investor) – and might only be accepted if it brings in further financial gains (interest paid by private borrowers in lending) or further improves the allocation of resources (technical assistance of private investors – meant to be strategic ones only and not financial ones).

In all fairness one must also acknowledge that the state recoups the gains but also – where they might exist – the losses of bank failures. The recapitalisation of the banking system was based on the foreign exchange reserves accumulated previously (capital was provided by PBOC through SAFE to the main banks, but the PBOC – as well as the local governments – also provided financial support to the rural cooperatives in need – mostly without requiring further budget deficits nor higher taxes on the public).

Because influence from the outside is largely impossible, the incentives for managers to do good in the interests of the state are only given by the penalty of being taken out of the framework – that is often not a powerful incentive because such a penalty is rarely used (only in strong corruption cases). In all other cases, the person to be punished might just been rotated to another institution or position. At the same time the stability of the system means that too high risk taking is not necessary either.

Maximising returns to the state is not an end in itself, rather ensuring stable and continuous flow of financial resources to ensure a perpetual power base is required. Corruption is acceptable up to a certain point – as long as the survival of the state is not endangered. From lending to state borrowers and a small public base, the banks can reap privileges in terms of continuity of their franchise and of their existence, by being rewarded for supporting the survival of the state. Not doing so would put bank gains at risk of not being earned (lending to SOEs is less risky than to private enterprises from which repayment might not be easily guaranteed). Taking too many risks in banking is thus not advisable – especially in view of the sizeable potential benefits. At the same time, regulation will not impede the development of the banks to generate profits (for example PBOC keeps a deposit and a lending rate – sufficiently one apart from the other so as to ensure a sound margin for banking business).

If we now return to a consideration of Figure 2.0 at the beginning of this part, in China we observe the same agency problems at each level of the graph – as in other countries. Each level has less information than the level below it which it wishes to control. The solution offered by the structure of China's banking system is that the permeation of the state at all levels reduces the incidence of information asymmetries to itself. Borrowers' managers and lending officers,[5] bank managers and regulators, regulatory officials and government officials, all emerge from the same apparatus and are chosen using analogous methods – this ensures that all are entrusted with the overarching goals of the state: maintaining stability and creating the necessary (financial) resources. Within that network, the information can flow freely and in case it does not, replacement of the key players or of the dilapidated resources is provided for.

The resolution of the information issue, however, does not preclude competition horizontally and vertically between layers and officials/managers. Competition exists because they follow their own particular interest (individually or at the level of the individual institution) in addition to being loyal to the Party. Such arrangement also allows for widespread corruption to take roots.

5.5 Does the current regulatory arrangement lead to more risk-taking?

A central question in the study of bank regulation is to understand what leads to higher risk taking. Assuming that higher risk taking always may have the downside of a higher probability of default by the bank (and thus being rescued by taxpayers' money), higher risk taking should be restrained – but by more or less regulations?

Chinese banks are operating in a sheltered market. With their poor incentives, they should take more risks to increase profits. But that is not the final goal. In China, banks' managers are driven not by the takeover threat but by the need to ensure a smooth career path. Excessive risk taking is not incentivised because managers of banks are being rotated from one position to another. They risk their own career rather than their bank's financial standing. That is the incentive for taking some risks and maybe even some bribes – but in a limited manner so as not destabilise the whole framework and the individual future prospects. Such risk aversion does not preclude some lobbying, however. Where rules appear too strict, banks do not refrain from lobbying in order to achieve more lenient regulations (as for example for the recognition of cross-holdings of subordinated debts into the capital adequacy calculation; Fang H., 2009).

However one question remains: why did a bank manager obviously take more risks before the 1998 crisis than after and also after the banks' restructuring exercises? It appears that the indicators used to judge on the managers' performance have changed. Before their performance was solely based on political adherence to the party line, but that requirement was enhanced by further financial indicators and compliance to issued regulations.

In conclusion we find that – while in other countries more state has meant largely poorer efficiency in banking and higher instability of the banking system – this does not seem to be the case for China. In China, the state capture of the banks appears to be more of a blessing than a liability. Control by the state has changed its tools and channels but has increased its scope.

5.6 Balance between centre and periphery

All is not well in China either: the current arrangement is not risk-free. Increasingly, power is being transferred to local authorities that have more leeway in enforcing the rules set by the central government. This issue is important when the regulators require the cooperation of local authorities to achieve their goals.

With the growing power of local authorities, the capacity of the central government has been eroded. At the same time, the growing transfer of power towards the periphery has also meant that the establishment of a truly private and independent alternative has been brought to a complete halt. The private and independent arrangements that have been able to exist to date (for example, foreign shareholders, international rating agencies, external auditors) owe their very existence to the necessity of the state having reliable information about the banking industry it wishes to control.

The private monitoring and governance arrangements are also to the benefit of the local authorities. They can draw more information and thus more control from such mechanisms.

A transition from socialist banking to a market-oriented system has failed to become a revolution because the underlying structures continue to serve the same purposes: that is solely the interests of the state. This was termed a 'trapped transition' by Minxin Pei (2006b). The banking system is geared towards producing better returns to the state. There is no incentive for further banking reforms other than those that ensure the current status quo can endure.

For the time being, the current mechanisms offer what the state requires, but it remains to be seen if in the long term such arrangement is still viable and still fulfils its purpose. As long as the state is not only a predatory one but also offers on balance growth and development (or even a safety net in times of crisis), it is likely that the status quo will not be challenged.

Thus the greatest danger to the status quo and to the system's stability is the state itself but only because it is losing effective control over competing levels of authority (centre versus periphery or local). The central government must manage the diverging interests of local authorities and ensure that these constituencies play a neutral role at least. Up to now the private and independent monitoring arrangements have been established at national level only. There is little control over the activities of local financial sectors.

Can the central authorities credibly convince the other layers of the state that only a limited independence and competition between them is feasible if all are to enjoy in the long term the fruits of the economic development as well as their achieved political power?

Box 1 The role of peripheral private and independent arrangements: foreign investors

Since 1991, when the Asian Development Bank acquired a stake in the Xiamen International Bank, foreign banks have started to buy stakes in the capital of Chinese banks. Most of the deals took place between 2004 and 2006, after CBRC raised the ceiling on individual stakes to 20% and overall on foreign stakes to 25% in the capital of any type of Chinese bank (including RCCs) in December 2003.[1] Further to this, in January 2006, CBRC announced that foreign investors can invest in 'up-to-now off-limits' A-shares.[2] Overall, individual foreign institutions' stakes range from 2 to 20%. As of end 2008, foreign investors had taken equity stakes in 31 Chinese banks (approved) and their equity participations amounted to some USD32.7 bln (a further USD45.5 bln were raised through market listings, Table B.1).

The interest in Chinese banks – depending upon the foreign investor – included all types of institutions, from the large commercial banks to the rural financial institutions but also with local entities – which were purportedly easier to handle (see tables in chapters on the respective bank types). Getting a share of the growing Chinese market is an understandable goal for the foreign investor and the domestic bank get fresh capital as well as better corporate governance, new technology and more exposure to international practices and funding.

Table B.1 Foreign investors in China (USD bln)

Year	Prior to 2006	2006	2007	2008	2009
Number of investors allowed	18	6	5	6	0
Amount invested	14.3	5.22	1.76	11.52	0.21
Amount raised in stock markets	11.39	29.90	4.22	0	3.93

Source: CBRC Annual report 2009.

Chinese observers were not uncritical of such entry, however (Yuan J., 2005, and Yu Y. and Luo D., 2005a and 2005b). In response to such critics and concerns over the usefulness of foreign practices, the adequacy of prices paid for 'Chinese jewels' and the stability of the financial system, regulators promptly clarified their stance over foreign entry.

CBRC's leaders gave five guiding principles for judging foreign investors:

- they should not get controlling stakes in large banks;
- negotiations should follow market principles;
- foreign investors should bring in strong management experience and technical skills;
- the investing institution should be a large financial institution; and
- the adequacy of the foreign investor should be tested in a strict review.

Further to these principles, minimum standards have been announced: investments should be for more than three years and for more than 5% stakes, the investing institution should bring forward a director to sit on the board; the institution should not have more than two strategic investments in Chinese banks and the foreign investors should bring technical and network support (*People's Net – Jiangnan Times*, 2005; Yu F., 2005).

According to the new licensing rules published in early 2006, foreign investors in Chinese financial institutions should have a long-term orientation, have a large asset base (at least USD10 bln for investing in a commercial bank, less in the case of rural institutions), have a good international credit rating, have been profitable in the past two consecutive years, show sound internal controls and enjoy a favourable (economic and supervisory) environment at home (References for laws 19).

Prior to its listing, ABC's chairman showed a self-confident stance that the search for foreign investors could be dropped (later on some benevolent foreign investors were taken on board nonetheless – albeit not as strategic but only as cornerstone investors[3]). Foreign investors' appeal was to communicate confidence and promote the standing of the institution.

Foreign banks are expected to bring capital and expertise, but not control. Control will remain in the hands of the state, for both smaller and larger banks. The state regularly reiterates its unwillingness to relinquish full control. Such assertions have been heard from central bankers, bank regulators and other high-ranking government officials. Most of the foreign influence is likely to be felt in the area of corporate governance – and to serve the interests of the state.

A further arrangement with foreign investors came in the case of Shenzhen Development Bank. In order to clean the bank's books, foreign investors were accepted to take a strong share of the business (the capital share was less than 20%, but the board director and staffing was partially in the hands of the investor). A few years later, the trick proved to be a success. The bank is clean and was sold at a great profit for the foreign investor as well. The local authorities did not need to pay too much for that.

Earlier foreign banks were signing partnerships to market their mutual funds through Chinese banks, because these possess strong networks that can help to achieve critical mass. But later Chinese banks were being allowed to create and promote their own mutual funds, and are making full use of this opportunity. Thus they have learned from the foreigners, and learned it so well that they can do by themselves, without any foreign help (EIU, 2006a).

The introduction of foreign investors and the opening up of the banking sector to competition will have little impact on the position of the Chinese state. Pei Minxin (2006a) writes that '[p]artial reforms have thus created a hybrid, albeit state-centred, system that allows these elites to perpetuate its privileges'. For him, even foreign entry into banks' equity is only a way for the state to strengthen itself. As two China observers mentioned,

> China's communist cadres have discovered that equity capital, like state banks' loans in the old days of central planning, does not have to be repaid. And while investors' funds do come with some strings attached, including international-standard accounts and disclosure requirements, this is a small price to pay considering how little control the state has had to relinquish in the process. (Mitchell T. and Lau J., 2006)

With their limited influence (at most a combined 25% of the banks' capital) over decisions in Chinese banks, foreign investors might as well settle for taking their dividends home (Table B.2) without much reforms (or only those reforms necessary to ensure steady investment gains) – without embarking on a full marketisation of the banking system, which is not in the interest of the state.

Table B.2 Gains of foreign shareholders (bln)

	ICBC		CCB		BOC	
	Date	USD	Date	USD	Date	USD
Capital injected by foreign shareholders	Apr-06	3.8	Aug-05	3	Jun-05	3.6
Capital injected by state	Apr-05	15	Jan-04	22.5	Jan-04	22.5
Share price at IPO	27/10/2006	3.14**	01/06/2006	2.82**	27/10/2005	2.18**
Share price at time where restriction are lifted*	20/10/2009	6.15**	27/10/2008	2.51**	31/12/2008	1.89**
Net gains per share (end-2008), when restrictions where lifted						
Number of shares						
– foreign investors		24.1		44.7		35.3
– state		236		133.4		179.7
Foreign shareholders' gains		4.93		1.99		1.10
State's gains		5.66		1.20		0.92

Notes: *Based on first trading day's adjusted closing (adjusted for dividends and splits), ** in HKD. Assuming that the number of shares held did not change over time and a constant exchange rate between USD and HKD of 7.75.
Source: Daily quotes from Yahoo Finance on 16 May 2010, Capital injections data from news sources.

Their impact on the banks' financials remains unclear. Some recent studies (Garcia-Herrero, 2008; Shen, C., Lu, C., Wu, M. 2009) appear to suggest that efficiency improves slightly – but the difference is insignificant. Level of NPLs or efficiency and returns are, however, poor indicators over the short time period of observations – especially in view of the positive economic environment. Assuming that the impact could be positive but rather limited appears realistic nonetheless – the quality of the partnerships rather than the percentage share of capital allowed might become the focus of regulators.

Conclusion of Part II

The case of China is interesting in many ways. It contrasts with previous views of regulatory arrangements. It does not confirm that political elites are solely interested in plundering riches from the institutions under their control. Instead the political authorities are also interested in their long-term survival as a group which is dependent on the unhindered flow of financial resources. Because the authorities have been fragmented through the reform process, the state has to rely on further mechanisms to ensure that it knows what banks are doing. This is ensured through higher transparency and powerful regulators. This is this combination which is unusual that ensures stability.

Furthermore in order to compensate for the generous implicit deposit insurance mechanism, supervisory power is high to ensure a timely prevention of deviations, the state also remains fully in control of the allocation of human resources (which provide an incentive solely for moderate risk taking) and finally private monitoring by auditors, rating agencies and foreign shareholders also limits negative spillovers. China is characterised by the concurrent strength of supervisory and private mechanisms at the same time. The political function through the regulators has established a restricted private monitoring and governance mechanism. This has the function to limit adverse consequences from the greater power enjoyed by regulators (for example higher incidence of corruption, reduced efficiency of financial intermediation, reduced banking system fragility).

While such an arrangement does not preclude corruption nor eliminate the rent-seeking behaviour of elites nor does it allocate – as we will see in the next part – more funds to the private sector (in that

China confirms the results of correlations analysed by Barth, Levine and Caprio (2006: page 189)), it does, however, sufficiently limit such negative effects on the overall development prospects and long-term survival. Thus the regulators are concerned with market imperfections and political failures only to the extent that they would put an end to the state as it is now.

Part III
Demand

Over the years, the Chinese miracle has continued to puzzle observers and researchers alike. How can such a flawed system, which does a poor job of financial intermediation, still support such rapid economic growth over the past 30 years?

It appears that it is actually because the state has such a pervasive role in the finance sector that economic growth could be supported. McGregor (2010: 169) writes, 'the decentralised nature of the Party and government system has been fundamental to the Chinese economic miracle'. In his view, the competition for business and economic growth between localities and regions is what explains China's economic dynamism. Each local government acts as its own boss, drawing its own guidelines or rules,[1] owning and directing its own banks, and so on. This leads to a distortion in the provision of financial services because funds are mainly directed at those deemed worthy of finance by the authorities.

6
Financial Intermediation

6.1 Definition and measurement

For an economy to grow, it is important that the allocation of funds is efficient and that financial intermediation runs deep (Cull and Xu, 2000). Poor financial intermediation can be the result of information asymmetries, loans rationing, the mispricing of transactions, poor monitoring of behaviour, a lack of monitoring and enforcement mechanisms for contracts, and so on. All other things being equal, banks (Table 6.1) should be in a better position to allocate funds than, for example, bureaucrats because of their expertise in the analysis and management of risks.

In order to secure successful and efficient financial intermediation, the administrative steering and control of financial flows should be either reduced to a minimum or scrapped completely.[1] Furthermore, a functioning resources allocation requires high levels of transparency and information disclosure so that market participants can be informed in a timely and thorough manner (Grimm, 2005). This information disclosure acts as a market discipline if stakeholders have the means to impose some kind of sanctions for the transmission of incorrect or misleading information.

The depth of financial intermediation in a country is generally measured as the percentage of total loans compared to GDP (Table 1.3). Higher GDP per capita and higher economic growth are both positively correlated with a deeper financial intermediation. The figures do not, however, indicate anything about the quality of the financial intermediation. Since the available resources should be allocated to the most efficient and productive uses, that sector of the economy that is most competitive and is growing most rapidly should also receive a commensurate part of the

Table 6.1 Local currency loans and deposits in China (year-end, CNY billion)

	2000	2002	2004	2005	2007	2008	2009
Total loans	9,937	13,129	17,736	19,469	26,169	30,339	42,562
Total deposits	12,38	17,092	24,053	28,717	38,937	46,620	61,201
Loan to deposit ratio (%)	80.3	76.8	73.7	67.8	67.2	65.1	69.5

Source: Based on data from www.pbc.gov.cn.

Table 6.2 Loans by economic sector and their share of GDP (%)

	2000		2005		2008	
	to GDP*	to loan portfolio**	to GDP	to loan portfolio	to GDP	to loan portfolio
Loans to agriculture	15.1	7.4	12.2	13.2	11.3	14.1
Loans to construction	5.6	2.5	5.5	3.4	5.7	2.9
Loans to industry	40.4	25.9	42.2	25.7	42.9	28.9
Loans to commerce	39	27.2	40.1	18.8	40.1	14.2
Other loans		37.0		38.8		39.9

* is the percentage that this economic sector contributes to GDP. ** is the percentage of short-term loans lent by financial institutions to this particular economic sector.
Notes: The National Bureau of Statistics publishes the contribution to GDP for the primary, the secondary and the tertiary sector and for the construction industry. The 'other loans' category is as stated in the PBOC statistics.
Sources: Data from www.pbc.gov.cn and www.stats.gov.cn.

funds in the financial system and the quality of the funds lent out should also be profitable (Table 6.2).

Financial intermediation is not only a function undertaken by banks. Capital and money markets, as well as venture capital for example, can also allocate funds to productive uses. Financial intermediation can also take some informal traits when family, friends or other unregistered entities, for example, support an enterprise financially (either with debt or capital).

6.2   Financial intermediation and financial infrastructure

A number of researchers have found that there is a low level of financial intermediation in China. Genevieve Boyreau-Debray (2003: 18) finds an 'inverse relationship between the rate of financial intermediation and the level of economic development among Chinese provinces, suggesting that factors other than economic fundamentals play an important role in lending decisions'. When analysing financial flows within China, they also find that 'the state-dominated financial system severely retards the efficient allocation of capital'. To a large extent the importance of SOEs in one region also determines the volume of financial flows (from government or banks).

Park and Sehrt (2001) also analyse whether or not the allocation of financial flows in China relies on policy motives. The tests they carried out show that policy lending is also strong in economically more developed areas and was stronger even after the formal ending of credit quotas[2] (and after the first bank bailout; see Lu et al., 2005). They further find that in coastal provinces the rate of financial intermediation is actually negatively correlated to the rate of economic growth. The allocation of financial resources reflects SOEs' financing needs: large financial flows are directed towards SOEs in the reform process (Cull and Xu, 2000; Zhang L., 2005). A more recent micro-level study also confirms these findings: the bias towards SOEs is still clearly evident, but can be reduced when foreign capital is admitted (Poncet, 2009).

Political affiliation also has a role to play: according to Du and Girma (2007), firms have a higher chance of surviving and growing if they have the right political connections (even though they might not be the most productive) at local or central level – whichever is required. This is even more pronounced in the case of firms in capital-intensive industries.

Financial intermediation is also biased against rural areas (Brandt et al., 2005b). This is even true for rural financial institutions. The reason for such discrimination is first that rural financial flows are static (each branch or cooperative has to rely on its own deposits for lending) and second that interest rates are capped (this remained in force in rural areas in 2004). This impedes the adequate remuneration of risk-taking activities and curbs the level of lending. Additionally, the older rural financial institutions tend to deposit their customers' funds with the central bank. In turn these funds help sustain high economic growth in urban areas where most banking activities take place (Chen X., 2009).

On the other side of the financial intermediation spectrum, deposits are widely available (Figure 6.1). Banks are highly liquid and gathering deposits is an easy task: due to cultural factors (such as the preference for low-risk investment products with stable, predictable and in some way guaranteed returns), the lack of social safety nets (for unemployment, illness, pension, accidents, and so on), the lack of alternative investment channels (lacklustre state of the stock markets, under-developed wealth

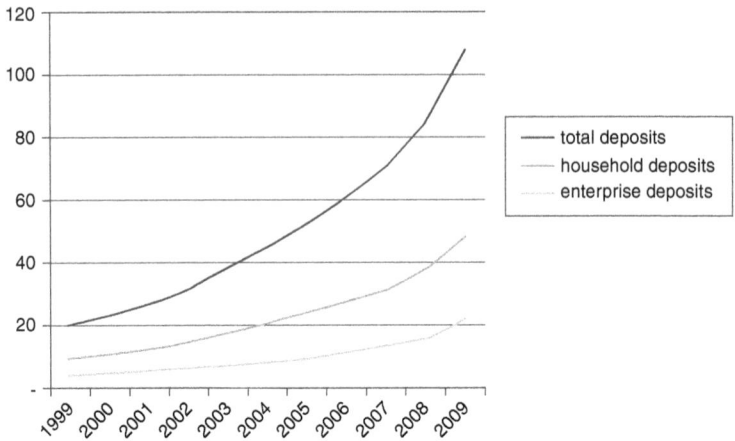

Figure 6.1   Deposits (CNY trn)
Source: Based on data from www.pbc.gov.cn.

management, highly volatile real estate markets, lack of corporate bond market, and so on), an implicit guarantee of banks' deposits and large banking networks spanning the country. In addition, until recently fixed interest rates were standard (meaning that shopping around for the best rates was a futile exercise) and Chinese have a high propensity to save (Chen X., 2005).

6.3   Enterprises financing

Chinese financial markets exhibit some peculiar features: enterprises cannot turn to debt or capital markets because of their limited capacity and development (EIU, 2010a; Box 2). For many enterprises and individuals, self-reliance or support from other financing channels (for example, inter-company lending, informal lending and authorities' support) have been the only means to participate and benefit from economic growth. Still the banking sector plays a central role and the economy grows at a high rate (Table 1.5).

The main borrowers of Chinese banks are SOEs, the private sector (mainly represented by smaller enterprises as well as collective enterprises) and private persons (Table 6.3).

State-owned enterprises

The SOEs are often large enterprises with structures inherited from before the adoption of the reform and opening policy. At the end of 2008, there

Table 6.3 Enterprises by ownership type, 2008

	Number of enterprises in industry, trade and construction		Loan volume by enterprise types at selected banks		
			CCB	Merchants	CITIC
State-owned enterprises	25,813	4.1%	47.7%	38.7%	35.0%
Joint-stock enterprises	106,075	16.7%	14.2%	12.5%	43.0%
Private enterprises	323,442	51.0%	19.1%	19.6%	7.0%
Foreign enterprises	84,897	13.4%	10.4%	17.5%	12.7%
Collective enterprises	31,088	4.9%	1.5%	0.0%	1.0%
Other enterprises	63,365	10.0%	7.2%	11.7%	1.2%
Total	634,680	100%	100%	100%	100%

Source: Based on data from www.stats.gov.cn and banks' annual report.

were more than 25,000 SOEs in China active in industry, trade and construction. After a policy of 'grab the big fish and let go small fish' (抓大放小), most SOEs of lesser importance have been privatised and reformed (Zhang L., 2005). The most important 161 companies are managed through the State-owned Assets Supervision and Administration Commission (SASAC).

In 2008, the more than 21,000 SOEs in the industry sector generated CNY14 trn in output and controlled assets amounting to CNY18.8 trn. According to the National Statistics Bureau, they produced combined profits of CNY906bln.

SOEs, both large and small, share a number of common challenges. They suffer from political interference (at both the local and the national level), have unclear lines of control (often controlled and managed by one or more ministries or administrative units), have poor creditworthiness and repayment incentives (no hard budget constraint and cannot go bankrupt), are burdened with policy and social goals (generate employment opportunities locally and shoulder social and tax payments) and lack professional management and functioning structures of corporate governance.[3] Thus the incentives to lead these enterprises in a commercial way are rather thin (Goodhart and Zeng, 2005) and the incentives for taking risks depend on the managers' interest in raising their personal career prospects.

Last but not least, large enterprises such as state-owned ones are attracted to bank loans because they are relatively cheap (MGI, 2006) and less cumbersome compared to debt markets. Banks are the preferred partners for financing not only because of pricing, but also because of the historical relationship that bonds them, because of the similar administrative structures that still exist and because of the shared interests on both sides.

Such conditions naturally influence negatively their lenders – traditionally, the SOCBs. While the riskiness of SOEs may be understood as low because of the high likelihood of being rescued, SOEs are partly responsible for the large volumes of NPLs in the SOCBs.[4] The SOEs remain a major liability of the financial sector (and not an asset).

Private and collective enterprises

According to a *Caijing* survey (Du J., Lu Y. and Tao Z., 2008), the non-state sector generates around 65% of China's GDP and accounts for 70–80% of its growth, but only 20% of formal bank loans find their way to this type of borrowers.[5]

Often, lending to private firms is seen as more risky because of their information opacity,[6] lack of collateral, and the absence of formal structures and good governance. Other factors also influence their access to loans: the operational and lending policies of banks (procedures often do not differentiate among borrowers, industries, and so on); the incentive mechanisms for bank managers (often based on stable interest income generation and the avoidance of bad loans); and the lack of widespread confidence in private enterprises (Zhang X., 2004a).

Private and collective enterprises lack collateral which would be required to enhance their creditworthiness in the eyes of Chinese banks. Collateral is often required in the form of land or buildings, the only type of collateral acceptable to many banks (OECD, 2005; Table 6.4). Some banks in the coastal areas use other forms of collateral on a trial basis, such as inventory and movable assets. These could develop in the future, as shown by PBOC projects.[7] With Chinese banks progressively relying more on cash flows for analysis and lending, the accessibility of credit for enterprises other than SOEs should become easier and enable the further penetration of local banks (OECD, 2005).

All other things being equal, collective enterprises such as TVEs fare slightly better. TVEs are established in villages or townships but their ownership form may be either private or collective.[8] These represent a strong inflow of financial resources for townships and villages which saw their revenues decrease as a result of fiscal reforms. The TVEs generate profits that can be transferred to the township. They make up 53% of the loan portfolio of RCCs (He G., Du X., Bai C. and Li Z., 2009).

The TVEs have a greater chance of getting a bank loan – at least with local financial institutions – because of the protection from local authorities. In the past enterprises in rural areas have often relied on their local

Table 6.4 Loan portfolios' collateralisation, 2008

	SOCBs average (%)	JSCBs average (%)
Unsecured loans	27.2	20.1
Loans with guarantees	21.2	31.9
Collateralised loans	38.0	35.6
Loans with pledges	13.6	12.4

Notes: Unweighted averages. JSCBs do not include Bohai Bank.
Source: Own calculations based on data from banks' annual reports.

governments to ensure sufficient funds. At the same time, these generated tax revenues and employment in their areas. However, they still suffer from the poor financial intermediation because most lending is directed towards urban areas. Banks implicitly analyse rural enterprises as being more risky and less worthy of loans. Apart from this bias, collateral is also an issue for TVEs. They lack the ability to provide collateral and require stronger support and guarantees from local authorities (Kwong and Lee, 2005).

Rural enterprises are characterised by Huang (2008) as entrepreneurial, market-oriented, and politically independent – for him these are the mainstay of healthy growth rather than their urban counterparts. Where rural enterprises found financial liberalisation, property rights security and some checks and balances on government bureaucrats, they have thrived – as in the 1980s.

Lending bias

The lending bias towards large SOEs is a continuing feature of the Chinese banking landscape, even though the banks have had time to promote reforms internally. There are a number of reasons for this.

First, the central authorities continue to dictate on an ad hoc basis which industries should be prioritised or discriminated against in lending (in the most recent example, the CBRC asked banks again not to lend to energy-consuming industries). Additionally, the five-year plans in recent years have highlighted in very concrete steps which industries should be prioritised: environmentally friendly industries, knowledge-based activities, enterprises controlling core technologies and resources, and so on (Naughton, 2007).

Second, despite often poor financials, the SOEs continue to enjoy strong support and backing can be expected in dire times – at both central and local levels. The banks fully know this and recovery can be expected to be easier – albeit not always faster. Local governments have a strong interest in keeping their pet enterprises afloat as they are pillars in the local economic development (in terms of tax revenues, job creation, and so on).

Third, once the financing needs of SOEs are met, the remaining funds can be used for other enterprises as well – thus a crowding-out effect exists (Poncet et al., 2009). SOEs further act as informal lenders by lending on some of the funds they received from banks.

Fourth, the financial health of most SOEs is bolstered by the fact that they continue to pay subsidised interest rates on their loans (Ferri and Liu, 2009). With lower costs, their profitability appears in a better light and they even are now required to pay dividends to their state shareholders (Mattlin, 2007).

Fifth, both the banks and the enterprises they finance are controlled by the state as their majority shareholder. Decision-making can be tilted towards required issues. State ownership also works when the ownership is only indirect.

Finally, the fiscal stimulus enacted in late 2008 is being implemented in large part by the banks. This led to an even more pronounced lending bias towards the SOEs. Many observers then wrote about '国进民退' – meaning that the government spreads its wings while the private sector retreats.

To ensure access to bank loans, private enterprises have to spend a considerable amount of their profits on a range of fees and entertainment. A survey of the investment climate in China published in 2006 shows that all enterprises have had to apportion part of their revenues to pay for entertainment fees (often a euphemism for payments to induce favours), as well as having to interact frequently with administration. However, the share of sales that is put forward for entertainment averages 1.0–1.5% for state-owned firms and 1.1–1.8% for small domestic firms depending on the firm's location (World Bank, 2006). The time spent with bureaucrats averages 58–89 days for SOEs and 30–45 days for small domestic firms – again depending on their location.

The financial intermediation function of Chinese banks is hampered by hidden information and hidden action (Longueville and Ngo, 2004). In fact, bank officers tend to build informal information networks to mitigate this risk, but the reliability of these is limited by the private interests of stakeholders in these networks (which may collude with those of bank officers). Other factors such as inappropriate incentives on both sides and limited risk pricing mechanisms in banks[9] also place a drag on the system.

The issue of hidden action is also a strong challenge in China. Credit monitoring and controls are under-developed at best and loan officers rarely check the use of loan proceeds or the progress of an investment project. In fact, they do not have any incentives to do so: there is little punishment for bad behaviour (such as loss of employment) and the bank will not be declared bankrupt when it accumulates losses. Where bank managers are responsible for their unit's profitability, discrimination against SMEs is much less likely to occur (Brandt and Li, 2003).

More stringent capital requirements have a potentially negative impact on the depth of financial intermediation: to comply with higher capital adequacy, one inexpensive way is to increase the portfolio of government bonds which carries a lower risk.

In the past few years, the Chinese authorities and regulatory bodies have stepped up their efforts to induce banks into lending to SMEs and private enterprises.[10] Since the SMEs and private enterprises are a large but loose constituency (without a strong cohesion or influence over the state apparatus), local and central government use supportive policies to ensure that those outside the state sector are also able to increase their revenues. Such actions function as a valve through which air can escape – or in that case enterprises can be reassured that their concerns are taken seriously. Government intervention does not target the resolution of market failures but rather uses a varied range of mechanisms to ensure control over an orderly financial system.

The more pervasive the interference and influence of the central authorities, the less liberalisation and free space will be available for private entrepreneurship to thrive and to find adequate funds for growth.

6.4   Informal financial intermediation

Because Chinese banks do a poor job of financial intermediation, enterprises and individuals turn to the informal financial sector.[11] This has grown in response to their financing needs.[12] Both, the formal and the informal financing tracks seem, however, to be necessary ingredients of China's economic success (Allen et al., 2005).

Informal lending has also developed because private funds have only a few good investment opportunities: lending informally can bring as much as 20% p.a. compared to the 1–2% in a bank's savings account.[13]

Informal lending in China takes various forms: loans from family and friends, pawnbrokers,[14] rotating savings and credit associations (ROSCAs) or hehui (合会) in their many different forms, money houses (钱庄), private equity or placement funds,[15] loans funds from SOEs, note discounting, land pawning and sharecropping, and so on (Tsai, 2001; Li and Hsu, 2009). Informal lending is especially lively in coastal areas and in Southern China. However, inner provinces as well as the North-East also see informal finance activities (Li and Hsu, 2007). It is not only the poorer strata of the population and smaller enterprises that benefit from informal arrangements – SOEs and wealthy individuals also make frequent use of informal finance. Not only do contract enforcement costs (for collateral and administrative requirements) raise the bar higher for those seeking appropriate financial products, but also interest rates ceilings continue to hamper the risk pricing and management capacity of commercial lenders.

Researchers have tried to estimate the scale of informal finance in China. The latest calculations are based on a large-scale survey in 2006 across almost all provinces and summarising the views of bank managers and entrepreneurs as well as government officials. The figures suggest that informal finance could account for around CNY1,505 bln (Li and Hsu, 2007: 57, 7) – that is around 8% of GDP. These figures appear large; however, prior surveys have also shown that informal finance is indeed very common – particularly in rural areas and for smaller enterprises. For instance, in rural areas, it could account for as much as 70% of all lending (Yao K., 2006) and 60–70% of SME financing comes from informal lenders in underdeveloped areas, compared with 30% in other areas (OECD, 2005). Informal lending can account for as much as 45–65% of all financing for large SOEs but 90% for small enterprises (Allen et al., 2004, 2005).

This hugely popular mechanism for financing needs remains a means of securing funds rapidly (four to six times more quickly as discovered by researchers in Nanjing and Shanghai; Li and Hsu, 2007) but a rather expensive one. Informal credit markets experience interest rates that can be much higher than those found in formal ones. A survey in Nanjing and Shanghai in 2006 found rates ranging from 8.4% by relatives to 15.3% by private lenders.

There can also be considerable variation in loan amounts: single loan amounts in Henan are at least CNY4 mln (Guo L., 2005) while another survey found that on average enterprises draw CNY10–30 mln (Niu M. et al., 2004). The purposes of such finance are becoming more diversified: from the original consumer orientation (including education, housing, individual farming) and the easing of short-term financial shortages (mainly for enterprises, both SMEs and TVEs) towards longer-termed productive operations (Niu M. et al., 2004). There is no reliable data for delinquency rates in informal lending, but these are assumed by most researchers to be quite low.

Informal lending has some important virtues in the Chinese banking market. Informal finance relies solely on creditworthiness, is flexible, convenient and produces easily understandable information (no need to understand procedures, requirements, and so on). Furthermore, informal lending makes a strong contribution to local economic development (Guo L., 2005) and gives information on realistic lending interest rates. Finally, it provides useful investment channels for idle funds and creates more impetus for reform in the formal lending system (Niu M. et al., 2004). But informal lending puts pressure on the sources of funding for formal banks, it represents foregone tax revenues for the authorities, the interest rates can be usurious, it breaches with official development policies (runs contrary to any controls that governments tend to set upon financial flows), and finally limits the regulatory role of the authorities (Girardin, 1997).

Local governments have long tried to curb or to forbid informal lending (Tsai, 2001); however, they have recently changed their attitude (Yu L., 2006) and have begun to monitor developments in informal lending (Balfour and Roberts, 2004; Li and Hsu, 2007). Having said that, attitudes still differ in regions and provinces and are also largely dictated by the liveliness of informal lending in that particular area and the attitude and support to private sector development of that particular local government (Tsai, 2001). Some authorities turn a blind eye as long as social disorder is avoided; others try to curb such activities when they compete head-on with local financial institutions which the authorities often own. Finally, other authorities tend to protect SOEs where these play a strong role in the local economy. Overall, there is no common or consistent pattern of treatment across China and the attitudes are determined not by central decisions and requirements, but rather by current local interests, historical developments under Mao (Li and Hsu, 2007) and authorities' understanding of how to apply central regulations.[16]

Still enterprises' growth cannot be explained solely in terms of the lively informal financing arrangements described above. Researchers using a World Bank sample from 2003 have found that private firms tend to grow more rapidly (with higher profits reinvestments and higher sales growth) when using bank finance (Ayyagari, Demirgüc-Kunt and Maksimovic, 2010) – which does not mean that banks are the secret behind China's growth. It seems banks can exert pressure (either on purpose or incidentally) on owners to spend their profits more on the enterprise the bank is financing than on other ventures that are worth investing in but which do not correspond to the loan purpose. Informal finance remains attractive – probably because of its flexibility and less narrow-minded supervision.

Box 2 Credit registry

In 1997 the PBOC established a centralised database for bank loans.[1] Within five years, the system covered almost the whole of urban China – but only in the case of corporate loans. Individual loans as well as trade credit were added at a later date. The nationwide credit registry finally became a reality in 2004 under the name of State Credit Bureau – under the aegis of the PBOC. The enterprise database and the registry for consumer lending were merged two years later.

As of December 2008, the database covered over 14 mln enterprises and 640 mln individuals. On any day, on average, the banks would make around 560,000 checks for individuals and 130,000 for enterprises.

The database includes information on the borrower (name, address, loan registration number, industry, some general financial data and pending law disputes), loan profile (amount, type of debt, currency, status of repayment based on the five loans classification, maturity) and on the collateral provided (guarantor details, mortgages, amount valued, as well as since recently account receivables used as collateral). A potential borrower will be required to present its loan registration card (provided by the PBOC) to the lending bank, which will then conduct an online check of the records of the borrower. When granting a loan, the bank will submit the necessary information about the transaction and the borrower to the PBOC. The information provided also covers payments to utilities companies (PBOC statistics show that as of June 2008 over nine million people were included).

In 2007, account-receivables information was added to the database for the first time, and by October 2008 there were around 30,000 accounts. The PBOC also increased its services to include information on SMEs and rural clients which had never before had a loan – in order to support information supply to banks. At a later stage it could include insurers and brokers – but should also be expanded to all non-bank financial institutions. Further the data included will also soon cover tax-related payments as well as those related to legal proceedings and offences.

Once more the main issue to be tackled in that respect is regulation. At the time of writing there is no final regulation on the credit registry and data protection[2] issues also remain open. Concerning the regulation of the credit registry (the draft regulation is ready) the main issue at stake is the responsibility of the management of the credit registry. While it might appear natural for the PBOC to take the lead, the merging of many data sources (legal, tax, and so on) means that much of the data also comes from other ministries and state departments which also want to retain a say in how the credit registry is run. Other authorities fear any monopoly over such wealth of data – that is, power. Then, to make things more complex, some of the data is held and gathered at the local level where some local governments have even established competing systems and databases (Wang P., 2010).

7
New Forms of Financial Intermediation

To expand the outreach and scope of financial services in China, commercial banks have been allowed to enter new business realms.

7.1 Microfinance and rural

Soon after Muhammad Yunus received the Nobel Prize for the creation of the microfinance institution, the Grameen Bank, the CBRC published a set of new regulations to ensure improved financial intermediation in poor and under-banked areas of China.

Microfinance institutions cater to the financing needs of the under-banked population around the world. Up to 2006, however, microfinance remained in China a small undertaking with non-government organisations or highly subsidised government on-lending providing the main services (there are around 300 such projects in China, He G., Du X., Bai C. and Li Z., 2009). Few were able to bank on that population in a profitable and thus sustainable manner.[1] None of them gained real scale in its operations. Microfinance was regarded more as a poverty alleviation tool for rural areas and unemployed urban dwellers than as an alternative financial intermediation mechanism (Situ, 2003).

One explanation was always that the under-banked are un-bankable in the eyes of commercial banks. However, lifting the restrictions on commercial banks to enter the microfinance arena has shown that they also have a genuine interest in advancing in that field. Not only did China lack the proper regulations, but its loan officers had to learn how to lend to such clients. The government funds forwarded by the RCCs also crowded out any commercially viable schemes.

In the market, potential seems high if one realises that by the end of 2006, there were 37,000 townships and 624,000 villages with a combined

Table 7.1 Yearly income of Chinese households (CNY, %)

	Rural households	Urban households	Rural income as % of urban income
1990	990	1,516	65
2000	3,146	6,296	50
2008	6,701	17,068	39

Source: National Bureau of Statistics.

population of 740 million and around 230 million households (He G., Du X., Bai C. and Li Z., 2009; Table 7.1). Loans came from formal institutions only for 38% of their needs; the remaining 62% were covered by informal mechanisms.

Microfinance in China is mainly a rural affair. While China has managed in the past to alleviate poverty on a large scale (albeit more in the 1980s than during the 1990s; Huang, 2008), the most recent past was characterised by rising income inequality and opportunities between urban and rural population, between coastal and inner provinces, and so on. At the same time, the question of food security has also become of paramount importance to the leadership. More than half the population account for just 15% in banking activities. In Chinese eyes the forgotten farmers have a huge potential for revolt and so access to development – and therefore to finance – are key to them sharing in the fruits of economic reforms and progress. Finally, realising that the rural credit cooperatives have done a poor job of catering to their customers' needs – with only 60% getting the required financing – and that a change could not be expected any time soon, the regulators decided to open up the markets: perhaps some contenders would bring in a better understanding of how to conduct business. In searching for measures to reduce inequalities and increase food security, the central authorities have produced between 2004 and 2009 a series of Number 1 Documents[2] concerning the sannong 三农 (agriculture, peasants, rural areas[3]) – this to highlight the importance of the issue. One leg of the measures to be implemented tackles rural financial intermediation.

In December 2006, the CBRC published a first set of regulations opening market access to rural areas to basically all commercial financial institutions – both domestic and foreign (References for laws 45, 46, 48 and 67). Other financial services issues were tackled either by the relevant regulatory authorities (for example, CIRC: SinoCast Banking Beat, 2010d) or by other banking regulations targeting specific financial products (for example consumer finance, and so on).

To deepen the level of competition, enhance financial coverage and respond to the unmet needs of 65% of farmers in rural areas,[4] CBRC proposed the creation of a special regulatory framework for establishing rural financial institutions: with lower entry requirements and thresholds but at the same time stricter supervision (低门槛、严监管). These entities can be in the form of 'rural funds mutual aid groups', 'loan companies' or 'township and village banks (VTBs)' (since June 2009, under certain conditions loan companies can upgrade themselves into VTBs: References for laws 66). They may be established at county, township or village level, with the approval of the CBRC. Their capital is provided by the rural population and rural enterprises for groups, by banks and cooperative banks for loan companies and by banks (also foreign ones), non-banks or individuals for banks. The range of products will depend on the entity: all can provide loans, but are barred from taking deposits – with the exception of VTBs. For regulators the new entities should, with their flexibility and sound mechanisms, enhance coverage of the banking-wise blank parts of China.

While not pertaining to microfinance in the strict sense of the word, these institutions are still a venue for serving the under-banked population and lending out small amounts.

Some Chinese and foreign banks indicated their interest at an early stage, and this could be the beginning of true competition in rural areas giving much-needed life blood to an almost dead patient (see chapter on rural financial institutions). The first village bank opened in March 2007 and within a few months a foreign one followed. Other lenders, including newly merged rural commercial banks, are opening VTBs, which can then rely on their shareholders' experience, network and systems. Farmers have also put their savings together to create mutual aid groups. They are in charge and the outlets offer simple products with quick processes and rates lower than informal ones.

The development of rural financial markets has shown that profitability can be achieved (CNY41 mln together cumulated until the first half of 2009) but the Ministry of Finance nonetheless still offers government subsidies (up to 2% of outstanding loans) when certain growth and prudential conditions are met (SinoCast Banking Beat, 2009a; Reuters News, 2009c). True commercialisation would enhance economic development by ensuring that resources are allocated according to demand. Authorities are pushing for further new institutions so that these are projected to reach 1,294 by end-2011 (CBRC, 2009a). The crucial question of creating sound incentives will be tested in the future: if one institution fails, then who will bear the risks and the losses?

Microfinance in the strict sense became a full reality with the enactment of the Guidance on Rural Microloan Business Promoted by Banking Financial Institutions in August 2007 and of the Guidance on Pilot Microloan companies in May 2008 (References for laws 46 and 48).[5]

Prior to this and starting as early as 1981, large UN organisations such as UNWDF, IFAD and UNFPA began microfinance projects in China. Later on the Rural Development Institute of the Chinese Academy of Social Sciences also implemented three projects – in Henan, Shaanxi and Hebei. Other donor organisations also joined the party, but it was only in the early 2000s that the RCCs made tentative inroads in the area. The Grameen model was often the choice of loan arrangement with its typical group lending at interest rates of around 8% p.a. (Rahman and Luo, 2010). Levels of repayment were poor (Brandt et al., 2005b). During these initial stages, microfinance lacked scale, proper regulations, outreach, and management experience.

It is only in recent years that commercial banks such as city commercial banks under the aegis and support of the China Development Bank (Bi and Shen, 2009), the RCCs for some and the Postal Savings Bank chose to enter microfinance lending by offering individual loans. Only those established as formal financial institutions under the supervision of the CBRC can offer savings products and money transfers as well (Table 7.2).

In common with many other regulations in China, those concerned with microfinance are highly detailed. For example, the loan size should be between CNY10–50,000 and CNY100–300,000 in less and more developed areas respectively. The guidelines also require financial institutions to streamline their operations and to reduce the administrative burden. The funds can be used for productive as well as consumer purposes (References for laws 46). Also interest rates are set at market rates by the institutions, but within the limits permitted legally.

Unfortunately, in terms of microfinance regulations, China has not gone much further. In fact, microloan companies can be established as long as the local governments in the regions in which they are active are willing to take responsibility for any possible losses and to supervise them independently. Thus few have come forward to date and the high level of uncertainty surrounding their future has also been a constraint on interested parties. They will have preferred other better regulated alternatives such as VTBs. The barriers for entry are then lower when registering with CBRC than under local rules (for example, in Beijing[6] the capital requirement is ten times higher; He G., Du X., Bai C. and Li Z., 2009). Despite restrictive local regulations, a newspaper article reported

Table 7.2 Selected MFIs in China (2008, CNY)

Name	Gross loan portfolio (in mln)	Number of active borrowers	Average loan balance per borrower	Portfolio at risk > 30 days	Capital/asset ratio	Deposits (in mln)	Return on equity
China Fund for Poverty Alleviation	15.7	26,878	584	0.76%	42.60%	0.14	−0.55%
Chifeng Zhaowuda Women's Sustainable Development Association	1.2	3,331	363	0.00%	32.65%	0.03	4.57%
Ningxia Yanchi Women's Development Association	1.2	4,244	287	—	2.98%	0.13	−6.49%
Opportunity International China	1.7	407	4,116	4.90%	27.33%	1.6	−0.97%
Rishenglong	4.5	457	9,846	2.13%	94.05%	0	12.47%
Sichuan Yilong Huimin County Bank	0.97	3,086	315	1.59%	68.77%	0.22	0.96%
Microcred	17.9	1,034	17,336	0.98%	99%	0	4.3%

Notes: As MFIs are free to report to MIX Market and the table only entails a selection of the largest ones, thus this cannot be considered a full market overview.
Source: MIX Market www.mixmarket.org and annual reports of the entities.

that – based on PBOC data – there were 1,334 small loan companies in China by end-2009 with loans outstanding amounting to CNY76.6 bln (SinoCast Banking Beat, 2010b). Furthermore, all non-bank microfinance projects remain in a grey area of regulation.

At least, under-banked Chinese have received more attention and a wider range of services: CBRC reported that by end-2009, the number of villages and townships that had no banking facilities declined from 2,945 to 2,792 within six months, and those without any financial services declined from 708 to 342 within the same period of time (CBRC, 2010).

7.2 Retail lending

Since the beginning of the liberalisation process in 1978, Chinese banks have had the opportunity to widen the scope of their financial products. One of the main growth areas in the Chinese banking system is retail banking.

Retail banking is relatively new to China and in recent years has been growing rapidly. In 2000, retail loans accounted for 5% of GDP, in 2004 they had increased to 13% and, finally, in 2009 they amounted to CNY5.5 bln (of which 88% are medium- to long-term loans), based on PBOC data. Most of these loans are residential mortgages, followed by other consumer loans (including credit cards lending) and automobile loans. The market for retail lending is dominated (as in the case of other types of lending) by the four SOCBs and to a lesser extent by the JSCBs (Table 7.3).

Such strong development can be explained mainly through the more consumption-driven economic growth in China and the growth of disposable incomes (especially in urban areas but now even in rural areas) as well as the growing usefulness of the credit registry which now also includes a large number of individual borrowers (Box 3).

According to von Emloh and Wang (2004), however, not all consumer segments are profitable: the more affluent customers account for 18% of customers and generate 40–50% of profits, but the less affluent 80% are unprofitable. The affluent customers are concentrated in coastal areas and have higher requirements in terms of level of financial services. This is an area where foreign banks can distinguish themselves.

Over the years and with more experience and a benign economic environment, there has been an improvement in the quality of the

Table 7.3 Retail lending in China (CNY bln)

	2007		2008		2009	
	SOCBs	JSCBs	SOCBs	JSCBs	SOCBs	JSCBs
Total loans	12,604	4,981	14,324	6,197	19,085	8,413
Total consumer loans	2,715	1,004	2,919	1,131	4,232	1,704
Mortgage loans	1,941	646	2,155	852	3,133	1,256
Credit card loans	289	42	116	108	161	144
Other consumer loans	470	95	647	275	936	299

Notes: The figures do not include the breakdown for Everbright in 2007, for Bohai in 2007–09, for GDB in 2007, for Zheshang in 2007 – this means that the breakdown does not always add up to the total. In the JSCBs only Evergrowing is not included.
Source: Banks' annual reports, 2007–2009.

Table 7.4 Non-performing loan ratios in retail lending (%)

	2006	2007	2008	2009
Retail loans	0.53	2.77	1.29	0.92
Credit cards	n.a.	2.63	2.39	2.83
Mortgages	n.a.	1.06	0.91	0.59
Automobiles		9.93	5.45	2.92
Others	n.a.	7.57	1.78	1.41

Source: CBRC (2007, 2008, 2009c and 2010).

commercial banks' retail portfolios. Credit cards remain somewhat a matter for concern, but the previously disastrous quality of automotive loans has improved to more sustainable levels – albeit not yet healthy ones (Table 7.4).

The first notices regulating retail lending were issued in 1998. More recently, strong growth prompted CBRC to issue a new *Provisional rule for managing personal loans* (References for laws 47). Principally, it increases the internal management requirements for personal loans in banks, for example requiring automatic drawing of the monthly repayments, further controls into uses of loans (does not apply to credit cards and to auto loans) and for larger loans (over CNY300,000 the funds should be disbursed directly to the receiver rather than the borrower).

Credit card lending

Bank cards have now become staple goods in China and the market is growing rapidly. According to a KPMG survey, there were some 142 million credit cards and 1,658 million debit cards in China by end-2008 (KPMG, 2009). For foreign banks, credit cards represent a great opportunity to reach out to high net worth individuals and urban consumers without having a widespread branch network similar to that of other domestic commercial banks. They also offer substantial data-gathering opportunities for the study of consumption patterns and behaviour. But that would be to reckon without the challenges of the Chinese market.

Cards in China come in three main versions: ATM cards, debit cards and credit cards. The majority of the issued cards are debit cards which enable the holder to withdraw money at ATMs and make payments that are immediately debited from current accounts. By the end of 2007, the purchase volume was 2.9 million and the cash volume 30 million (KPMG, 2009). There are quite a large number of cards in circulation, but the level of card purchases is relatively low (around one-third of all cashless purchases; Ren, 2010) as cash remains king and almost a third of all cards remain unused (card penetration ranges from 45% in the largest cities to 17% in smaller locations). In 2001, a new type of debit card was introduced, called 银联 (yinlian), which enables the holder to withdraw and pay at all points of sales terminals and ATMs in the country (at a cost per transaction, but at least proving that it was possible to link all institutions). At the turn of the century, the largest issuers were the SOCBs, with a market share of 90% (Worthington, 2003; Yan M., 2005). These have steadily lost ground to the more aggressive and efficient joint-stock commercial banks such as Merchants Bank.

Credit cards account for only a small share of all plastic cards. The first credit cards were introduced in 1979 by BoC as an agent for large foreign international banks. In 1985, BoC proceeded to introduce its own domestic credit card. In 1987–1988 it signed agreements with Master-Card and Visa. At the end of the 1980s, the other SOCBs had followed suit with the introduction of their own cards. In 1996, PBOC promulgated regulations with regard to credit card management. Credit limits are granted to individuals in full-time employment. With the integration of China into the world economy, the monopolist China UnionPay (CUP)[7] – controlling the country's payment and settlement system – has signed agreements with over 90 countries, so that its credit cards can be used abroad as well.

Now the urban infrastructure is increasingly supportive of card transactions: more than 1.35 million merchants accept the cards, with 2.1 million points of sales (POS) and 1.9 million ATMs (by mid-2009; PBOC, 2009c). But the system is not yet fraud-proof. PBOC statistics reveal that in the first eight months of 2009, fraudulent cases had increased over twofold – to 6,362 cases involving CNY440 mln. One security against this is that credit balances are limited to CNY50,000 per card, independently of the borrower's creditworthiness. With the financial crisis, the bad debts in credit card lending also rose: by over 100% in each quarter of 2009 to reach 3.4% of total retail debt in September 2009 (Ren, 2009; the ratio dropped slightly in the last quarter). Another security is now that criminal charges can be brought against those defaulting on credit card debts for more than three months. Finally, the banks can now rely on a credit registry with large amount of data from which they can monitor the repayment behaviour of (potential) clients.

China's credit card market lags behind the country's level of economic development. On one hand, this can be explained by the high propensity to save in China. On the other, it can also be explained by the difficulty in recovering debts. Despite these impediments foreign banks appeared inclined to believe that great market opportunities still existed. While margins appear high, low levels of card usage and card spending mean that profitability can only be reached with high issuance volumes. Thus far, the growth has been supply-driven and cards are often a promotional exercise. Profitable margins can be a reality only once customers do use their credit cards for revolving credit. Furthermore interchange rates are not the result of market forces but rather are limited by PBOC (1.4% or 0.2% for the issuer and CUP respectively in most cases, KPMG, 2009).

Since 2003 a number of foreign banks (such as the partnership between HSBC and Bank of Shanghai) have chosen to enter the credit card market through strategic partnerships with Chinese banks . Then with the WTO membership, most foreign issuers and banks hoped to enter the market directly, but they were delayed in this when the regulators stipulated that they should first establish data processing centres (EIU, 2010a).

Consumption lending

The regulators have also created an opening solely for consumption lending. The State Council had previously required regulators to support growth and in particular to spur domestic consumption to help change the structure of the Chinese economy away from solely export-led growth. These consumption loans companies can be registered since July 2009 (References for laws 59). This new type of financial institutions will surely increase the level of market competition – but probably first in the larger urban centres where it is easier to reach borrowers.

These institutions are registered and supervised by the CBRC and cannot take deposits; they loan only small amounts for consumption purposes. They can also serve as agents for other financial products such as insurance or investment funds deemed suitable by regulators. The loan amount to an individual client is limited to five times his or her monthly income. Entry barriers are lower, but the level of supervision remains tight: the companies need to comply with a CAR of 10%, 100% loan loss reserves and a balance on investment not over 20% of total assets. Investors must show a clean and profitable record for two years (foreign ones additionally need to have had a representative office or branch for at least two years). The registered capital must not be below CNY300 mln.

Already three such companies with local capital have been approved (by the Bank of China, the Bank of Beijing and the Bank of Chengdu), with a fourth foreign one awaiting approval (CBRC, 2010).

Automobile finance

Automobile lending is also a growing area of consumer lending. Automobile loans amounted to CNY158 bln in 2008 with SOCBs lending

CNY 74.3 bln, JSCBs CNY31.1 bln and auto financing companies CNY31.8 bln (PBOC, 2009a). To date in China only large commercial banks and nine foreign carmakers (Volkswagen, Toyota, Daimler Chrysler, Ford, Peugeot, Volvo, Nissan, GM and Fiat) offer such loans. As at end-2008, the nine AFCs had total assets of CNY38 bln. The quality of these assets is quite low (see Table 7.4). Additionally, only 10% of carbuyers are said to use automobile financing (Asia Pulse, 2010) and insurers have withdrawn from this type of business.

The 2004 regulations on car loans require that the maturity of these should not exceed five years (or three years for used cars); the loan amount is also capped according to the use to which the car will be put (private or commercial). Individuals have to make a down payment of at least 50% of the car price (References for laws 57 and 58).

To increase liquidity and growth in that market, regulatory authorities have allowed the issuance of the first car-loan-backed securities (by GMAC–SAIC joint venture for CNY1.9 bln) and of the first bonds.

Real estate lending

Real estate lending is highly correlated with the authorities' assessment of the market. This is a strong example of bureaucratic meddling and regulatory interference since its inception – this, however, did not impede strong growth.

Residential mortgages accounted for CNY4.76 trillion at the end of 2009 (Xinhua Chinese News, 2010) a 43% increase over the year. These have seen strong growth rates, with an average of 30% p.a.

The growth in real estate lending has paralleled the growth in the prices of real estate. High rates of growth are of concern to the authorities and have prompted them to intervene through a variety of administrative measures. In April 2005, in an attempt to curb real estate lending, 16 Shanghai lenders were ordered to cease any short-term consumer real estate lending business, preferential interest rates were removed (that is, for first-time buyers, the 10% reduction on the base rate was removed and the base rate for second-time and other buyers was 6.12% and only higher rates were allowed), and lenders were allowed to finance only up to 70% of their mortgages (PBOC, 2005a). Further cooling measures such as taxation (increasing the tax burden when a property was resold within five years) and prudential requirements (including increasing the risk weight for some real estate loans in the capital adequacy calculation) were also introduced in May 2006 (Yu N. et al., 2006).

A similar pattern can be observed in the propping up of the market. To prevent a freefall in real estate prices, which happened to coincide with the broader economic downturn, regulators relaxed their stringent rules on mortgage lending. In late October 2008, the PBOC and CBRC issued joint notices reducing the down payment for residential purchases to 20% from the previous 30% (this was retained for larger apartments) and the downward limit on interest rates to 0.7 times the PBOC benchmark rate (for first-time buyers). Meanwhile, the MOF declared that from November 2008 the deed tax for first-time purchases of flats of less than 90 square metres in size would be lowered to 1%. Stamp duty would also be scrapped. On average, first-time buyers can reduce their costs by 9%.

Then with the fears of a renewed overheating[8] growing in 2009, the authorities went the other way again. For second homes, discounts which were possible at the beginning of 2009 were scrapped completely: the interest rate variation from the benchmark can be as high as 1.1 times and the down payment is at least 40% (basically a return to November 2007 requirements) (EIU, 2010a). Finally, the monthly repayments should not exceed 50% of a borrower's monthly income (in reality, this is difficult to assess because banks have relatively few means for checking borrowers' true incomes). In addition, the preferential interest rates for property lending were removed as a means of cooling down developments in the property markets.

Part of the growth in real estate lending is also related to the active role local governments play in economic development in their region (The Economist, 2010c) which rely on land sales and taxes for up to 17% of their revenues. For many local governments, it is thus important to keep prices high and lending on this side also high. Cooling down this market would have to involve broadening investment opportunities for idle funds of enterprises and individuals, because real estate is often the sole financial investment available to them.

Box 3 Interbank bond market

An interbank bond market is of paramount importance to banks. It can help them to manage their portfolios and their balance sheets (reducing gaps and mismatches in maturities, for example), ensure that risks and rewards are better balanced, price financial transactions and indicate the state of the economy. The prices in bond markets are also important signals to banks and normally influence the pricing of debts to other borrowers such as enterprises. Despite all these positive features, the Chinese bond markets remain fully under-developed and thus play only a side role: interbank rates are more influenced by administrative measures than by markets. This is also true for the interbank bond market – although it appears more developed than the other two bond markets.

Hindering the development of a fully functioning bond market is the competition between bond and loan markets because SOEs can borrow from banks at subsidised rates, there is no need for them to turn to bond markets where issuance can be lengthy and costly. Secondly, market players in the interbank bond market do not often trade their holdings and prefer to keep them to maturity (because of low issuance prices), and most large banks are capital exporters while smaller ones and other financial institutions are importers. Finally, the Chinese bond markets are highly segmented with the interbank bond market being the largest of the three (additionally, there are governed by multiple regulators; Liu, Hui and Zhang, 2010).

A first bond market exists on the stock exchanges. The securities traded include T-bonds, corporate and convertible bonds – for spot and repo – and the trading takes place between small institutional investors and individuals. For historical reasons the market is off-limits to financial institutions (they have only recently been able to participate in underwriting). A second bond market is the smallest of all three and is an OTC T-bond market for retail investors.

The third one is the interbank bond market. This was created in 1997 for financial institutions with the intention of reining in the excesses of the previous years and trades are OTC (over the counter). The market is quite lively and most of the trades are by financial institutions, although other institutional investors are also allowed there. The trades are for spot and repos. Liveliness is also relative – in fact, credit risk is low so that real risk management has little meaning here. Finally, most issuance is short term in nature so that closing maturity gaps can be a futile exercise. In future all bond types could be traded here – as the

PBOC regulations say but that remain open as regulators disagree on how to proceed to halt segmentation.[1]

To underline its commitment to the enhancement of market conditions, the PBOC has issued various regulations relating to the relaxation of entry barriers and controls and it also introduced a new benchmark interest rate for the interbank market in early 2007: SHIBOR (Shanghai Interbank Offered Rate) based on the CNY lending rates of 16 leading banks for different maturities – from overnight to one year. However, the benchmark has yet to be used in lending to bank customers. Further, the benchmark is not influenced by market operations of the central bank nor by bank reserve requirements, but rather by changes in the deposit and loan rates set by the PBOC. Thus these short-term rates cannot yet be used for asset pricing.

Conclusion to Part III

Chapters 6 and 7 have shown again that the Party is pervasive in all realms of the economy – and the private sector is no exception. This is actually a two-way infiltration: private entrepreneurs need to interact with bureaucrats in their daily business so that they spend much time courting them, at the same time the Party has promoted private entrepreneurship within its ranks (inviting entrepreneurs to become members,[1] sending (retired) members to chair boards in private enterprises, for example).

The expansion of the means of financial intermediation has provided a useful valve to introduce more ways of getting a loan to more borrowers. The widening of product and customer scopes has not only had a positive effect on a large share of the population, but has also improved the performance of the banks and thus of the return on investment to the state.

Part IV
Supply

Having provided an extensive discussion of the lending activities that are common to all or most banks in China, we can now turn to the analysis of individual types of banks.

While no two banks are exactly alike, Chinese banks can be grouped into different types and their specifics can be analysed. Such analysis is unable to catch all the differences between banks, but has the advantage of giving a deeper and more detailed picture of the broader banking industry in China. Interestingly, the last few years have broadened and changed the types of active banks, and as a result, we can distinguish four broad types:

1 Large commercial banks, including the state-owned commercial banks (SOCBs) and the joint-stock commercial banks (JSCBs).
2 Smaller local banks, such as city commercial banks (CCBs).
3 Foreign banks.
4 Rural financial institutions, among which are rural credit cooperatives (RCCs) and the Postal Savings Bank.

Chinese banks had a successful year in 2009 with profits rising to CNY603 bln (compared to CNY532 bln in 2008). NPL ratios fell overall from 17.9% in 2003 to 1.6% in 2009[1] and finally in 2008 the NPLs were fully covered by loss provisions. Equity capital surged to CNY3.7 trn (a mere 5.3% of assets) and 239 financial institutions were able to show a capital adequacy ratio of 8% at least. The total assets of commercial banks amounted to CNY70.3 trn (a 26% increase since 2008). The financial institutions under CBRC supervision (including commercial banks, policy banks and NBFIs) held CNY61 trn in deposits and CNY42.6trn in loans. The commercial banks employed 2.7 mln people spread across 3,675 institutions (CBRC, 2010).

8
Large Commercial Banks

The banking industry in China is dominated by large commercial banks. They also play the role of market leaders in innovation and financial intermediation capacity.

8.1 Market shares and coverage

Between them the four SOCBs[1] – sometimes also called the Big Four – hold a 47% market share, compared with 53% in 2005. While they are losing ground to the joint-stock commercial banks, they remain strong market players. There are also visible throughout the country with branch networks spanning all areas (Table 8.1). The joint-stock commercial banks (JSCBs[2]) have gained market share, reaching 19% in 2009 (up from 15.5% in 2005). Their branches are spread all over the country, but concentrated in main urban centres.

8.2 Historical developments and business scope

Historically, the four SOCBs went along a different path from that of the JSCBs. The SOCBs are essentially offspring of the PBOC when China was still a mono-bank country. When they were separated from PBOC they represented departments of that institution with sector specialisations. This explains their names: BOC specialised in foreign trade and exchange, CCB in construction and engineering and ICBC in commerce and industry, while agriculture was the mainstay of ABC. The banks' commercialisation was slow and it is still much an ongoing process – although the progress achieved in the last few years is staggering for the financial performance at least. The banks remained for a long time – and still are to some extent – arms of the authorities and thus policy

Table 8.1 Branches and employees, 2009

	Number of branches	Number of employees
ICBC	16,394	389,827
ABC	23,624	441,144
BoC	10,961	262,566
CCB	13,384	301,537
BoComm	2,657	79,122
SPDB	565	21,877
CITIC	618	24,000
Everbright	35	19,217
Minsheng	434	26,039
Huaxia	349	12,301
Merchants	739	40,340
GDB	549	14,522
Industrial	503	22,004
SDB	302	9,887

Source: Banks' annual reports.

lending was pervasive.[3] This also saddled the banks with underperforming and unsustainable business and deprived them of their financial and commercial independence.

In each of the cases the reforms ran along similar lines. First, the better ones, BOC and CCB, were tackled. Then came ICBC and, finally and, more recently, ABC. For each, the authorities first transferred non-performing loans to the respective asset management companies, and then recapitalised the banks with foreign exchange reserves managed by Huijin.[4] After such financial restructuring, the authorities opened the banks to foreign investors which served as anchors prior to the stock market listings. Meanwhile, the banks had to restructure their management, processes, activities and controls internally in order to face more serious questioning by the markets.

The reform process at ABC took longer for a number of reasons. First, the bank was in worse shape (NPLs[5] and graft were quite widespread) and much more had to be done to get the bank to run like a commercial bank. Second, the issues at stake in this instance were of paramount importance to the Chinese leadership. The servicing of rural areas is a challenging issue, involving both market principles and politicised development goals (the State Council put a precondition for the restructuring: achieving 'facing *sannong*, integral restructuring, commercial operations, possible listing'; Hu C. and Zhang M., 2010). The bank transferred its bad assets into a subsidiary bad bank and restructured its activities around the principle of 'one bank, two systems'. An urban segment operates along commercial lines while the rural one serves a development purpose and would be subsidised where necessary by the first segment. In any case the bank has to have a certain amounts of loans going to rural activities.

Compared to these, the JSCBs fared better as they were never directly under credit quotas or policy lending instruments. Most of them were established in the late 1980s and early 1990s (the last one, Bohai, opened its doors in 2006; BoComm was re-established in 1986) to boost the competition in the banking industry. Such a start under more auspicious conditions enabled them to grow more healthy portfolios and business (Table 8.2).[6] They are often seen as innovators and have carved strong niches. They are also often touted as more customer-oriented and more efficient.

All large commercial banks are universal banks that offer similar products and services. At the beginning their main products included bullet loans and deposits. With time, they have also learned to enter into retail markets, have become agents for fund and insurance products, transfer money, offer trust investments and a wider range of fee-generating products. Deposits and loans still remain the mainstay of the banks (see table). With time, the banks will also need to review their earnings strategies: adding to the safe '三大一高' ('do high margin, large customers and large projects business with high concentrations') some smaller niches or business innovations.

Some of the JSCBs have already carved strong banking niches: Minsheng is a leader in SME lending while Merchants is strong in the area of credit cards. Overall, most of them still cater to large corporates and, albeit to a small extent, to local enterprises and individuals. To expand their offerings they have also taken the route of acquiring other financial institutions in China: BoComm and Merchants have acquired smaller city commercial banks and established rural institutions, BoComm also acquired in 2009 a small insurance company, others again ventured in the trust industry.

The large commercial banks have all made tentative overseas ventures. Some were as audacious as to either purchase foreign banks or at least acquire significant stakes in them. Others have preferred opening new branches to follow their customers. Foreign ventures help them to gain further skills. In 2007 ICBC acquired Bank Halim Indonesia, a 20% stake in South Africa's Standard Bank and 80% of Macau's Seng Heng bank. This was followed in 2009 by the acquisition of ACL Bank of Thailand and a 70% stake in the Bank of East Asia Canada in 2010. ICBC also used organic growth to expand its operations in the Middle East. CCB has preferred a policy of branching out and has restricted its acquisitions

Table 8.2 Trends in large commercial banks (CNY bln, %)

	SOCBs			JSCBs		
	2007	2008	2009	2007	2008	2009
Total assets	26,584	31,279	39,043	9,432	11,724	15,326
Net loan portfolio	12,604	14,324	19,085	5,026	6,262	8,506
Loan loss reserves	1,066	438	512	119	143	167
Non-performing loans	1,105	410	356	109	92	90
Customer deposits	21,935	25,799	31,955	6,992	8,493	11,382
Capital	694	1,855	2,126	474	572	726
Subordinated debt	135	135	279	94	161	175
Net loan portfolio	12,604	14,324	19,085	5,026	6,262	8,506
NPL ratio (%)	*8.01*	*2.87*	*1.87*	*2.02*	*1.22*	*0.89*
Basel I ratio (%)	*13.00*	*12.88*	*11.73*	*10.99*	*10.89*	*10.48*
Net profit	257	321	387	78	111	123
Return on equity (%)	*9.76*	*17.33*	*18.19*	*16.62*	*18.63*	*15.34*
Return on assets (%)	*0.96*	*1.01*	*0.98*	*0.68*	*0.77*	*0.69*

Note: Figures in italic are averages (unweighted), otherwise the sums.
Source: Banks' annual reports.

to closer destinations such as Hong Kong, Taiwan or Vietnam. The more courageous of the JSCBs took a hit during the financial crisis: Merchants' acquisition of Hong Kong's Wing Lung Bank was impaired and Minsheng's acquisition of the American UCBH was a total loss.

8.3 Shareholding structures

All large commercial banks are now structured as shareholding banks (the latest one being the ABC in mid-2009). The SOCBs, however, still show a majority shareholding by the state – through either Central Huijin Investment Co.[7] or the Ministry of Finance, or both (Table 8.3). The state does not hold such large direct shares in the JSCBs – although it still remains overall and indirectly the majority shareholder. The sole private bank is Minsheng.

Table 8.3 Shareholding structures of the SOCBs as of end-2009

Bank name	Huijin share (%)	State (others) (%)
BOC	68	NSSF 3.3
CCB	57	other SOEs 3
ICBC	35	MOF 35, NSSF 4
ABC	50	MOF 50*

Note: The state shares are since the reform of the state shares listed as well – at least they can potentially be sold. The remaining shares are held by other shareholders (foreign or on stock markets) * before ABC's listing.
Source: Banks' annual reports.

With the exception of GDB, Hengfeng, Zheshang and Bohai, all of the large commercial banks are listed on the stock exchanges of Shanghai and/or Hong Kong.[8] Some of the JSCBs were listed long before the SOCBs could even dream of being listed anywhere.[9] The largest among them also belong to the largest worldwide in terms of market capitalisation (PwC, 2010a): ICBC leads the group with USD246 bln. Together, ICBC, CCB, BOC, BoComm, Merchants, CITIC and Minsheng have a market capitalisation of USD765 bln (end-2009). The listings have had positive effects on bank efficiency in the short term (Luo D. and Yao S., 2009).

Most of the banks can now also boost foreign shareholders (Table 8.4). Foreign shareholders – albeit being limited to a single share of 20% or a combined 25% – have been invited to help steer the SOCBs before their listings. The JSCBs have also profited from that.

8.4   Governance and transparency

From a regulatory point of view, the large commercial banks all face the same rules and laws (previously some exceptions in relation to regulatory requirements were made for SOCBs). All banks now publish their financial statements using the same standards and requirements (from the CBRC and from the stock market oversight).[10]

Although increasing numbers of managers are being recruited competitively and their professional background is becoming more important in making a choice, the senior management in these banks is still appointed by the state and the Communist Party (Table 8.5). To remedy shortages of professional managers, banks have – in some limited cases – recruited foreign executives to their senior management teams (see chapter on corporate governance).

Table 8.4 Equity stakes by foreigners, 2008

Chinese bank	Foreign investor	Foreign stake (%)
SOCBs		
Bank of China	Li Ka-shing Foundation	0.48
	Fullerton Financial Holdings Pte Ltd	4.10
	Asian Development Bank	0.20
	Bank of Tokyo-Mitsubishi UFJ Ltd	0.19
China Construction Bank	Bank of America	11.0
	Fullerton Financial Holdings Pte Ltd	5.88
Industrial & Commercial Bank of China	Goldman Sachs, American Express and Allianz	5.15
Agricultural Bank of China	Standard Chartered Qatar Investment Authority Kuwait Investment Authority Rabobank, ADM	0.4
JSCBs		
Bank of Communications	HSBC	18.60
China Bohai Bank	Standard Chartered Bank	19.99
China CITIC Bank	Banco Bilbao Vizcay Argentaria (BBVA)	15.0
	Mizuho Corporate Bank	0.17
China Everbright Bank	Asian Development Bank	1.9
Guangdong Development Bank	Citigroup	20.00
	IBM	4.74
Huaxia Bank	Deutsche Bank and Sal Oppenheim	17.12
Industrial Bank	Hang Seng Bank	12.78
	International Finance Corp	2.73
	Tetrad Ventures	4.00
Shanghai Pudong Development Bank	Citibank Overseas Investment Corp	3.78
Evergrowing Bank	United Overseas Bank	12.06

Note: With the financial crisis, some cash-strapped foreign investors have sold their stakes in the SOCBs (for example, UBS, Royal Bank of Scotland, or Bank of America) – the figures have not been adjusted for that. The figures include only those investments at inception (not those bought on the stock markets).
Source: Media reports; bank annual reports.

While personnel decisions remain with the Communist Party, the banks are under the supervision of the CBRC, the rights on the banks' assets remain with the Ministry of Finance (for the Big Four; for the others, mostly with large SOEs – some under SASAC) and the capital is held by the country's sovereign wealth fund.[11] The high number of parties involved makes conflicts of interests inevitable and increases confusion with all remaining stakeholders (including the banks themselves).

Most senior positions are filled with party members and the chairman or the bank president is always the secretary of the party committee. A high value is placed on party loyalty and this is the indicator of choice for managers' performance. To recruit managers that are loyal to the party but still show a minimum of financial industry experience, the managers are rotated around the banks and regulatory agencies (Table 8.5). This practice could also be observed in the past: in 2006, Zhang Jianguo moved from BoComm to CCB, Chang Zhenming moved in parallel from CCB to CITIC Group, Chen Xin changed from Bank of Shanghai to SPDB. In addition, Xiang Junbo moved from PBOC to ABC and Yang Mingsheng changed from ABC to CIRC. Minsheng Bank – supposedly a private bank – is also prone to party interference (EIU, 2008). Then Minsheng also recruited a Hong Kong banker, Eddy Wang, to its team. The rotations do not only take place within the industry, executives also move up and down from other ministries and regulators.

The musical chairs have continued since then – culminating in the recruitment drive sponsored by the powerful Organisation Department since 2008 (Tucker and Anderlini, 2010). The authorities are offering a USD147,000 bonus for all Chinese-born but foreign-educated managers to staff its banks. One prominent example was the appointment of Zhang Hongli from a chairman position at Deutsche Bank (China) to a vice-president position at ICBC (Wen J., 2010). Such bonus payment to attract managers is necessary to compensate for the lower levels of executive pay in China (Box 9). In fact, the chairmen and presidents of BOC, CCB and ICBC received between CNY755,000 and CNY911,000 for 2009, as published in the respective annual reports.[12]

Longer-serving managers also appear to enjoy a high level of trust with the authorities and as a result their banks are able to venture abroad more quickly (for example, Jiang Jianqing from ICBC and Ma Weihua at Merchants).

Finally, it is important to note that the internal structures of these banks are not lean. These banks have many hierarchical layers and each layer has decision-making power in relation to lending and many other areas of business. For example, branches at ABC have multiple layers of loan approvals – three layers (operational, managerial and committee levels) – and all need to sign off a larger loan and at each level at least a department and a senior manager are involved. In addition, the committees for loan approval have power but no responsibilities: they cast

Table 8.5 Chairmen's and presidents' previous positions (selection)

Bank name	Chairman's name and other previous positions	President name and other previous positions
ICBC	Jiang Jianqing* Member of Central Committee of CPC, PBOC	Yang Kaisheng Huarong AMC
BOC	Xiao Gang Member of Central Committee of CPC, Orient AMC, PBOC	Li Lihui Vice Governor Hainan, ICBC
CCB	Guo Shuqing* Member of Central Committee of CPC, SAFE, PBOC, NDRC	Zhang Jianguo ICBC
ABC	Xiang Junbo* Member of Central Committee of CPC, PBOC	Zhang Yun –
Industrial	Gao Jianping* –	Li Renxing PBOC
Huaxia	Wu Jian* ICBC, BoComm	Fan Dazhi Smaller NBFIs
Minsheng	Dong Wenbiao PBOC	Hong Qi BoComm
SPDB	Ji Xiaohui* ICBC, Shanghai municipal government	Fu Jianhua CCB
BoComm	Hu Huaibang CBRC, PBOC	Niu Ximing ICBC
Merchants	Qin Xiao CITIC	Ma Weihua –
Everbright	Tang Shuangning* CBRC, PBOC, CCB	Guo You SAFE, PBOC

Note: The selection should not suggest that all other banks' senior managers have similar career paths. The positions show only the name of the institution – other than their current institution, the positions held might have been numerous and at different levels of hierarchy. The list entails only presidents and chairmen of the boards as of end-2009. The information does not include other positions held in universities and other non-bank or non-government institutions.
* Those with an asterisk are also mentioned as Party Committee secretaries in the annual reports. This information is given in a few annual reports only.
– Means that the person did not held any positions in other banks or authorities.
Sources: http://www.chinavitae.com/index.php and banks' annual reports.

only secret votes and their decisions are not linked to pay (Zeng J. and Liang H., 2008). Reforms have brought vertical hierarchies and more business responsibilities to each management position, but outside influences and graft remain.

8.5 Financial performance

The performance of the SOCBs has improved considerably over recent years and is now comparable to that of JSCBs. SOCBs have basically managed to close the gap in terms of efficiency, financial performance and productivity (Luo D. and Yao S., 2009; Table 8.6).

This is certainly not only the result of reforms and restructurings within the banks, or the result of stock market listings, but also the result of improvements in the banks' environment (with more private enterprises and better protection of property rights: Hasan, Wachtel and Zhou, 2006).

For 2009, the results, however, reflect the financial turmoil – but not in the same way as for other banks in the US and Europe. Most banks posted better results – but that is also an artificial result of provisioning and impairment recognitions (Dong Y., 2010b) – which were lower than in 2008 (which then reflected the toxic assets held by some banks for example). It is also the result of margins that improved in the last six months of 2009 – especially compared to 2008.

Bank margins are heavily determined by PBOC's decisions over lending and deposit base rates and market concentrations, so that the banks have few worries over their long-term profitability (Table 8.7).

The banks during the financial crisis in 2007–09

The banks' exposure to toxic assets came to light during the financial crisis (Table 8.8). But once the provisioning was done, attention turned elsewhere.

The main impact from the financial crisis was the government's fiscal stimulus enacted in late 2008. With the banks the main conduit for stimulating the economy and saving China from a worldwide slump, the banks have seen their loan portfolios increase strongly.

The first negative effect was a drain on earnings – mainly because the first instrument used were short-term discounted bills with low margins. This short-term effect ended in the third quarter and was soon

Table 8.6 Efficiency of banks compared (CNY mln)

	2004		2009	
	SOCBs	JSCBs	SOCBs	JSCBs
Assets/employees	14	41	28	56
Assets/branch	261	1,162	607	2,252

Sources: www.stats.gov.cn and banks' annual reports.

Table 8.7 Performance of SOCBs and JSCBs in 2009 (CNY bln, %)

	ICBC	ABC	BOC	CCB	BoComm	Merchants	CITIC	SPDB	Minsheng	Industrial	Everbright	Huaxia	SDB	Zheshang	Bohai	GDB	Hengfeng
Total assets	11,785	8,883	8,752	9,623	3,309	2,068	1,775	1,623	1,426	1,332	1,198	845	588	163	118	666	214
Net loan portfolio	5,583	4,011	4,797	4,693	1,802	1,162	1,050	911	868	692	632	419	356	86	69	367	93
Loan loss reserves	145	127	113	127	38	24	15	18	15	10	16	11	4	1.0	0.8	14	1
Non-performing loans	88	120	75	72	25	9	10	7	7	4	8	6	2	0.0	0.1	9	0
Customer deposits	9,771	7,498	6,685	8,001	2,372	1,608	1,342	1,295	1,128	901	800	582	455	121	102	544	133
Capital	679	343	545	559	164	93	107	68	89	60	48	30	20	9	5	22	10
Subordinated debt	75	50	74	80	50	30	15	19	1	10	22	10	8	2	1	5	2
Net loan portfolio	5,583	4,011	4,797	4,693	1,802	1,162	1,050	911	868	692	632	419	356	86	69	367	93
NPL ratio (%)	1.54	2.91	1.52	1.50	1.36	0.79	0.95	0.80	0.84	0.54	1.25	1.50	0.68%	0.01%	0.10%	2.40%	0.38%
Basel I ratio (total capital in %)	12.36	10.07	11.14	11.70	12.00	10.45	10.14	10.34	10.83	10.75	10.39	10.20	8.88	11.06	10.21	8.98	12.00
Net interest income	246	182	159	212	67	40	36	34	32	27	20	16	13	3.10	1.81	13	3
Fee & commission income	55	36	46	48	11	8	4	2	5	3.12	3.16	1.02	1.18	0.22	0.13	2	0
Operating profit before provisions	190	114	126	164	49	25	22	20	21	18	24	8	8	1.45	0.81	6	1
Net profit	129	65	85	107	30	18	15	13	12	13	8	4	5	0.87	0.26	3	1
Return on equity (%)	19.05	18.96	15.65	19.11	18.37	19.65	13.61	19.41	13.62	22.29	15.88	12.43	24.59	9.98	4.90%	12.92%	11.77%
Return on assets (%)	1.10	0.73	0.98	1.11	0.91	0.88	0.82	0.81	0.85	1.00	0.64	0.44	0.86	0.53	0.22	0.43	0.56

Source Banks' annual reports, author's own calculations.

Table 8.8 Exposure to the financial crisis at ICBC, BOC and CCB (bln USD)

	ICBC	BOC	CCB	Total
Subprime mortgage bonds	1.20	3.27	0.24	**4.71**
Alt-A bonds	0.60	1.38	0.29	**2.27**
other related bonds	0.06	0.00	0.00	**0.06**
Lehman Brothers exposure	0.15	0.07	0.19	**0.42**
Fannie Mae and Freddie Mac exposure (incl. bonds guaranteed by both institutions)	1.70	9.95	1.50	**13.15**
Dubai loans*	0	0	1.03	**n.a.**
Total	**3.71**	**14.67**	**2.23**	**20.61**

* According to Dong Y. (2009), Chinese banks (not only the SOCBs) participated between 2002 and 2009 in over USD9 bln in loans to Dubai and related companies (that is the total loan amount granted by the syndicate, not the combined amount lent by Chinese banks alone). The data for Dubai loans is as of December 2009.
Note: Some JSCBs also reported some losses in toxic assets.
Source: Banks' quarterly reports, September 2008 and Xinhua China Money, 2009.

replaced by a more important issue: capital adequacy. While CBRC raised the capital and provisioning requirements, and restrained the issuance of subordinated debts, the bank's capital base eroded in face of strong loan growth (32% in 2009). As the issue became more acute for all banks, they faced additional uncertainty in respect of the feasibility of raising additional capital (banks hoped to raise a combined CNY300 bln in 2010): Chinese capital markets were already under strain, highly volatile and the banks make a large share of the market capitalisation.

The final issue to be tackled here is the quality of the loan portfolio. The quality of the new loans is not yet clear and nor is it apparent to what extent the reforms of the risk and control management have trickled down to the lower-level branches. The strong growth in loans will have an impact, especially on infrastructure-related lending which is more long term in nature. This increases concentrations but also allowed some banks, such as BOC, to restructure their loan portfolios. For now the bankers believe that their NPL ratios will remain below 5% until 2014 (PwC, 2009c).

8.6 Challenges ahead

The financial performance of SOCBs has improved dramatically since 1999, much of this thanks to the largesse of the central authorities.

The sustainability of the reforms will be tested, among others, in terms of asset quality. Repeated efforts have shown that accounting can help to clean up books in the short term; however, strong economic growth coupled with excessive lending could rapidly transform the banks' books into non-performing ones. It remains to be seen if the alleged internal reforms and restructurings can be maintained.

All banks also face common challenges. While the corporate governance structures are theoretically in place, since most of the banks' shares are state-owned ones (either directly or indirectly through SOEs), conflicts of interest do arise. The large and controlling presence of the state in these banks damages the efficient functioning of the corporate governance structures. Despite being partly listed on Chinese stock markets, most of their shares remain in the hands of the state and outside investors are not yet in a position to have a positive influence on the banks' corporate governance.

9
Smaller Local Banks

The smaller urban local banks include mainly city commercial banks as well as a dwindling number of urban credit cooperatives. City commercial banks (CCBs) are local financial institutions that were set up in the reform era under the aegis of local governments. Most of them are headquartered in urban centres and their development is clearly linked to their narrow scope and environments.

9.1 Market shares and coverage

Over the years the city commercial banks have been able to achieve a slight increase in their national market share: from 5.5% in 2004 to 7.2% in 2009. This is not only the result of an increase in their number, but also the result of strong growth in their asset bases (from CNY15 bln per institution in 2004 to CNY40 bln in 2009).

Considering just their national market share would be unfair since expansion beyond their locality is off-limits for most institutions; and for the best-in-class it has only been possible since 2005. Each of them ranks within the first four or five banks in its local area. May Yan (2006) has illustrated that on average they have a banking asset market share of 8.5% in their localities and, in general, rank just behind the SOCBs.

Historically, CCBs have been limited to expansion within their own particular locality. It is now the case that healthier banks can apply for branches outside their localities provided they have at least CNY50 bln in total assets, equity capital of at least CNY1 bln, NPL ratios lower than 6% over the past three years, ROA of at least 0.45% and ROE of at least 10%. The largest 33 CCBs have successfully applied for such extensions for over 100 new (sub-)branches (CBRC, 2009c).

While the CCBs normally market themselves as the 'local economy's bank' or the 'locals' bank', the structure of their loan portfolios reveals a different picture. On average, in 2005, only 38.6% of surveyed CCBs' portfolio went to SMEs or to individuals. Later statistics show that regulators' pressure to increase lending to SMEs had some impact in 2008 with the SME loan portfolio growing to 71% of all loans – in 2009, however, with the implementation of the fiscal stimulus only under half of the loans actually went to SMEs. Local governments often find in CCBs' strong financial support for their large infrastructure projects. The lending decision for the large credit limits is often not based on commercial grounds. During 2009, many CCBs increased their exposure to local governments.

To venture beyond their borders in terms of geography and of products or markets, the CCBs have also started to establish some of the new financial institutions permitted in rural areas (Xinhua Economic Focus, 2010). But the challenges remain strong: from human resources to adequate systems, proper management of risks and internal controls – all issues that become even more pronounced when going abroad.

9.2 Historical developments and business scope

Most of China's CCBs were established in a process beginning in 1995 and involving the mergers of some 2,200 UCCs and urban cooperative banks.[1] The first was the Shenzhen City Cooperative Bank, established in June 1995. CCBs were created in the first place to provide financial services to SMEs, individuals and (perhaps most importantly) governments in their locality (Zhong J., 2004). Most of them no longer carry the name 'city commercial bank'; they are more likely to be called 'Bank of' a certain locality (over 60 of them have made this change to their names; Xinhua Economic Focus, 2010).

Over the 15-year periods since their formal establishment, one can distinguish three phases of development. The first phase is characterised by the reduction of historical risks (in some cases CCBs faced payment crises) which included for most the restructuring of their capital base, and the stripping out and disposal of NPLs; the second reform and development phase related to when they became the main finance provider of local residents and SMEs; the third entails the upgrading of systems and procedures (*China INFOBANK Limited*, 2005b). Not all CCBs are in the same development phase and some are taking longer than others.

The urban credit cooperatives belong to a soon to be extinct type of financial institution which was a side effect of early reforms.[2] The better performers were allowed to be merged together to form city commercial banks (CBRC, 2008). With the help of their local authorities, 13 of them were further able to resolve their non-performing loans issues (taking off their balance sheet some CNY13.9 bln in NPLs). Still 289 of them were closed or had to stop business between 2003 and 2007. During that time a further 76 failed institutions were merged with other better-run banks. Later on, the remaining ones used their retained earnings, fresh capital and other fund-raising instruments to replenish their capital bases. By 2009, there were only 11 UCCs left to be resolved – probably through restructurings – and an additional 12 had been closed in the course of 2008.

A new breed of CCBs has emerged as the result of mergers among former city commercial banks, urban credit cooperatives and even rural financial institutions (for example, Jiangsu Bank and Huishang Bank). As mergers of bad banks do not necessarily lead to the creation of better banks, internal restructurings and reforms have also been used in order to prune the most poorly performing businesses. Merging the banks was nevertheless hailed as a long-term solution for China, but the main issue to be tackled is government interference. This cannot be reduced because the banks are still fully in the hands of local authorities and the relationships remain. Politicised lending practices will endure.

9.3   Shareholding structures

On average local governments own 75% of the capital of CCBs (KPMG, 2005), directly and indirectly.[3] While May Yan (2006) shows that direct ownership for major CCBs is only at 23% of capital on average, one should take full account of the other government-owned enterprises which are also their shareholders. Part of this ownership was set up in 1995 when the local Finance Bureaus were allowed to use part of their budget to invest in around 30% of CCBs' equity. Further to this, a rule had been set by the PBOC that a single enterprise cannot own more than 10% of the capital and that a single individual cannot own more than 2% (*China Industry and Economy Information Net*, 2005). The local government, as a result, often has the final say in running the bank and taking strategic decisions.

As in the case of the four SOCBs, the state in form of local and provincial governments has played a strong role, both as a shareholder and as a financial supporter in case of technical insolvency (Table 9.1).

To diversify the shareholding structures and expand their capital bases, the banks have also auctioned their shares (SinoCast Banking Beat, 2009f).

Table 9.1 Financial support from local governments to CCBs, 1994–2004

In CNY bln	1994–2004
Compensation for losses	7.13
Stripping of NPLs	12.18
Disposal of non-performing assets	39.88
Total	*59.19*

Source: Based on Xie D. (2005).

Local authorities have also invited other shareholders, such as foreign ones (Table 9.2), other Chinese commercial banks (EIU, 2010a), large Chinese corporates or the China Development Bank, a policy institution which has, for example, helped Beibu Bank.

Each of the CCBs is a limited liability entity with a unified structure and management. Some of them had managed to list their shares in Shanghai (Ningbo, Nanjing and Beijing CCBs) before the securities regulator put an end to that venue.

9.4 Governance and transparency

The CCBs need to comply with the same regulations as other commercial banks when it comes to the issues of asset quality, capital adequacy, information disclosure and risk management. The minimum capital required is lower at CNY100 mln, compared with CNY1 bln for JSCBs and CNY50 mln for rural commercial banks.

Regulatory agencies have increased their pressure on local governments to progressively release local banks from their grip and influence. CBRC and the Chinese government have encouraged CCBs to improve their capital adequacy and their loss reserves, to establish prudential operational mechanisms, control-related parties' transactions, reduce lending concentrations, and strengthen information disclosure to improve transparency, implement restructuring plans and the overall level and competitiveness of each institution (CBRC, 2004a, b).

Financial statements should be published according to the new Chinese Accounting Standards which are quite close to the internationally recognised IFRS. The banks should also publish their annual reports on their websites, but at present only 64% do so (SinoCast Banking Beat, 2009d).

The CCBs are ordered into six groups according to their performance and financial standing by the CBRC. The sixth group is composed of

Table 9.2   Foreign investors in CCBs (up to 2009)

Chinese bank	Foreign investor	Foreign stake (%)
Bank of Beijing	ING Bank	16.07
	International Finance Corp	4.04
Bank of Chengdu	Hong Leong Group	19.99
Bank of Chongqing	Dah Sing Bank	17.00
Bank of Dalian	Bank of Nova Scotia	19.99
	International Finance Corp	5.00
Bank of Hangzhou	Commonwealth Bank of Australia	19.99
	Asian Development Bank	4.99
Bank of Jilin	Hana Bank	19.70
Bank of Nanjing	International Finance Corp	3.28
	BLNP Paribas	12.61
Bank of Ningbo	OCBC (Singapore)	15.34
Bank of Qingdao	Intesa Sanpaolo	19.90
	Rothschild Group	5.00
Bank of Shanghai	HSBC	8.00
	International Finance Corp	7.00
	Shanghai Commercial Bank (Hong Kong)	3.00
Bank of Tianjin	ANZ Banking	20.0
Changsha Commercial Bank	BRED Banque Populaire	20.00
Jinan City Commercial Bank	Commonwealth Bank of Australia	11.0
Nanchong City Commercial Bank	DEG (Germany) and Sparkassen International Development Trust	13.30
Urumqi City Commercial Bank	Habib Bank	19.90
Xi'an City Commercial Bank	International Finance Corp and Scotiabank	16.4
Xiamen City Commercial Bank	Fubon Financial Holding	19.99
Yantai City Commercial Bank	Hang Seng Bank	20.0

Source: Media reports.

'failed institutions' which have been closed or stopped business (CBRC, 2009c).

Local governments influence the CCBs not only financially, but also by choosing senior managers and directors. Most of these are chosen because of their political allegiance, rather than their managerial and banking skills (Li Z., 2005). The human resources issue is aggravated by the fact that most CCBs' staff come from the old UCCs and have relatively low levels of education (staff with specific finance educational backgrounds make up only 30% of all staff) and performance records (Lu M., 2005). Finding good staff locally can be a challenge in second-tier cities.

The CCBs cooperate with their peers in some limited areas, such as through a clearing centre, for loan syndication, funds and bonds investment management, credit card issuance and training in international banking business (*The Asian Banker*, 2005b; *Financial News*, 2005c).

9.5   Financial performance

Before 2004, city commercial banks as a whole showed a quite alarming picture. Some had NPL ratios of around 60% and a small number of them had negative equity capital on their books (Zhang J., 2005). Apart from CCBs with negative equity, the majority of them showed on average that the loan volume to their ten largest clients amounted to 200% of their equity (Zhong J., 2004; *China Industry and Economy Information Net*, 2005; Zhang J., 2005; Yan M., 2006). Of accumulated net profits amounting to CNY1.5 bln in 2003, only CNY0.3 bln remained after dividend payments (represented a 80% payout ratio). While most in the 2005 survey had formally established a risk management function, only two institutions really used the developed risk management guidelines in their daily business (*Financial News*, 2005c; SCDRC, 2005).

The average figures (Table 9.3) hide some large and persistent disparities because of differences in the degrees of local government intervention, in enforcement of the same regulations, in commercial cultures and in limits fixed internally by some banks for certain regions (Zhou X., 2004a).

Another important factor in accounting for the discrepancy in performance is the quality of ownership of CCBs. A survey (*Financial News*, 2005a as well as SCDRC, 2005) found that banks' profitability is influenced not so much the percentage of shares held by local governments as rather the level of revenues of the relevant local government. Where

Table 9.3   Efficiency of CCBs (CNY)

	2004	2006	2009
Assets per bank (in bln)	15.23	22.95	39.72
Assets per employee (in mln)	n.a.	22.75	31.95

Source: Own calculations based on CBRC 2007 and 2010.

local governments can rely on abundant revenues because of strong economic development or a large economic centre, the banks tend to show
lower levels of NPLs. This is also confirmed by another research exercise
based on PBOC data (Shih et al., 2005b). Overall, where economic activities are supported, where private enterprises strive, where SMEs can
find guaranteeing institutions for their loans, where individual incomes
are higher, where local governments make efforts to protect the rights of
enterprises and individuals, CCBs tend to show a healthier development
and sounder financial situation.

More recent figures for the CCBs' performance show a brighter picture
(Table 9.4). However, some CCBs are still run badly (Li P., 2009): one
of them – and probably no exception – shows that its lending to the
local government's investment company amounted to 44% of its capital
and that the exposure to its ten largest borrowers was 177% of equity.
Additionally, 42% of its loans had no collateral at all (only 26% were collateralised while 16% were based on guarantees or pledges respectively).
Finally, the deposits over one year constitute only one-seventh of the
loans of over a year. Concerning risk management, credit analysis was
not thorough, monitoring was poor and some rules and regulations

Table 9.4 Performance of city commercial banks (CNY bln, %)

	2004	2006	2008	2009
Number of CCBs	112	113	136	143
Total assets	1,706	2,594	4,132	5,680
Total liabilities	1,647	2,472	3,865	5,321
Market share of banking assets	5.5	5.9	6.6	7.2
Total loans	905	1,400	1,422	2,890
Total deposits	1,434			4,650
NPLs	106	65	48	38
NPL ratio	11.7	4.8	2.3	1.3
Coverage ratio			114.0	182.2
SME loans		403	1,012	1,380
SME NPL ratio			3.5	
Capital adequacy	2.7	8.6	13.0	13.0
Total equity	58	122	267	359
Net profits	9	18	41	50
RoE	14.2	14.9	15.3	13.8
RoA	0.5	0.7	1.0	0.9
Number of employees		113,999	150,920	177,765

Source: CBRC (2007, 2008, 2009c and 2010).

were not complied with. The bank did not have an appropriate exposure management system and approvals came sometimes after disbursement. To make matters worse the bank even has an agreement with the local authorities – its main shareholder – to take over the non-performing assets for which it had itself approved the loan.

9.6   Challenges and opportunities

Capital adequacy is a substantial headache for CCBs. Since their main shareholders are local governments and they need to decrease their dependency on them, increasing capital from existing shareholders is not a solution. Another possible solution would be to turn to capital markets; however, their current operating state makes access to such financing problematic. Thus the only remaining option is either to attract new shareholders (foreign or domestic private investors) or to issue subordinated debt (Zhang J., 2005; Zhou W., 2005).

Foreign entities are happy to enter the market at relatively lower costs (albeit with often too little shares). For local private enterprises, the incentives are lower since most CCBs have relatively low ROAs and they can find other more rewarding investment opportunities (Zhou W., 2005) and finally because they are also often borrowers in these banks. The introduction of new shareholders will drive the formation of new interests and reform current interest structures (Zhou W., 2005). This in turn can lead to significant changes internally and in risk management.

The second issue concerns the internal corporate governance structure of CCBs, which has a decisive influence on their healthy long-term development. This is supported by the evidence from the reform years. Since CCBs have been transformed into their current form, their profitability has improved, thus showing that legal ownership has had a positive influence on their results.

The last issue concerns the diversification of shareholdings. While large stakes ensure a more stable development, large shareholders can also advance their own interests at the detriment of smaller or minority shareholders. Concentrated large shareholdings also favour related-parties transactions.

Box 4 Public–private oversight mechanism: Central Huijin Investments Co.

At first Central Huijin Investments Co. (Huijin) was only established as a conduit to recapitalise the Bank of China and China Construction Bank with the country's foreign exchanges reserves. It has now graduated into a wholly state-owned investment arm[1] of China's sovereign wealth fund, China Investment Corporation. Its capital amounts to USD110 bln (CIC Annual report, 2008 and 2009).

Following its investments in BOC and CCB, it has dipped further into the financial sector by acquiring large strategic stakes in other banks (for example, ICBC, BoComm, Everbright, CDB and ABC) and insurers (for example, China Reinsurance, New China Life and Sinosure). Investments in the securities industry are managed by its subsidiary, China Jianyin Investment. Other state investments in the financial sector are managed only by the Ministry of Finance.

To manage the company, the central authorities first appointed Xie Ping as chief executive. An outspoken and reform-minded banker, Xie Ping has been more recently replaced by Peng Chun from BoComm (Hu C., 2010). It also employs other managers – all active and professional. Such banking background is necessary because Huijin does not intend to act solely as a finance investor – it is also active in management oversight and allegedly requires the implementation of certain corporate governance instruments.[2] In fact it has to produce a return on its investments and must rely for that on appreciation of its investments on stock markets or on the payment of dividends. Because of this approach, it is sometimes labelled a 'commercial government agency'.

But what threat can Huijin be if the banks believe – probably correctly – that bad behaviour will not be sanctioned strongly because rescue would come forward at any time. A first test came with the recapitalisation exercises for 2010: Huijin agreed to reinvest the dividend payments from its investors to allow for a stronger capital base and thus to forego covering its own costs. Can market-minded technocrats really change party loyalists' minds and behaviours?

In addition, journalists reported that Huijin's say in banks and banking reform is actually less strong than assumed: it has to compete with CBRC, PBOC, and the Ministry of Finance (which also compete between themselves) and to advance some of its views which run contrary to those of MOF and PBOC. And because it also uses funds from the state to invest (which come from SAFE which is itself under the PBOC umbrella), it has few rights to decide where investments would be appropriate and no final say over which managers to appoint. It is a prolongation of the state's arms in implementing policy goals[3] – as a 'policy financial platform' (Hu C., 2010).

10
Foreign Banks

10.1 Market shares and coverage

Foreign banks, in the past five years, had a market share hovering around 2% of all loans.[1] For foreign currency loans in China, they had a larger market share of 20%. The same holds for the Shanghai market. A survey by McKinsey has shown how difficult it can be for foreign banks to secure market share in China: large branch networks still play an important role and Chinese customers are loyal to their banks, with banking relationships lasting on average between nine and 12 years (Bekier and Lam, 2005).

Those foreign banks with the strongest presence in China are HSBC, the Bank of East Asia, Standard Chartered and Citigroup. Many foreign banks have started to expand into inland regions but remain concentrated in coastal areas. Above all they are well capitalised – a sound base for expansion – and enjoy the backing of their parents institutions (in terms of knowledge, strategy and systems, and so on). Luo Ping (2003) thinks that their influence on the Chinese banking system is relatively small as they remain niche players.

10.2 Historical developments and business scope

From 1978 foreign banks have been allowed back into China. However, in the period up to 2006 their business scope and geographic range was limited due to restrictive Chinese regulations, most of which have been eased gradually over the years.

Foreign banks were attracted into China mainly because of the potential business opportunities, as shown by Leung et al. (2003). With improvements in the regulatory and legal environment, increasing numbers have established operations. However, the prospects and the environment are not the sole aspects factored into the foreign management decision: other factors to take into account include bank size, support and commitment to a China strategy from the headquarters and the international network of the organisation.

With the implementation of WTO commitments beginning in 2006, foreign banks could expand their business scope in terms of products, customers and geography.

In the late 1990s, foreign banks were granted licences to make CNY-denominated loans, and from 1998 they were allowed access to the interbanking market for refinancing. By the end of 2005, foreign banks could provide both CNY- and foreign currency-denominated financial products. Foreign banks had established their expertise in certain areas: trade finance, money market products, foreign exchange and derivatives dealing (Metcalfe, 2005). Until the late 1990s, foreign banks could only offer financial services to foreign customers, joint-ventures and foreign enterprises. Their main customers are still international companies, joint-ventures and large state-owned companies with a foreign background (Metcalfe, 2005). Until 2006, foreign banks were also limited to 25 cities.

With the entry into the WTO, China dropped a large number of limitations towards foreign entrants. To be able to enjoy the same rules and regulations as other Chinese commercial banks, foreign banks need to register a subsidiary.[2] Registration requires CNY1 bln in capital[3] (with an additional CNY100 mln for each branch), a healthy banking group backing the entity (and at least USD10 bln in assets), previous profitability and experience in China, and compliance with the requirements for risk management and internal controls. Many banks have registered a subsidiary under the new rules, but have also kept their previous operations running, to benefit from both sides.

Since this time the banks have been able to expand or to open up new niches, in areas such as wealth management, trade finance, debt capital markets, and acquisition financing.

10.3 Shareholding structures

Since China's entry into the WTO foreign banks can choose between full incorporation in China, establishing a branch or a representative office[4] as before, or indirect entry with an equity stake[5] in a local bank. While the branch option was the choice before 2006, thereafter banks have preferred the first or the third option. Meanwhile the third option which was seen as a feasible alternative (Tables 8.4 and 9.2) has been shown to be no less difficult because of restrictions on the stakes that can be acquired (Box 1) and thus the difficulty in infusing one's own practices and knowledge (during the financial turmoil many large investors sell their stakes in the Big Four after realising that the money would be better spent elsewhere).

10.4   Governance and transparency

Apart from the rules with which all banks in China have to comply, foreign banks are also subject to other specific regulations (References for laws 60). Further to these, foreign banks need also to comply with provisions that apply to foreign enterprises in general (Wei W., 2005) as well as with those for foreign investors (References for laws 63).

In early 2006, licensing requirements were brought more or less into line with those for Chinese institutions, and the requirements for business lines and for the qualifications of directors and managers are broadly similar (Tables 2.2 and 2.3). Licensing is already a level playing field. Prudential ratios are the same for all banks.

Nevertheless some restrictions remain – the only consolation being that these also apply to Chinese banks:

- Liquid assets must make up more than 25% of liquid liabilities.
- Assets of a branch by currency should amount to more than the liabilities in the corresponding currency.
- 60% of the bank's operating capital shall be invested as follows: half in forex deposits and the other held in local currency government bonds or times deposits maturing in less than six months.
- SAFE requires a foreign off-shore debt quota of 40%.
- Interbank market loans can make up a maximum of 150% of the branch's capital.
- A loan to deposit ratio of 75% must be complied with (up to 2011; potentially the most difficult issue in compliance).

10.5   Financial performance

Although the foreign banks have only a small market share, their operations are efficient, they have high growth rates, they play an important role in certain areas (such as settlement services and foreign exchange

Table 10.1 Foreign banks' performance (CNY bln, %)

	2004	2005	2006	2007	2008	2009
Number of banks			14	29	32	37
Total assets	582.29	715.45	927.87	1,252.47	1,344.78	1,349.23
Total liabilities	532.91	653.01	853.16	1,135.30	1,202.81	1,181.85
Market share of banking assets	1.84	1.91	2.11	2.38	2.16	1.71
Total loans			473.75	644.00	762.13	686.67
Total deposits				443.10	597.40	
NPLs			3.79	3.22	6.097	6.18
NPL ratio			0.8	0.5	0.8	0.9
Coverage ratio						139.66
Capital adequacy					18.45	21.22
Total equity	49.38	62.45	74.71	117.17	141.97	167.38
Net profits	2.35	3.66	5.77	6.08	11.92	6.45
RoE	4.8	5.9	7.7	5.2	8.4	3.9
RoA	0.4	0.5	0.6	0.5	0.9	0.5
Number of employees			16,724	31,343	27,812	32,502
Assets per bank (mln)			66,276	43,189	42,024	36,466
Assets per employee (mln)			55	40	48	42
Number of outlets	188	207	224	274	311	338

Note: The figures for 2006–2009 cover only the banks that are locally incorporated under the rules issued from 2006 onwards.
Source: CBRC 2007, 2008, 2009c and 2010; own calculations.

lending), and they have a strong influence on the markets (CBRC, 2005a). The banks have been found to have a limited impact in China – mostly on the JSCBs but much less so on the Big Four (Xu D. and Feng Q., 2008).

Their profits are limited in China (Table 10.1), but the value of their investments is growing (Financial Times, 2010).

The banks during the financial crisis in 2007–09

With the squeeze on liquidity squeeze as a result of the financial crisis, foreign banks in China also faced a much harsher environment: their own parent companies were themselves in dire straits and Chinese banks were reported to be reluctant to lend funds to them. The CBRC had to reassure market players that foreign banks were healthy. Then, in order to ensure a more independent flow of liquidity, the banks were allowed to issue renminbi-denominated bonds on the interbank market.

10.6 Challenges ahead

With all the progress that has been made, the expectation was that soon the banks will take over in China. But that has yet to take place.

Foreign executives still complain about the lack of transparency in regulations (they contend that they are not being treated on an equal footing), that branches are approved slowly on a case-by-case basis, that the credit culture is weak and that the interbank market fails to fulfil its proper role. Nevertheless, they all remain upbeat about the Chinese potential (PwC, 2010b).[6] The largest banks (HSBC, Standard Chartered and Citibank) have also established rural entities (see the following chapter on rural financial institutions).

11
Rural Financial Institutions

For a long time rural areas have been served by a small number of formal financial institutions: the ABC, the RCCs, the postal savings system (Box 5) as well as the Agricultural Development Bank of China[1] (ADBC), a policy bank. Their main role is to provide financial services to local farmers and agricultural enterprises and to support the economic development of rural areas. Since the level of financial intermediation has remained poor in rural areas, CBRC opened competition to other institutions such as village and township banks, loan companies and mutual aid finance groups (see chapter on new forms of financial intermediation). At the same time the reform of the RCCs has produced rural commercial banks and rural cooperative banks.

11.1 Market shares and coverage

Rural financial institutions make up around 11% of the total banking assets, a proportion that has remained relatively stable in recent years. However, to better reflect their standing and their rural positioning, one should consider their presence in those areas. By 2007, ABC, ADBC, rural cooperatives, the PSBC and the new rural FIs had loans outstanding of CNY7.7 trn, according to CBRC – but not all loans service the rural economy. By 2009, the amount of loans to agriculture stood at CNY9 trn. For example, RCCs in Fujian province are the lender of choice for agriculture, accounting for 96% of all such loans in the province (even though their loan portfolio makes up only 9% of all loans in Fujian; Wu W., 2009).

The RCCs benefit from a close relationship to their target markets and are still often the sole financial institution in these under-banked rural areas. Their loan portfolios are heavily geared towards agricultural lending.

Box 5 Postal savings

In March 2007, the Postal Savings Bank of China (PSBC) was established as a commercial bank. It had previously been – as was frequently the case in other countries – a part of the post office's network under the name of China Postal Savings and Remittance Bureau. The owner remains the China Post Group (which is under the supervision of the Ministry of Finance, not SASAC), but the bank's supervisor is CBRC.

With a commercial bank licence, the bank is now able to lend funds – the goal is mainly to reach out to rural areas. Before 2007, the bank was separated from PBOC to take only deposits. These were then guarded at the PBOC for a subsidised rate of 4.6% p.a. (the rate was later adjusted to be closer to that of other financial institutions). Now PSBC's deposits are deposited with other rural institutions, policy banks and invested in government bonds. By end-May 2009 the postal system sat on deposits amounting to CNY2.2 trn so that from that point of view it is China's fifth-largest bank.

Its operations are carried out through a network of over 36,500 outlets (two-thirds of which are located in rural areas). Through the network, the bank acts as an agent for wealth management, mutual funds, insurance and foreign exchange services. Another strength of the bank is its remittance service for which it cooperates with Western Union. Now the bank is also using its strong network to loan small amounts to farmers and other rural enterprises. The bank's loan portfolio amounted to CNY30 bln in 2008 (CNY60 bln were disbursed). The absence of legacy lending gives the bank the chance to have a fresh start but does not yet guarantee a healthy development in the future.

The bank faces a number of challenges. It is difficult to diversify investment channels because of the lack of safe alternatives, the lack of investment experience of the savings system staff, and the absence of proper risk management mechanisms. Then, transparency is a weak point (Table B.3): no financial statements are available – even though since 2008 the bank is supposed to publish them in accordance with the new Chinese Accounting standards. Thirdly, the bank is also expected to fulfil development goals in the rural areas, and this could have an impact on its loans. At least for now, the deposits it received from the rural areas will be used for rural areas – in contrast to the past when bank deposits were mainly used in urban areas. Finally, the corporate governance mechanisms are not supported by a professional owner or strong credit culture and processes. The bank is run under an administration which can interfere at any time (even though it now boosts a board of directors (BoD), a supervisory board (SB) and senior management). With such a wafer-thin equity base and a rather poor profitability, the bank has no margin of error in lending.

Table B.3   Performance of the PSBC (CNY bln, %)

	2009	2008	2007
Number of branches		19,912	20,441
Number of employees	132,536	116,759	109,403
Total assets	2,704.51	2,216.29	1,768.75
Total liabilities	2,671.34	2,194.19	1,756.79
Market share of banking assets	3.43	3.55	3.36
Total equity	33.17	22.10	11.96
Net profits	3.22	0.65	0.65
RoE	9.7	2.9	5.4
RoA	0.1	0.0	0.0
Equity/assets	1.23	1.00	0.68
Assets per employee (mln)	20.41	18.98	16.17

Source: CBRC (2007, 2008, 2009c and 2010); author's own calculations.

All rural financial institutions bear to diverging extents the marks of a double pressure: being sustainable, and at the same time being a conduit for government rural policy (this resulted in high non-performing loans: according to CBRC the NPL ratio for agriculture – the mainstay of RCCs and ABC – was 47% in 2007).

For example, the creation of the new rural financial institutions is one of the pillars of the Chinese government to enhance financial intermediation and services in rural areas, to ensure a proper economic development to close the gap existing between livelihoods in urban and rural areas (a list of initial institutions as established can be found in Li L., 2008).

11.2   Historical developments and business scope

The RCCs were re-established in the early 1980s[2] to ensure financial intermediation and to direct financial funds to rural areas. They first functioned out of the ABC framework and in competition with the semi-formal but now defunct rural credit funds (RCFs[3]). Under the ABC leadership, RCCs suffered from a number of inefficiencies:

- Deposits were not priced profitably, so that the expense of managing large numbers of small accounts became prohibitive.
- The RCCs were required to fund a great part of the ABC with their own funds (20–30% of their deposits).
- Loans-to-deposit ratios were lower than that for the rest of the financial institutions because of large deposit requirements at the ABC.
- High operating costs were the result of inefficiency and large branch networks.
- The operating model of RCCs did reflect that of ABC (geared towards large agricultural clients) rather than the needs of their own customers (smaller enterprises and farmers) (Watson, 2003).[4]

ABC played diverse and conflicting roles with the RCCs: depositor and drawer of funds, supervisor and leader. ABC and not their own customers was given preferential treatment by RCCs.

In the mid-1990s, the rural financial system was overhauled: ABC and RCCs were made independent from each other and RCFs were closed (Zheng Y., 2003). The newly won independence of RCCs (they were directly supervised by PBOC) brought higher efficiency and even profits in some cases (but also NPLs from ABC).

Today, RCCs customers include rural farmers, rural enterprises, as well as local authorities. Products and services are reduced to the simplest ones and innovation is not supported by the authorities. RCCs do not orient their lending specifically towards their members. Statistics show that while there have been increases in the deposits held by farmers, the loans to them have decreased continuously over the same period of time. This is because RCCs are unwilling to lend without collateral and because collateral often cannot be provided by members (He Z., 2004).

In most cases the RCCs lend short-term facilities (most of them under one year and none of them over three years): supply is not adapted to the requirements of farmers who would prefer longer maturities loans with different repayment schemes (Xie P. et al., 2005a).

The network of RCCs reaches out to the lowest administrative level in China: branches and outlets can be found in urban centres, townships and villages. Nevertheless, RCCs are limited to operations within their own local regions. The geographical restrictions have had negative effects: first, it made local authorities' interference in the daily operations of RCCs easier (especially since the 1990s when local governments depended on tax revenues from local enterprises for their economic development); second, it hindered the establishment of a market discipline mechanism and created a strong monopoly (which created 'too important to fail'-institutions); third, it destroyed the opportunity to achieve economies of scale; and fourth, it weakened the RCCs' risk withstanding ability (because of a small capital base and undiversified activities) (Liu M. et al., 2005).

The continued poor performance of RCCs meant that the regulators have tried to reform them on a number of occasions. Finally, in 2003 the latest plans were put on the table: in August of that year a process began in eight Chinese provinces that is still ongoing. The focus of the reforms is three-pronged: ownership, capital structure and operating model. First, proper shareholding structures were established (previously the RCCs were cooperatives only in name[5] and control was in the hands of managers). Local governments are not allowed to interfere in their operations. Then, the RCCs had to choose between three distinct operating forms: rural commercial bank, rural cooperative bank or rural cooperative credit union.[6] The first form carries the highest capital and prudential requirements – thus it is no wonder that most choose the latter option. With that option only the lower administrative levels of operations needed to be consolidated. Finally, the CBRC also required local authorities to help resolve the wealth of bad loans, required the constituting RCCs to give the reform impetus and that investors with the PBOC smooth the way for capital injections (Zhang Y., 2009d).

Most managed to stay afloat – as a bank or as a union. The remaining institutions were closed or merged. Reforms, however, have not gone as far as to remove employees and managers nor local governments. Thus internal controls remain weak and government funds are still needed to ensure a stable basis.[7] Rumours in the press show that it might not yet be the last supper (Zhang Y., 2009a). To enhance their standing, mergers have been used. Many have also been able to open up branches and outlets outside their original locality or province.

Finally to facilitate and broaden the scope of business operations new ways of doing business have been permitted (PBOC Rural finance research group, 2008). These include: lending to farmers' cooperatives, loans with pledges on agricultural production purchase orders, loans collateralised with rights on farmlands (for example, growing fruits and flowers) and small loan amounts (where administrative procedures are reduced to allow for faster repeat lending of limited amounts).

11.3 Shareholding structures

The RCCs' 'cooperative' structure created highly scattered and diversified holdings which on the one hand guaranteed no controlling ownership but at the same time meant that individuals had little chance to exert any influence, so that they rapidly lost interest in taking their oversight function seriously. While the ownership structure of RCCs was formally organised around the cooperative members, it became clear over time that the RCCs were controlled from inside, by insiders (He Z., 2004).

Even though the RCCs are collectively owned, members did not contribute voluntarily to the RCCs' capital and cannot withdraw from their investments (Dong and Featherstone, 2004). Their right to choose managers is hindered by the influence of local governments (Schlotthauer, 2003). Around half of the generated profits were further transferred to the local authorities' public funds (10% for social security, 10% for educational purposes and the remaining 30% were distributed to the collective).

To cope with the above issues, early reforms introduced new owners, such as enterprises. These had larger stakes but in a number of cases these created controlling stakes that by no means lead to a power balance between shareholders. Still, in most cases the incentives for taking up an oversight function for holders of RCCs' capital are almost inexistent due to the strong interference of central and local authorities (Yang X. and Shen S., 2004).

Finding new shareholders to instil a fresh wind is difficult. Foreign souls – although invited (Zhang Y., 2009b) – were interested but the challenges are often very daunting so that few have come forward. To date only the Australia and New Zealand Banking Group (ANZ) and Rabobank have taken equity stakes. In an attempt to promote further investments the International Finance Corp. of the World Bank has also chosen to invest.

Clear and strong ownership would help to restructure the shareholding structures of RCCs since they have to comply with a maximum of 10% for a single shareholder. It would also help them in lending to their purported stakeholders rather than as in 2009 to local government finance platforms, real estate projects and other potentially highly polluting activities (Zhang Y. and Fang H., 2009).

The other new rural financial institutions have found it much easier to find new shareholders. Investors prefer clean books with no legacy lending – even though the interference of the authorities is still very much a reality. ICBC and CCB have shown interest and also some city commercial banks have established village and township banks around their localities. Even foreign investors, such as HSBC, Citibank and Standard Chartered, have opened their own subsidiaries, branches and outlets (EIU, 2009a).

11.4 Governance and transparency

The RCCs were previously regulated by the ABC (between 1983 and 1996), then by PBOC (before 1983 and between 1996 and 2003) and are now under the supervision of CBRC. RCCs do not have an effective independent and specialised control institution (as, for example, the one that overviews and checks the accounts of Genossenschaftsbanken in Germany, Liu M., 2004).

In 2003 and 2006, the regulatory authorities issued rules with regard to the management and licensing of RCCs and other rural financial institutions (References for laws 14, 23, 24 and 25). According to these rules, rural financial institutions (just as any other banks in China) are responsible for their risks, gains and losses and should conduct their business free from any interference, especially that of local authorities. Rural financial institutions are also required to establish proper corporate governance structures (see Annex).

The RCCs' hierarchies and structures are modelled on the same administrative hierarchies that can be found in local authorities – the last reform did not change this.[8] This ensures a quick and easy channel for influencing decisions and helping to resolve the financing difficulties of farmers – a central point of concern in the eyes of the authorities. This is reinforced by the fact that managers are nominated by the authorities (Yang X. and Shen S., 2004).

The reforms provided a real financial effort to reduce historical burdens and in most cases real reforms of the capital structure were implemented (Xie P. et al., 2005c). The heightened competition in the rural areas as well as reforms imposed upon old institutions have all led to enhancements of the rural markets but have also pushed regulatory capacities to the very limit (Li L., 2008).

11.5 Financial performance

Even as a monopolist in most rural areas, the RCCs were not in a position to produce high net profits. Most were weighed down by NPLs, interest rate controls and low levels of efficiency. In many cases, the value of assets was lower than that of the liabilities and insufficient to repay debts (资不抵债).

Table 11.1 Interest rates differentials compared to PBOC benchmark for rural financial institutions, 2007

Institution types	Times to benchmark (% of institutions)				
	0.9–1.1	1.1–1.3	1.3–2	over 2	Weighted rate
RCCs	6.6	9.8	73.5	10.2	1.6
RCoBs	11.3	13.3	72.2	3.2	1.47
RCBs	27.5	29.7	42.8	0	1.29

Source: PBOC Rural finance research group, 2008.

Asset quality is a challenge for RCCs (some still show NPL ratios of more than 30%; Zhang Y., 2009d). By the end of 2005 the NPL ratio at RCCs for the four loan categories was on average 14.8% (CBRC 2006b). While recent falls in NPLs are a welcome signal, the decreases follow mainly the strong growth in lending experienced by RCCs (Xiao Z., 2006), thus not hinting at a sustainable and long-term change in lending practices and controls.

Interest rates are an important factor and incentive mechanism for the generation of profits (Table 11.1). Shen and Cheng (2004) estimate that RCCs would need, depending on their location, to charge between 8 and 16% p.a. in order to be fully sustainable – instead of having their interest rates capped at 2.3 times the central bank's benchmark. In practice the interest rates charged range from 4.5 to 8% p.a. (Xie P. et al., 2005a,b,c). Territorial restrictions in moving funds from one RCC to another aggravate the lending distortions in rural areas.

In an effort to improve their loan portfolios, the PBOC gave them a choice between re-lending facilities to be repaid without any further conditions or special bills with conditions but which did not need to be repaid. Special bills were the preferred option, amounting to CNY153 bln in 2008. The conditions require them to keep half of the NPLs, to follow the redemption and assessment procedures of the central bank, and to make progress on the internal controls, information disclosure and corporate governance fronts. The bills have not been the cure for all, but at least for some of them.

The RCCs and all other rural financial institutions need to comply with the new Chinese accounting standards, to classify their loans according to the five categories and to comply with capital adequacy requirements.

To help with the development of the financial infrastructure, PBOC has supported the development of a central clearing system for RCCs (Ma D., 2010). In addition, there has been promotion of bank cards and links to the credit registry.

To prove their worth, the new rural financial institutions have been able to show profits (Table 11.2). For example, in 2010 HSBC was able to announce that its rural subsidiary had become profitable.

By end-2010 the RCCs are required – by CBRC – to reach a capital adequacy ratio of 8%, a loan portfolio quality ratio of 10% and coverage of loan reserves to NPLs of at least 70% (Zhang Y. and Fang H., 2009). Further, the CBRC also expects a RoE of 15% and a RoA of 1% (Zhang Y., 2009d). The cooperatives have a long way to go (by mid-2009 more than 700 unions still had negative equity on their book – but nevertheless continued to expand their lending rapidly, writing CNY138bln in loans with as little as CNY1bln in equity).

The newly established financial institutions fare much better (Table 11.3).

To help with profitability, the authorities offer subsidies (SinoCast Banking Beat China, 2009a) and tax breaks (The Wall Street Journal Asia, 2010a).

11.6 Challenges ahead

It is not easy to lend into agricultural markets. Seasonality in output and widespread geographical dispersion requires highly efficient business models. Transaction costs are not the only issue; externalities also abound and the lenders have only limited influence over the issues of loan use, diversification and the economic environment (Jia X., 2008).

The most important and strongest challenge for RCCs and for all new rural financial institutions is to be able to maintain their profitability while simultaneously enhancing their services to rural areas. As such, profit orientation does not necessarily clash with their focus on development. The banks need to be fully responsible for both their decisions and their losses. Although RCCs have a definite lending advantage in rural areas because of their knowledge of local markets and borrowers, they typically do not capitalise on this.

The most important source of risk to rural institutions is the interference of governments – at both the local and the central level. Decisions at the micro and the macro level cannot be said to be taken independently – especially when it comes to the financing of local projects.

At present there has at least been an increase in the level of competition in rural areas following the creation of new rural financial institutions. This might force RCCs to re-think their operations and to clean up their books. However, it will not solve all of the outstanding issues.

Table 11.2 Performance of RCCs and their reformed offspring (CNY bln, %)

	2003	2006			2009		
	RCCs	RCCs	RCBs	RCoBs	RCCs	RCBs	RCoBs
Total assets	2,650.92	3,450.28	503.81	465.36	5,492.50	1,866.12	1,279.12
Total liabilities	2,664.62	3,300.54	478.91	435.87	5,258.06	1,754.57	1,194.03
Market share of banking assets	9.2	7.9	1.1	1.1	7.0	2.4	1.6
Deposits	2,405	3,884					
Loans	1,713	2,624					
NPL ratio	29.37	29.93			12.1		
Capital adequacy	−6.75				4.3		
Total equity	−13.7	149.74	24.9	29.49	234.44	111.55	85.09
Net profits	−0.55	18.62	4.09	5.37	22.79	14.9	13.49
RoE	0.0	12.4	16.4	18.2	9.7	13.4	15.9
RoA	0.0	0.5	0.8	1.2	0.4	0.8	1.1
Number of employees	628,000	634,659	20,003	37,188	570,366	66,317	74,776
Number of institutions	34,909	19,348	13	80	3,056	43	196
Assets per employee (mln)	4.22	5.44	25.19	12.51	9.63	28.14	17.11
Assets per bank (mln)	76.33	170.59	36,839.23	5,448.38	1,720.57	40,803.95	6,091.99

Note: the capital adequacy and NPL ratio are not for June 2009 but for December 2009.
Source: CBRC (2007, 2008, 2009c and 2010); PBOC Rural finance research group (2008); author's own calculations.

Table 11.3   Performance of new rural financial institutions (CNY bln)

	2008			2009		
	VTBs	LCs	MAFGs	VTBs	LCs	MAFGs
Number of institutions	91	6	10	148	8	16
Number of employees	1,629	45	52	3,586	75	96
Capital		4.20			7.00	
Deposits		6.46			26.90	
Loans to *sannong*		1.40			6.60	
SME loans		1.88			9.10	
Profits					0,04	

Note: *Sannong:* agriculture, farmers and rural areas.
Source: CBRC (2007, 2008, 2009c and 2010).

In fact, they are likely to remain the main conduit for policy lending as they are still the mainstay of China's rural banking industry. The threat of being closed down or squeezed out as an institution because of poor performance is still unlikely, meaning that pressure does not build to prevent another failure.

Conclusion to Part IV

The performance of all banks in China has improved in recent years, with years of efforts to reform them finally bearing fruit. The return on investment to the state is not yet positive, however.

The state cannot stand on the sidelines and simply enjoy the fruits: the low-hanging and easily reachable reforms have already been introduced. What now remains is the much harder task of addressing other risks, such as portfolio quality, corporate governance, capital adequacy and overall withstanding ability. These represent continuing as well as future challenges for China and their long-term resolution is paramount if the state is to enjoy a guaranteed flow of resources from the financial sector.

Part V
Risks

Interviewed at the time of ABC's IPO, Liu Mingkang stated that the SOCBs had just completed the easier part of their homework and now needed to concentrate on four specific issues: corporate governance, risk management with Basel II, information systems and innovation capacity (Zhang M., 2010d). All of these areas are inexorably linked to a change in mindsets, systems and culture. These resulted in the banks' poor past standing as shown by large amounts of bad loans, poor capital adequacy and flawed to non-existent corporate governance. As the banks' standing has improved, so have their prospects in the wider world and their ability to withstand crises. These latter two aspects embody the latest changes to the industry but nonetheless carry risks.

12
Non-performing Loans

One major and long-standing issue in the Chinese banking industry is that of non-performing loans (NPLs). This problem is common to most banks, but was particularly acute in those banks which are older and where state shares carry greater weight. The highest NPL ratios were found in SOCBs, some CCBs and rural financial institutions (Table 12.1). While the situation has largely improved across the industry (albeit probably not system-wide[1]), the outlook remains bleak where the roots of the problem have yet to be tackled.

As for many banks in previous years their NPLs have exceeded their equity, the banks were technically insolvent and were kept afloat only to avoid bank runs. Apart from weighing down a bank's profitability, high levels of NPLs also have the effect of reducing a bank's creditworthiness (which may lead to a rating downgrade or greater hurdles or costs in raising funds), increasing potential bank and system failure (through contagion) and negatively impacting economic reforms.

12.1 Estimating the level of NPLs

The level of NPLs at the turn of the century is still unclear. Stakeholders and observers of the banking systems have mentioned figures that diverge quite strongly (Table 12.2): in 1999, the then Governor of PBOC, Dai Xianglong, said that 20% of all loans were non-performing; in 2001, he revised this figure to 26.6% and in 2002 to 30% if calculated by western standards (Lardy, 1999). A government researcher (mentioned by Shih, 2009: 27) put the ratio at 30% in 1996 and 28% in 2001. In the late 1990s and early 2000s, the estimates of NPLs ranged from 20 to 35% of GDP or 20 to 40% of all outstanding loans (Schmitz, 2004). Well-informed

Table 12.1   NPLs holdings in China

Bank type	Bln CNY (%)					
	2005			2009		
	NPL amount	NPL ratio	Share of NPLs	NPL amount	NPL ratio (%)	Share of NPLs
SOCBs	1,072.48	10.49	81.66	362.73	1.80	72.94
JSCBs	147.18	4.22	11.21	63.72	0.95	12.81
CCBs	84.17	7.73	6.41	37.69	1.30	7.58
Rural commercial banks	5.71	6.03	0.43	27.01	2.76	5.43
Foreign banks	3.82	1.05	0.29	6.18	0.85	1.24
Total	1,313.36	8.61	100	497.33	1.58	100.00

Source: Based on data from www.cbrc.gov.cn.

Table 12.2   NPLs and GDP (CNY bln, %)

Year	NPL ratio (%)	GDP	Total loans	NPLs to GDP (%)
1999	20, 20–40	10,699	9,373	18, 18–35
2000	26, 20–40	11,598	9,937	22, 17–34
2001	30, 20–40	12,560	11,232	27, 18–36

Note: The table shows for different NPL ratio estimates to what volume of NPLs they correspond.
Source: GDP: IIF statistics, loan amounts: PBOC.

observers even put forward that 50% of all loans was non-performing by the turn of the century (Studwell, 2002).

RCCs in China fared even worse: in 2001 an investigation showed that in the reviewed provinces, the NPL ratio reached an average of 45% and a maximum of 67% (Xie P. et al., 2005d). In December 2005, the President of ICBC disclosed the bank's NPL ratio for 1998 (based on the five-tier classification) at 47.5% (Jiang J., 2005). Later data show that NPL ratios reached 25%, 23% and 15% for ICBC, BOC and CCB respectively in 2002 (Kudrna, 2007).

Exact figures for NPLs were difficult to come by for a number of reasons:

- Poor standards for the reporting of bad debt levels (each branch knows how much bad debt is acceptable and the numbers are not double checked).

- Classification of loans according to the four-tier (where the classification requirements are less stringent and usually NPL levels are understated[2] – according to Tang Shuangning, the introduction of the five loan categories basically 'created' CNY600 bln in bad loans: Hu C. and Zhang M., 2010).
- A large number of loans are rolled over even though the borrower cannot repay the principal (these are then still counted as performing).
- Existence of loans with large outstanding amounts where new loans are granted to avoid large write-offs in case of borrower bankruptcy.
- High number of inefficient SOEs and commercially unviable projects.
- Loan classification standards are not always followed in a stringent manner[3] (WB, 2003).

Overall, the NPL ratios have improved but in individual cases this has yet to become a reality (Table 12.3). For example, a PBOC staff member reports for Jincheng city in Shanxi province that by the end of the first quarter of 2008, the NPL ratio in the city (across all commercial and policy banks as well as cooperatives) amounted to 17.8% – with the policy banks showing an NPL ratio of 25% and the RCCs 46% in March 2008. Reductions in this ratio stem almost only from the 'SOCBs' restructurings (Li P., 2009). The banks' loan portfolios were also highly skewed towards three local industries (power, chemical and coal industries).

12.2 Classification standards for NPLs

Until 2004, China used a nationally devised classification for NPLs, referred to as the four-tier classification. This old classification emphasised loans over borrowers (a defaulted loan did not require that another loan from the same borrower would be treated as non-performing), principal over interest repayments, and the occurrence of a default event over the true riskiness of the borrower/transaction (Huang et al., 2005). Since 2004, it uses the five-tier classification, in line with international classification standards (Table 12.4).

It should be noted that international current practices with the five-tier categories classification standard still leave some leeway in judging into which category a particular loan should fall. As a consequence, bank managers can still, albeit to a lesser extent, report the NPL volumes that are deemed acceptable. In addition, some banks consider collateral in categorising loans – so that overdue collateralised loans are still recognised as performing in the first year of being overdue (Holland, 2009).

Table 12.3 Non-performing loans in China

	ICBC	ABC	BOC	CCB	BoComm	Merchants	CITIC	SPDB	Minsheng	Industrial	Everbright	Huaxia	SDB	Zheshang	Bohai	GDB	Hengfeng
2009																	
– NPL ratio (%)	1.54	2.91	1.52	1.50	1.36	0.79	0.95	0.80	0.84	0.54	1.25	1.50	0.68	0.01	0.10	2.40	0.38
– Reserves coverage ratio (%)	164	105	151	176	151	253	149	246	206	255	194	167	162	–	–	156	212
– Equity coverage ratio (%)	–1,191	–5,316	–1,427	–1,023	–1288	–647	–2135	–625	–1,133	–1,018	–630	–701	–1,355	–869	–681	–434	–2,519
– Reserves to portfolio (%)	2.61	3.16	2.35	2.70	2.10	2.04	1.44	2.02	1.76	1.39	2.49	2.57	1.11	1.17	1.22	3.88	0.82
– Top 10 borrowers' concentration (%)	20.90	22.47	28.00	18.94	22.15	28.82	39.52	25.04	34.01	38.71	0.48	33.99	40.85	39.89	7.46	56.43	30.53
2005																	
– NPL ratio (%)	4.69	25.08	4.62	3.84	2.34	2.58	4.14	1.97	1.30	2.33	–	3.04	10.56				
– Reserves coverage ratio (%)	54	5	81	67	70	111	80	142	101	91	–	69	38				
– Equity coverage ratio (%)	27	845.99	8	11	7	–5	13	–20	–0.5	4	–	21	203				
– Reserves to portfolio (%)	2.61	1.29	3.86	2.63	1.66	2.95	3.42	2.88	1.34	2.15	–	2.16	4.16				
– Top 10 borrowers' concentration (%)	35.4	n.a.	25.6	28.38	26.26	42.56	46.49	32.48	43.6	39.43		38.2	122.2				

Definitions: NPL ratio = amount of NPLs at the end of the year/gross loan portfolio amount at the end of the year; Reserves coverage = reserves for loan losses/ amount of NPLs; Equity coverage = (amount of NPL–reserves for loan losses)/total equity at the end of the year; Reserves to portfolio = reserves for loan losses/net loan portfolio.
Source: Own calculations based on data from banks' annual reports.

Table 12.4 Four-tier and five-tier loan classification

	Before 2004		Since 2004	
Performing	Performing		Standard	
	Overdue	Missing repayment on the principal not on the interest	Special mention (SM)	Borrowers currently still able to service the debt but some factors could impede repayment
	Doubtful	Within two years after payment period, still no payments	Substandard	Borrowers unable to cover principal and interest in full from normal operating income and losses possible (overdue >3 months)
Non-performing loans	Unrecoverable/ loss	Only in the unlikely event that the borrower is declared bankrupt or liquidated	Doubtful	Collection of principal and interest in full is improbable, significant losses certain, collateral to be collected (overdue >6 months)
	–	–	Loss	Considered uncollectible, after exhausting all collection efforts or instituting legal proceedings

Note: The amount of time written in parenthesis is for guidance only (the number of days overdue is an important indicator for the bank but no limits is stated in the regulation).

Loans which are overdue with other departments or other financial institutions should also be categorised under 'special mention'. Restructured loans shall be classified at least as sub-standard.

Source: Marshall et al. (2004a); WB (2003); own research. Rules for laws 10.

Regulations have also been issued to monitor and manage NPLs (References for laws 26 and 50). NPLs and assets should be monitored and assessed on a regular and systematic basis. Special attention should be given to the largest NPL levels and volumes, to large exposures and related parties' transactions. Reporting on NPLs should be made on a monthly basis to CBRC and should cover basic information and situation on the loans (amount, maturity, trends, area, industry, and so on), write-offs, concentrations, quality of newly disbursed loans, analysis of the reasons and trends in quality of new NPLs, and measures taken to improve or to resolve uncovered issues.

According to the directive on loan loss provisions for bank loans (References for laws 51), general provisions shall be raised for 1%, 2%, 25%, 50% and 100% for each of the five loan categories under the new classification (altogether coverage of NPLs with provisions is required to reach a minimum of 150%). But the banks now need to comply with IAS 39 in China so that they also use historical data and experience to judge the amounts to be raised on a portfolio basis. Additionally, the banks raise specific provisions depending upon the concrete situation of a single loan or subportfolio (for the non-performing categories the provisions may be 20% higher than the norm). These are entirely dependent on the bank's own assessment[4] of the borrower's repayment ability in the future ('objective proof' such as late payments, heavy financial difficulties, bankruptcy, are required to raise the loan loss provisions). The general provisions are tax deductible while specific ones are not.

12.3   Reasons for the emergence of NPLs

In a speech, the PBOC governor, Zhou Xiaochuan (2004a) stated,

> [...], 30% of the NPLs resulted from state planning and administrative intervention, 30% were due to defaults of state enterprises after state banks provided financing based on state policy, 10% came from structural adjustments as a result of state orchestrated closures, mergers and restructurings of enterprises, 10% stemmed from intervention of local governments including poor creditor protection in the judicial and enforcement process, while 20% was due to the inappropriate internal management. In addition, factors, such as poor credit culture, intentional defaults and inadequate application of accounting standards, can be found in all above categories. One striking truth is that many of these causes are related to legal, judicial and enforcement practices.

The emergence of NPLs is highly correlated with the practice of policy lending. For many banks, government interference and credit quotas meant lending to politically motivated schemes, independent of creditworthiness or the level of risk. For example, Guangdong Development Bank's loan portfolio quality was much worse in Guangdong than at its other branches (Lu Y. and Long X., 2005).

Xie Ping (2006), the former general manager of Central Huijin Investment Co., thinks that NPLs emerged as a result of widespread and common collusion between banks, local authorities, their employees, regulators and asset management companies (AMCs, see Box 6). Collusion entails all activities that ensure that responsible persons are not made responsible when it comes to the creation of NPLs. Collusion is useful to those who use it because the cost–benefit–risk equation is in equilibrium: the risk of being discovered is low and the cost attached to it is lower than the expected benefit from collusion, the benefits depend on the breadth and the depth of collusion, because the deeper and broader the collusion, the lower the risk of being caught. Another incentive is when NPLs are disposed of: because NPLs are difficult to value and the information is opaque, the chance of achieving a high price on an NPL sale is high, especially when collusion is at play. Internal collusion within banks, for example, also serves as a method to stand against always higher performance requirements set by authorities for banks.

In their internal structures, banks did not have strong internal controls and credit cultures. Loan monitoring was also ignored and there were no sanctions for bad lending decisions (no bankruptcy was allowed for banks and borrowers). Sanctioning mechanisms would have increased the learning effect and strengthened responsibility and decision-making within the banks. NPLs never represent a danger to bank managers (even during an economic downturn). Because of the lack of incentives for banks to manage their risks, enterprises were also not required to reduce their leverage (and few intended to repay loans: Chen X., 2005). Furthermore some regulations hindered the development of adequate loan loss provisions (LLP) (anything above 1% of the outstanding loans in provisions is not tax-deductible) and set interest rates below the real cost of loans (Lou J., 2000).

12.4   Resolving the NPL issues

The central government's response to the NPLs issue emerged progressively. First, it created the four AMCs, each corresponding to one of the SOCBs. Then, it injected cash on more than one occasion, mainly in the SOCBs (Table 12.5). Local governments have also injected some funds into the banking system and helped create asset recovery companies.

For the other banks, mainly CCBs, the only options were to resolve NPL issues either in collaboration with local authorities through the creation of special entities which take over part of the NPLs (in 2004, local governments spent a total of CNY23.3 bln to buy NPLs from CCBs; *Xinhua's China Economic Information Service*, 2005b), or by themselves through the creation of specialised loan work-out and recovery departments.

Table 12.5 Non-performing loans disposals at state-owned commercial banks

| Year | In bln CNY | Asset Management Companies | | | | |
		Huarong	Great Wall	Oriental	Cinda	Total
1999	Volume of NPLs bought	407.7	345.8	267.2	350	1,370.7
	Loans from Central Bank	94.7	345.8	116.2	3	559.7
	Received from	ICBC	ABC	BoC	CCB, CDB	
	Debt securities from bank	313			347	660
	Financing for NPLs purchase	407.7	345.8	116.2	350	
	Average interest rate (%)	2.25				
2000–2001	Volume of NPLs bought				44.5	44.5
	Loans from Central Bank				44.5	44.5
	Received from the Central Bank, CCB and CDB					
2004	Volume of NPLs bought				320.1	
	Loans from Central Bank				160.5	
	Received from BoC and CCB 278.7 and from BoComm 41.4					
2005	Volume of NPLs bought					459
	Loans from Central Bank					459
	Received from ICBC and spread among all four AMCs					
	Average interest rate (%)					2.25
Total	**Loans from Central Bank**					**1,223.7**
	Volume of NPLs bought					**2,194.3**

Note: Additionally, the costs to the central authorities were higher if one factors in the successive capital injections amounting to a total of CNY732 bln between 1998 and 2008 for the Big Four. Taken together, the disposals and the injections have cost the authorities around 10% of today's GDP – and that does not entail the reform costs of other financial institutions.
Source: Based on Yu, N. (2005d).

These departments are more likely to deal with recent NPLs. Banks have tried to avoid the outright sale of NPLs as it would mean that they need to recognise a loss. However, as the recovery value and probability of loans declines with time, it would be best to sell soon so as to recoup as much value as possible.

Higher competition, market-driven commercialisation but, most importantly, official pressures made loan reductions necessary. These reductions were achieved mainly through disposals, sales or selective write-offs of NPLs (Table 12.6). Fresh inflows of capital have enabled the largest NPL holders (that is, SOCBs) to write off or sell their NPLs. A large volume of NPA has technically changed hands, but is still in the system (see Box 7).

To decrease the level of NPLs in a sustainable manner, Xie Ping (2006) notes that banks should introduce monetary incentive mechanisms (and not government-related), truly independent check and balance mechanisms within banks (internal audit, credit controls, and so on), strengthen the role of independent external auditors, increase the level of sanctions and strengthen internal controls. However, in many cases banks have found short-term fixes to resolve their NPL issues.

Table 12.6 Write-offs and NPL disposals in China for selected banks (CNY mln)

Bank name	2003	2004	2005	2006	2007	2008	2009
ICBC	n.a.	50,500	27,547	11,144	8,171	12,373	11,866
BOC	n.a.	186,900	4,783	3,684	6,798	5,575	9,038
CCB	158,817	6,342	3,784	3,329	6,445	6,579	6,845
ABC	n.a.	n.a.	6,081	16,123	3,242	717,560	1,070
BoComm	8,831	33,382	312	1,147	1,122	1,927	2,804
Merchants	468	303	745	328	528	667	738
CITIC	n.a.	3,035	3,519	3,685	3,072	931	1,326
SPDB	n.a.	509	977	1,163	780	599	814
Minsheng	121	404	511	437	792	1,328	1,345
Industrial	86	335	576	990	451	860	298
Everbright	n.a.	n.a.	n.a.	2,336	3,981	14,850	561
Huaxia	378	481	800	1,014	1,500	2,054	1,987
SDB	0	835	599	564	2,302	10,607	175
Bohai				0	0	0	0
GDB	n.a.	n.a.	n.a.	58,000	460	1,093	557
Zheshang					0	0	0
Hengfeng	n.a.	n.a.	n.a.	n.a.	174	466	84

Notes: The figures for the three SOCBs in 2003–2004 and BoComm in 2004 include transfers of NPLs to the AMCs (the same holds for Everbright in 2008). Bohai and Zheshang as new banks did not have to make any disposals or write-offs up to now.
Source: Based on banks' annual reports.

One special feature of the Chinese banking system is the rolling over of loans without any clean-up practices, called 'lending new to repay the old' or 借新还旧. The loans are normally for a one-year period (often also as a way to bypass administrative rules not to extend medium- or long-term loans) and are rolled over at the end of each year, with no concern for the creditworthiness of the borrower, or capacity or willingness to repay the loans. First, the structuring of these loan facilities is carried out poorly. Second, the likelihood of monitoring and recognising NPLs is reduced to a minimum. This creates poor discipline on the part of the banks and on the borrowers, but at least it does not increase the amount of NPLs.[5] The banks use such devices flexibly: if a loan amount is needed to reach targets, it can be extended by a few days after the end of the reporting period (Wen X., Zhang M. and Fang H., 2009).

Banks have also employed other methods to significantly decrease NPL levels: in certain cases they have extended the maturity of NPLs or have transferred loans from the original borrower to the guaranteeing entity and so on (*China Business*, 2003b). For some observers (interviewed in the above news article) the banks' impetus for decreasing NPL levels came simply from an administrative requirement from the regulators.

For Chinese regulators, the challenge of dealing with NPLs is still very much an ongoing concern. The pressure is now coming from newly disbursed loans and especially those disbursed at the onset or during the financial crisis.

12.5   New loan quality

In December 2005, the President of ICBC disclosed the bank's NPL ratio for newly disbursed loans after 2000 at 1.6% (Jiang J., 2005). New loans seem to have a better quality if ABC's portfolio can be of any guide (Table 12.7).

With the improvement of SOEs' performance as well as the increasing number of private enterprises which exhibit better efficiency and performance, the number and volume of NPLs have been decreasing (Figure 12.1).

The increased close supervision of NPLs in banks by CBRC has also helped raise awareness and induced efforts to reduce NPL levels.

Another reform that will surely reduce further the number and volume of future NPLs is linked to changed incentive mechanisms. On one side, managers are increasingly being recruited in a competitive way in the job market. On the other side, banks – mainly BOC and CCB – have required officers and managers to take responsibility (Zhang X., 2004b): large NPL ratios or volumes can become a reason for reducing remuneration or for

Table 12.7 New and old loan quality at ABC

Year	2007	2008	2009
Old loans (% of total)	33.2	11.8	7.2
Old loans NPL ratio	65.08	12.68	10.49
New loans (% of total)	66.8	88.2	92.8
New loans NPL ratio	3.13	3.23	2.33

Source: ABC IPO prospectus, 2010.

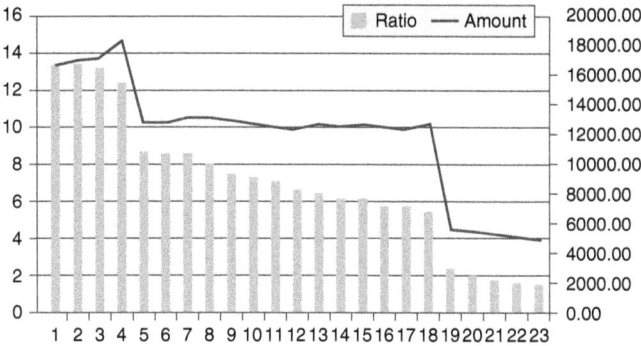

Figure 12.1 Decrease in NPLs in China (in % and 100 mln).
Note: The figure above highlights well the impact of loan disposals on asset quality and that the decrease in the NPL ratio was mainly achieved by loan growth.
Source: Based on data from www.cbrc.gov.cn.

asking a manager to step down. Further to this, banks are now required to implement due diligence guidelines from CBRC when assessing borrowers and transactions risks (References for laws 8).

But two other developments have made increases in NPLs a renewed concern. These were first the introduction of long-term[6] (Table 12.8) and thus riskier lending (which also became available to SOEs, even less concerned with risks and repayment) and second the financing of large government projects (Box 8) from state budgets to banks' loan books.

However, the recent period of rapid loan growth that banks have just experienced could distort the quality of real assets (for example, in real estate lending, wholesale and trade as well as in manufacturing, the NPL ratios published by banks are consistently higher than the overall NPL ratio[7]). Under good economic growth conditions, banks normally tend to be less prudent in lending and thus the amount of new NPL from these is difficult to come by (only ABC in its listing prospectus published NPL ratios for new and old loans). In addition, the rapid growth

Table 12.8 Short-term loans at main commercial banks (%)

	ICBC	ABC	BOC	CCB	BoComm	Merchants	CITIC	SPDB	Minsheng	Industrial	Everbright	Huaxia	SDB	Zheshang	Bohai	GDB	Hengfeng
2007	44.6	n.a.	43.3	42.1	n.a.	n.a.	66.7	70.7	51.7	n.a.	61.1	63.4	63.0	73.6	n.a.	76.1	82.8
2008	43.7	47.1	43.7	43.0	62.0	63.7	68.7	60.7	57.6	53.2	60.1	73.1	66.1	77.0	n.a.	73.1	85.5
2009	37.6	41.8	37.4	37.6	40.1	53.8	59.7	54.9	54.6	40.1	48.6	55.3	56.3	65.0	n.a.	54.8	70.0

Note: Short term means a maturity of less than one year.
Source: Own calculations based on data from banks' annual reports.

in retail loans also accounts for an important part of the reduction in the ratios of NPLs.

A report by the AMC Cinda (CINDA Asset Management Company Research Center, 2010) expects the 2009 loan surge to lead to an increase in NPLs in 2012–13. Their analysis is based on survey questionnaires principally with SOCBs and JSCBs. These show 64% of the respondents believe that the ratio will increase. Bad loans are likely to be concentrated in infrastructure, real estate, retail mortgages and export sectors. A PwC survey of Chinese bankers showed that most expected their NPL ratios to rise, but they also believed that it would be possible to keep them under 5% (PwC, 2009c).

The numbers of special mention loans could hint at future NPLs (Table 12.9).

Moreover the rate at which loans move from the special mention category to the next (doubtful – counted as non-performing) is quite high. In 2009, special mention loans amounts which became non-performing was on average[8] 14% (12% and 18% for 2008 and 2007 respectively) – but the situation can be very different in each bank (for example the ratio ranges between 6% and 49% in 2009).

Another worrying development is the recurrent overcapacity in some industries such as, for example, steel production, power generation and cement (Table 12.10). While central authorities have tried to curb investments in these industries (mostly energy and infrastructure related), the efficiency of such administrative mechanisms is low because local governments often act against them.

Table 12.9 Special mention (SM) loans in main Chinese banks (CNY bln, %)

	SOCBs			JSCBs		
	2007	2008	2009	2007	2008	2009
Special mention loans	605.3	1,012.9	893.6	148.5	164.4	128.1
– as % of gross loans	5.9	6.9	4.6	6.8	2.4	1.5
– NPL ratio with special mention loans (%)	9.6	10.7	6.8	5.1	4.0	2.6
– NPL ratio without special mention loans (%)	2.9	2.9	1.8	10.1	1.2	0.9
– as % of capital	87.2	54.6	42.0	40.8	34.2	19.5

Notes: The figures for JSCBs never include Everbright and for 2007 do not include Hengfeng either. The figures are based on total and not on averages.
*Accounts for the special mention loans fully as if they were non-performing ones.
Source: Own calculations based on banks' annual reports.

Table 12.10 NPL ratios by industry sector (%)

Industry sector	2009	2006–2009 averages
Agriculture	4.52	26.30
Mining	0.38	2.77
Manufacturing	2.54	6.28
Power generation	1.41	2.02
Construction	1.32	2.66
Transport & communication	1.29	1.75
Computing	2.62	4.21
Wholesale & trade	2.71	9.50
Hotels & catering	4.82	12.05
Finance	0.08	0.59
Real estate	1.93	4.20
Commercial services	0.9	5.34
Research & technology	2.98	7.98
Environment & public facilities	0.37	1.02
Other services	1.68	3.78
Education	2.29	2.93
Health & social	1.61	3.55
Culture & entertainment	3.24	9.21
Public management	0.44	3.38

Source: Author's own calculations based on CBRC (2007, 2008, 2009c and 2010).

The enactment of the fiscal stimulus relying on the banks to forward funds has also heightened risks (Table 12.11). It is not a question of if NPL ratios will increase – but rather one of when and to what extent (Reuters News, 2009a).

Other established lending practices have the potential to create further NPLs: the decentralised system for the granting of loans (which lowers the oversight and control over quality, decreases the consistent application of practices, increases the likelihood of outside influence, and de-links lending and macroeconomic conditions), the high reliance on guarantees from related companies as collateral (meaning a greater chance of systemic risk because of interlinked and reciprocal guarantees) and the high reliance on bullet repayment loans (which reduces financial discipline with borrowers and de-incentivises loan monitoring) and, finally, the still widespread rolling over of loans[9] (Ramos R. et al., 2005).

In order to stem the flow of new NPLs, the regulators have issued frequent and repeated warnings to banks not to lend to local government financing platforms, to energy-consuming businesses or to any

Table 12.11 Risky credit exposures (in % of respective loan volume)

	ICBC	ABC	BOC	CCB	BoComm	Merchants	CITIC	SPDB	Minsheng	Industrial	Everbright	Huaxia	SDB	Zheshang	Bohai	GDB	Hengfeng
Top 10 borrowers	2.67	2.48	3.28	2.39	2.73	2.95	4.26	2.61	4.15	4.25	0.05	0.35	3.66	5.24	0.77	5.08	0.40
Real estate	8.2	11.4	7.5	8.1	7.4	6.6	4.8	8.7	11.7	9.8	10.6	8.2	7.4	16.0	10.8	7.8	2.4
Manufacturing	15.4	23.6	21.6	18.1	21.8	18.0	21.7	21.8	13.8	15.9	14.6	29.1	20.2	23.3	32.7	22.8	35.9
Trade	5.1	6.1	14.8	3.3	8.4	7.5	8.8	9.5	4.1	6.3	7.5	12.6	11.5	10.4	5.4	15.1	11.1
Residential mortgages	16.9	13.3	18.5	19.2	12.9	26.3	11.8	15.0	11.3	22.1	15.6	6.8	27.3	1.4	0.0	13.3	0.8
Trust loans	5.0	0.0	0.0	13.0	6.5	6.1	5.3	12.1	3.8	5.2	5.0	4.1	2.5	0.7	0.0	4.2	0.9
Restructured loans	0.6	0.5	0.6	0.4	0.3	0.2	0.3	0.1	0.3	0.2	0.7	0.2	0.5	0.1	0.0	0.9	0.0
Loans overdue less than 90 days	0.3	0.0	0.3	0.1	0.2	0.1	0.4	0.0	0.4	0.2	0.1	0.1	0.4	0.0	0.0	0.0	0.0
Unsecured or guaranteed	48.4	n.a.	53.3	47.5	55.0	51.7	n.a.	50.5	53.9	49.2	0.0	49.6	41.7	48.6	n.a.	55.3	42.6

Source: Own calculations based on data from banks' annual reports.

Table 12.12   Loan loss provisions in banks

Year	2003	2004	2005	2006	2007	2008	2009
Loan loss provisions (% of NPLs)	19.7	14.2	24.8	34.3	39.2	117.9	155.4

Source: CBRC (2010).

sectors which are believed to be in a bubble state (such as real estate[10]). Compliance with maximum exposure limits and concentration will be enforced and banks are required to review again their internal controls and conduct assessment of their loans' performance after disbursement (Asia Pulse, 2009d and CBRC, 2009b).

At the same time they have also required higher loan loss provisions by banks on their loan portfolios (Table 12.12). Even local commercial banks can boost a ratio of 182% as a whole. The CBRC has changed its rules to require 150% as a minimum instead of previously 130% and 100% (CBRC, 2010).

12.6   NPLs and systemic risk

Older NPLs have now been transferred away from the banks' balance sheets, but remain in the financial system. AMCs still have large amounts of NPLs on their books. These represent a further challenge and a potential liability for the central authorities. Based on CBRC data from 2006 the AMCs could still hold around CNY400 bln in NPLs. CBRC estimated in 2009 that the banking system still had CNY518 bln NPLs (PwC, 2009b).

In addition, more NPLs can be found on PBOC's books (Li T., 2008). Li Tong estimates, for example, that by the end of 2007 the total NPLs held by all banks, the AMCs and PBOC could amount to CNY3.9 trn (of which one-third is held by PBOC and another third by the country's commercial banks). The PBOC non-performing loans stem from the PBOC practice to lend funds to institutions that enable them to write their NPLs down, from taking over failed institutions and borrowings to AMCs – none of these loans was ever expected to be repaid. The system-wide NPL estimate of CNY3.9 trn corresponds to 15% of real GDP or 35% of foreign exchange reserves in 2007.

In May 2006 Ernst & Young (E&Y) (E&Y, 2006) published its estimate of the amount of NPLs remaining in the banking system: USD900 bln (including pre-1999 NPLs and potential new ones), more than the official foreign exchange reserves. Following strong criticism from PBOC, the report has been withdrawn rapidly.

As long as the country continues to show strong economic fundamentals such as a dynamic private sector, a high percentage of self-financing in enterprises, capital account controls, a high propensity to save (with most savings left in financial institutions), a high level of foreign exchange reserves and low levels of public debt (Melka and Xu, 2004), China is unlikely to feel the pinch from its NPLs.

Once economic growth cannot support such a situation, then NPL levels will be experienced to the full. In future, the only sure way to establish a sustainable level of new NPLs is to have appropriate control mechanisms, corporate governance structures and best practices in risk management. All of these need to be supported by professional and committed employees (Melka and Xu, 2004). A number of researchers agree that as long as the Chinese authorities have the financial resources to support the banking system and to pay for resolving its insolvability, then the systemic risk of the banking system remains rather low (Melka and Xu, 2004 as well as Longueville and Ngo, 2004).

Looking at the current state of NPL in China, one cannot say that the NPL issue has been thoroughly resolved. Transfers have taken place, which led to large reductions in the levels of book NPLs. The prevention of new NPLs requires adequate credit policies and building up a strong credit culture. All such soft facts and structures are still missing in practice. No one can be sure that the next economic boom would not bring more new NPLs.

If as in the financial crisis in 2009 the authorities wish the banks to increase their lending and that it should directed to earmarked projects in order to ensure smooth economic development, then the authorities need explicitly to foot the bill – and the banks can make that sacrifice in their loan portfolios (Yang Q., 2009).

Box 6 AMCs and NPL sales

In 1999, following the Asian financial crisis, the Chinese regime established four[1] Asset Management Companies (AMCs) to deal with NPLs in state-owned banks (one AMC for each of the SOCBs). Initially such schemes were not made available to other banks. The purpose of these AMCs was to help restore the originating bank's loan portfolio quality, to clean up the banks' balance sheets, to centralise the disposal of NPLs, to opt for faster methods in resolving the NPL issue and to sell some NPLs in open auctions.

The state-owned banks have transferred in 1999 an initial CNY1.4 trn of NPLs to the AMCs. For loans originating before 1996, the AMCs purchased NPLs at face value from SOCBs supported by central bank cash. In return, banks received notes issued by the AMCs to the PBOC (carrying interest) and, consequently, the PBOC funds the losses incurred on the NPLs (Griffiths, 2005). Further NPLs sales to the four AMCs paid 50% of the face value in cash and the bidding AMC transferred the recovered amount to PBOC later (Yan M., 2005).

The AMCs have a range of other possible means to deal with non-performing assets: legal disposal, sales of collateral, debt restructuring, debt for equity swaps, sales of asset bundles, and disposal by a trust or liquidation. Initially, most loans were sold through auctions and securitisations. Most NPL sales were bundled for a small number of investors (including foreigners) in private bidding processes. The disposals of NPLs have now been largely restricted (PwC, 2005 to 2009), despite the large amounts of NPLs in the banking sector and also the willingness of foreign investors to participate in the distressed debt market (PwC, 2004c; Shih V. et al., 2005a; PwC, 2006). Restrictions, such as the lack of open sales and the high minimum prices set by the authorities, have made further deals more difficult. Then the banks also began their own sales, competing with the AMCs. A strong impediment to NPL sales is the requirement that they should not be sold below their net book value. A final blow was dealt by the protectionism of local courts and the restrictions on real estate purchases for foreigners which culminated in a Supreme Court guidance in March 2009 suspending the resolution of new and current NPL sales (PwC, 2009b).

Additionally, debt–equity swaps[2] have had a perverse effect: they restored the SOEs' balance sheets, reduced their indebtedness to normal levels and stripped the pressure from interest repayments

(Steinfeld, 2005). Thus the SOEs were actually able to seek loans from SOCBs, which had previously sold their old debts with these companies to the AMCs (the SOEs are then meeting the required financial ratio standards, they have shown that they receive the state's support and finally the banks help AMCs out, by providing cash to the SOEs taken over by AMCs).

The recovery rates were initially 27% (2003) but subsequently this fell to 21% (2006). Up to March 2005, AMCs had resolved on average 49% of all NPLs they had taken over (Table B.4). The better loans were then been sold out, thus began a difficult period where recovery rates decreased and no further information was published.[3]

Table B.4 The fate of NPLs transferred to AMCs (CNY bln, %)

	2003	2004	2005	2006
Book value of non-performing assets & debt–equity swaps	1,600	1,588	1,579	1,563
Recovery in cash and non-cash	142	172	206	236
Losses in disposal	371	507	639	899
Cumulative resolved assets	512	679	845	1,135
Resolution ratio (%)	3.20	4.28	5.35	7.26
Recovery ratio (%)	8.86	10.83	13.07	15.09

Note: Recovery includes asset sales and other (non-)cash means. Cumulative resolved assets include as well losses incurred in disposing them. The resolution ratio is the relation between the NPAs and the cumulative resolved assets and the recovery ratio reflects the relation between recovered assets (by any means) and the NPAs.
Source: CBRC, 2007.

The AMCs enjoyed favourable taxation, fees structures and support in the courts and could thus dispose more efficiently of bad assets. However, they were still facing a number of basic challenges, ranging from their unclear status (ownership, supervision, guidance come from different ministries and administrations), cumbersome approvals for sales, questionable valuation standards, limited rights in the companies taken over,[4] and the fact that their future is far from certain.

To live beyond their original ten years, the AMCs have lobbied authorities hard to expand the scope of their business, moving into insurance, securities brokerage, trust investments and private equity. With regard to the bonds issued to the banks, they lack the funds to repay these, so that the bonds have been rolled over for another ten years, the SOCBs have invested just below 50% in their capital (effectively taking them over but not placing them on their own balance sheet) and recapitalisation exercises are now beginning (Cinda AMC received USD2.2 bln in July 2010).

Box 7 Trust loans and loan transfers

Asset-backed securities (ABS) did a useful job for the banks in managing their risks before they fell out of favour with the onset of the financial crisis in 2007. Since then, any type of loan transfer has remained cautiously watched at best. China has followed another route. Because ABS were slow to take off in China (EIU, 2010a), the banks turned to other innovations. In April 2010 the authorities preferred to establish a loan transfer platform under the aegis of the PBOC.

But in order to adjust their loan portfolios and manage their risks and liquidity, banks did not wait that long. In collaboration with trust investment companies, they structure wealth management products, in which an individual invests into a company and the bank acts solely as an agent. The funds of the investor are simply forwarded to a chosen company and the banks pocket the intermediation fees. Trust companies help to structure the products – this is less expensive than setting up SPV structures as in ABS transactions and helps them to circumvent the fact that they cannot take deposits (but can invest in equity). Local government projects also used such products to fund specific needs. Because the risk of default is not carried by the bank, the so-called trust loans are booked off-balance. In 2009 almost CNY800 bln in such trust loans were issued publicly (Bai, B., 2010). According to the SOCBs' and JSCBs' annual reports, in 2009 they had a combined CNY1.4 trn in trust loans outstanding (excluding BOC, ABC and Bohai which do not publish relevant information; Table B.5).

Through the use of such products, the banks can grow without having to raise further expensive capital and can adjust their balance sheet structure at year end as necessary. They also earn additional fees and can retain their borrowers. Finally, they can bypass any regulatory limits and restrictions on lending and capital adequacy or liquidity. This did not please the CBRC which published a *Notice on standardising the cooperation between banks and trust companies* (References for laws 64) in December 2009. The *Notice* first requires banks not to structure trust products on their own borrowing clients. In addition, banks are required to book these products on their balance sheets and thus to apply the lending and concentration limits as well (provisioning will also be required and thus drag down earnings and margins on these products). These requirements put an end to most of the volume of that market (*The Wall Street Journal*, 2010b).

Table B.5 Trust loans in main Chinese commercial banks (% of net loan portfolio)

	ICBC	ABC	BOC	CCB	BoComm	Merchants	CITIC	SPDB	Minsheng	Industrial	Everbright	Huaxia	SDB	Zheshang	Bohai	GDB	Hengfeng
2007	3.9	20.8	n.a.	12.0	10.4	10.4	3.9	10.5	4.3	16.0	5.0	3.4	2.6	1.3	n.a.	4.8	0.9
2008	5.4	n.a.	n.a.	12.7	9.6	8.8	5.3	8.9	3.9	6.2	6.3	3.0	3.9	0.9	n.a.	4.7	9.2
2009	5.0	n.a.	n.a.	13.0	6.5	6.1	5.3	12.1	3.8	5.2	5.0	4.1	2.5	0.7	n.a.	4.2	0.9

Source: Banks' annual reports, own calculations.

In fact, it has never been clear who would bear the losses of default. Trust companies and investors fully expect the banks to implicitly guarantee at least the principal. In order to avoid social disorder the authorities would certainly pressure the banks into forwarding more loans to such defaulting clients.

Banks will have to think over true sales again or use repo-like (also called buy-back) transactions to transfer loans (Li T., Wen X. and Zhang M., 2009b). The promised establishment of a loan transfer market in three years' time seems a long way off – especially if banks have to wait for it to become lively in trading and efficient in managing balance sheets before they can turn to it.

Box 8 Local government financing

In 2009 – for the first time in 15 years – local governments won the right to issue their own bonds. By law local authorities are not authorised to run a deficit as they are pleased. Central authorities are far too aware that they would otherwise spend recklessly and leave the bill to be settled by the central government. In 2009 Chinese local authorities issued some CNY200 bln in bonds.[1]

However, it should not be thought that in previous years local authorities have sat on the sidelines without any funds to finance their pet projects. Over the years they have used a number of different schemes to access bank loans. First, they took up financing through fully-owned international trust and investment corporations (ITIC). These went bust spectacularly in late 1990s.[2] The end of that story soon opened out into a new venture type – no less unsuccessful.

In May 2006, CBRC, in collaboration with other ministries, issued a further notice to constrain the growth of the so-called 'bundle loans', that is fixed investment loans provided to local governments with their (illegal) guarantees (Guo Q. et al., 2006b as well as Sun M., 2006). While it is prohibited by law for local governments to guarantee investment projects, they have in many cases given de facto guarantees (or letters of comfort) which in case of failure could trigger a series of domino-like defaults (Zhang Y. and Li Z., 2006).

The current arrangement is to create a financing platform managed by a wholly owned company under the local authority. The risks linked to these platforms are the same as before with ITICs or bundle loans. The structure is only slightly different to circumvent new curbing regulations. For now, the volume of loans to these platforms is estimated at CNY7.7 trn[3] by CBRC (Anderlini, 2010b and McMahon, 2010b), with only 70–80% relying on some kind of sustainable source of loan repayment. As before support to these platforms cannot be guaranteed, although the authorities might have an interest in keeping such structures afloat. To make things worse, it is only recently that banks started approving such loans at provincial branch levels (before that approval was more decentralised).

The recurrent reappearance of such similar structures (sometimes only involving a change of names) and the eagerness of local authorities in investment projects can be explained for financial reasons: local governments can only run a deficit or take on debt once this has been approved by local people's congresses. Thus they can only steer economic development and investments through companies that are fully under their control, which they often guarantee in front of lenders (the guarantee is backed by the fact that these authorities hold a monopoly over local resources and are the legitimate anchor for economic and social development – which banks happily support). Additionally, the resources allocation system between central and local authorities does not enable them to finance easily the projects on which they are required to spend money (health care, housing, and so on). Finally, the fiscal stimulus enacted in late 2008 has also given provided the correct impetus for the banks side and the government to lend and invest on a greater scale. There is certainly a true need for better infrastructure and communication means, but there are also undoubtedly a number of flawed and uneconomic projects.

The platforms often finance infrastructure or public utilities projects. Others are linked to housing and communication or transportation. By mid-2009 the number of such platforms had soared to over 8,000 (Zhang M., 2010b), with a negative RoA (Duan Q., 2010). The loans proceeds should normally be repaid through land sales revenues, tax revenues, government subsidies and other revenues from the projects themselves – but sometimes (Caixin, 2010) the funds amount to three times the revenues. The lack of a steady stream of revenues is not only the sole issue: another challenge is the very poor capitalisation of such venues – especially those created to fund capital expenditures. To enhance the platforms' standing, some local authorities put up land as collateral – the value of which is highly dependent on the real estate market – or ask other local authorities or subsidiary firms to issue cross guarantees – thus increasing only the systemic risk. Bankers fear that if financing stops, then the platforms will not be able to repay and fall into the non-performing category (as a side effect of the 'lend new to repay old loans'-practice) (Caijing Magazine, 2009a).

On 13 June 2010, the State Council issued a Notice (References for laws 56) to put an end to the financing structures (Zhang M., 2010c). The notice is solely the result of a number of previous warnings issued by authorities and regulators. While the details still need to be worked out in full, the banks are first required to '逐包打开、逐笔核对、重新评估、整改保全' ('open one by one, audit one by one, reassess, improve to save from further damage'). Public welfare projects – that is, any project that does not have sustainable revenue flows – should no longer be financed at all. The remaining platforms should enhance their standing through better corporate governance structures, capital replenishments, and commercial operations. The notice also repeated that guarantees of local authorities are worthless – but that did not stop lending previously either.

Banks have taken a more passive stance – waiting for the regulators to tell them concretely which platforms are fine, which are not and what to do with them. Since the notice deals only with the current state of affairs, history is likely to repeat itself once again – until government debts are recognised and tried. Where there is demand, there will be supply – so it would be better to formalise that demand.

13
Capital Adequacy and Risk Management

13.1 Capital adequacy

Chinese banks have generally been undercapitalised (Table 13.1) – especially considering the fact that adequate provision has not been made for their loan losses.

The Basel capital ratio has only been published by banks in recent years and this trend is increasing as banks are pressured into compliance by regulators (and, to some extent, by stock markets and shareholders). After their second recapitalisation exercise, all SOCBs can now boast capital ratios that are above the required minimum.

Now most of the Chinese banks are compliant with the minimum 8% Basel I capital adequacy ratio[1] (Table 13.2). The table, however, cannot be understood as all banks being compliant, since it includes only commercial banks (that is, SOCBs, JSCBs, CCBs, RCBs and foreign banks).

In 2008 and 2009 all large commercial banks were sufficiently capitalised, even after taking into account losses and provisions (Table 13.3).

In the past, the central goal in the banking sector was the gathering of deposits. Therefore the loan-to-deposit ratio was the single most important performance indicator: it was the criterion for the payment of bonuses, for the development of business targets and for judging the effectiveness of branch business. All relied heavily on this single figure because, in the absence of an efficient money market, asset growth could be achieved only through deposit growth (Harner, 2004a). Furthermore, each branch had to be self-sufficient in terms of funding because deposit transfers between branches, across provinces were forbidden. Regulation and compliance were all based on the loan-to-deposit ratio (set at 75%) (Figure 13.1).

Table 13.1 Capital ratios at Chinese banks (%)

	2003	2004	2005	2006	2007	2008	2009
SOCBs	4.06	4.25	4.57	5.59	5.62	6.15	5.45
JSCBs	3.30	3.13	2.99	3.50	4.67	5.00	4.78
CCBs	3.41	3.42	4.06	4.69	5.64	6.46	6.32
RCBs	1.22	4.78	5.14	4.94	5.41	5.75	5.98
RCoBs			6.42	6.34	6.35	6.51	6.65
UCCs	0.27	1.14	1.55	2.74	4.89	5.84	6.36
RCCs	−0.52	2.38	4.20	4.34	4.30	4.26	4.27
PSBC					0.68	1.00	1.23
Foreign banks	9.82	8.48	8.73	8.05	9.36	10.56	12.41
Chinese banks combined	**3.25**	**3.66**	**4.10**	**4.87**	**5.16**	**5.59**	**5.19**

Definition: Equity/assets = total equity at year end/total assets at year end.
Source: Own calculations based on data from CBRC (2010).

Table 13.2 Compliance with Basel I ratio in China

Year	2003	2004	2005	2006	2007	2008	2009
Number of banks compliant	8	30	53	100	161	204	239
% of banking assets compliant	0.6	47.5	75.1	77.4	79	99.9	100

Note: The total number of commercial banks included here is 240, so that one bank remains incompliant.
Source: CBRC (2010).

Table 13.3 Recapitalisation cost of banks (2009, CNY bln)

	SOCBs	JSCBs
Equity	2,126	726
Loan loss reserve	512	167
NPL amount	356	90
Recovery rate of NPLs (%)	20	20
Actual loan losses	284	72
Capital surplus (deficit)	2,354	821
Total loans (gross)	19,597	8,673
Required Basel ratio 8%	1,568	694
less: existing surplus capital	2,354	821
Required new capital	0	0
plus: existing deficit	0	0
Recapitalisation cost (surplus for growth)	0	0

Note: SOCBs include ICBC, BoC, CCB and ABC.
Source: Own calculations based on Hu 2002, data from banks' annual reports.

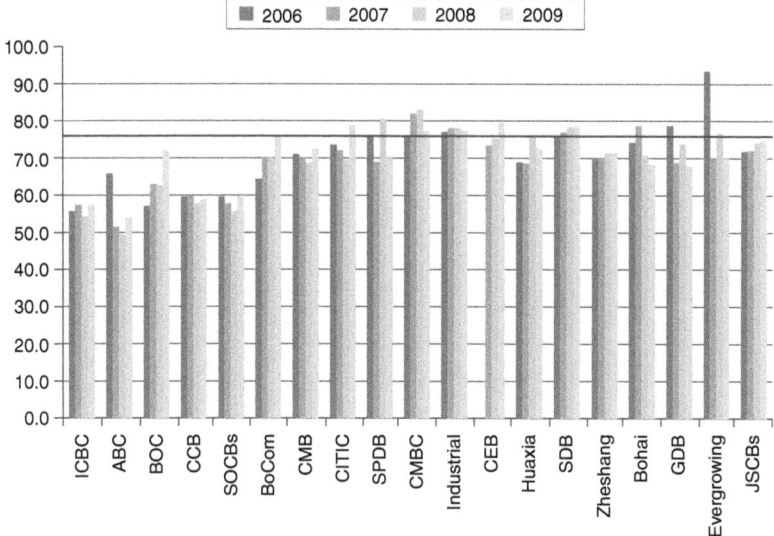

Figure 13.1 Loan-to-deposits ratio at selected Chinese banks
Definitions: Loan deposit ratio = net total loan amount/total deposit amount.
Source: Own calculations based on data from banks' annual reports.

As a consequence, the concepts of capital and capital adequacy were not on the mind of neither bank managers nor bank regulators and capital constraints were unheard of.[2] Such strong deposit growth disregarding asset quality and capital adequacy also favoured the building up of NPLs.

13.2 Basel I in China

Thus, in February 2004 when the CBRC issued a regulation on capital adequacy for commercial banks, this was seen by many observers as a revolutionary measure (References for laws 28 and Marshall et al., 2004a). The PBOC had previously published a minimum CAR of 8% (prescribed in the earlier *Commercial Banking Law*) but did not give any detailed calculation methods or definitions of its components, and in addition adherence was not enforced. Thus the *Regulation governing capital adequacy of commercial banks* was, in a number of respects, a fundamental and 'dramatic step' (Desombre and Chen, 2004). The level of enforcement is strong: at least the public has never heard of any non-compliant bank being sanctioned, although the pressure to comply was always high.[3]

Table 13.4 Basel I ratios of main Chinese banks (%, 2009)

	ICBC	ABC	BOC	CCB	BoComm	Merchants	CITIC	SPDB	Minsheng	Industrial	Everbright	Huaxia	SDB	Zheshang	Bohai	GDB	Hengfeng	Total
Basel I ratio	12.36	10.07	11.14	11.70	12.00	10.45	10.14	10.34	10.83	10.75	10.39	10.20	8.88	11.06	10.21	8.98	12.00	*10.48*

Source: Banks' annual reports, as published by the banks, based on total capital.

The new regulations took into account Basel I and Basel II rules as well as the prospects of Chinese banks soon facing foreign competition (through the entry to the WTO in 2007).

The transition from a quantitative growth (based on attracting deposits or on a funds constraint system) to a qualitative growth path (reflecting the quality of the assets held or a capital constraint system) took place formally until the end of 2006. At the same time the banks were required to increase levels of provisioning.

The main elements of the new regulation are outlined here. Capital adequacy calculations must take into account provisioning for (loan) losses. Capital is defined in two tiers and long-term subordinated debt shall not exceed 50% of core capital and tier 2 shall not exceed the amount of tier 1 capital.

Risk weightings promulgated by the CBRC are somewhat different from those advocated in the Basel I accord. The Chinese regulators have scrapped the Organisation for Economic Co-operation and Development (OECD) club rule and replaced it with a more Basel II-like approach: claims on sovereigns and overseas banks shall be weighted according to externally available ratings from international credit rating agencies. Claims on the Chinese government are treated as if China was rated better than AA− (China as a sovereign is currently rated by Standard & Poor's with A+/A-1+). Otherwise risk weights are similar to those promoted under Basel I for on-balance and off-balance sheet exposures. Risk mitigants are recognised in the sense of Basel II. A further important step taken by the regulators is the removal of the preferential treatment of SOEs (Table 13.5). They now receive the same risk weights as other enterprises. Furthermore, debt issued by AMCs in exchange for NPLs carries a 0% risk weight to incentivise the disposal of NPLs.

Market risk is also taken into account in the capital adequacy calculations. This recognises the increased level of financial market activities in China. This applies only to banks with trading positions exceeding the lesser of 10% of the bank's on- and off-balance sheet assets or CNY8.5 bln. Operational risk is not taken into account in the new capital calculations, but is addressed in another document.

Information disclosure and supervisory review are based on Basel II requirements. The BoD or president of the bank is responsible for capital adequacy and senior management is responsible for its implementation. Supervisory review is undertaken through on-site review and off-site surveillance. Banks are categorised into three groups depending upon the adequacy of their capital (CAR > 8%, CAR < 8% and CAR < 4%). For each group CBRC has a range of measures at its disposal,

Table 13.5   Changes in loan risk weightings (%)

	Until 2003	Since 2004
Loans to central-level SOEs	20	50
Loans to provincial-level SOEs	50	100
Loans to sub-provincial SOEs	70	100
Loans guaranteed by very large SOEs	50	100
Loans guaranteed by large SOEs	70	100
Loans collateralised by land rights or residential buildings	50	100
Issuance of bankers acceptance drafts	70	100
Bonds of policy banks	0	20*

Note: *Change for CDB only/starting from 2011 onwards.
Source: References for laws 28.

ranging from requiring management improvements to the complete suspension of activities. Principles are basically similar to those of pillar 2 in Basel II, but they lack the rigour and level of detail of the Basel standards. Disclosure is the responsibility of the BoD and should include details on risk management policies, their scope of application, capital, capital adequacy, and credit and market risks. Disclosure to all relevant stakeholders is required within four months following the end of the accounting year.

Capital adequacy is now the responsibility of the BoD, and stringent sanctions apply to those banks that are undercapitalised.[4] Any inadequate levels of capital should be dealt with by the BoD through a special action plan. This made banks more efficient, more disciplined and more market-oriented. To comply with the above regulations, banks had to improve asset quality, dispose of NPLs and raise fresh capital, either by looking for new shareholders (through IPOs, for example), pressing the present ones for new capital or issuing long-term subordinated debt and hybrid bonds (Table 13.6). These three alternatives are increasingly also available to smaller banks. Capital management is becoming a reality and a necessity for Chinese banks.

With the unfolding of the financial crisis in 2008, the CBRC pushed up the capital and provisioning requirements (for the latter see the previous chapter). Large banks must comply with an 11% CAR and smaller ones with 10%. Most banks already comply with this. At the same time the banks also tried to restructure their own balance sheets with various means such as trust loans, loan transfers (Box 7), and expanding loans to industries and areas they previously did not reach out to (Zhang M. and Dong Y., 2010). Additionally, information disclosure will become

Table 13.6 Sources of capital for Chinese banks (%)

	2006	2007	2008	2009
Stock market issuances	23	47	9	4
Retained earnings	10	28	23	52
Subordinated debt	12	10	17	32
Others	22	9	20	12
Government recapitalisation	33	6	31	

Source: CBRC (2007, 2008, 2009c and 2010).

broader in quarterly reports by the banks to CBRC each quarter (Reuters News, 2009d).

In line with the efforts of regulators around the world to redefine the meaning of bank capital, the CBRC also issued additional regulations on the issuing of subordinated debts (Fang H., 2009 and references for laws 55). Following the increased use of subordinated debts (in the first eight months of 2009 the banks had issued a combined CNY232 bln – more than three times the figure for the whole year of 2008) and intense lobbying[5] by the commercial banks, CBRC settled for a compromise which requires banks, starting from 1 July 2009, not to recognise cross-holdings of subordinated debts as capital for the purposes of CAR calculation. Furthermore, the notice requires the bank to cap long-term subordinated bonds issuance to 25% of the lender's core capital and that those lenders with a CAR below a 7% threshold (5% for those non-nationwide banks) should not be allowed to make use of subordinated debt to replenish capital. This will increase the investors' base as well as the quality of the banks' capital.

As a result, at end-2009 and in the first half of 2010 the banks produced a large number of refinancing plans and raised fresh capital on domestic stock markets. Because the banks intended to raise funds for the next years' growth, the pressure on stock markets was very high (Bai X., 2010).

13.3 Basel II in China

The new capital accord (Basel II) could have a potentially strong impact on Chinese banks and their environment. This is mainly due to the fact that Basel II and the whole risk management framework are in stark contrast to the current reality of the Chinese banking sector. Ba Shusong (Ba S., 2005b) sees challenges for China with Basel II, ranging from capital and risk management to data and disclosure, as well as organisational structures, incentive compatibility (between banks and regulators), market-oriented supervision and the fostering of financial innovation.

Previously, the CBRC had stated clearly that it will initially concentrate on implementing Basel I requirements and will thus not require Chinese banks to comply with the new Basel II rules for now. '结合国情, 积极参照' was the motto (that is, 'according to the national situation, participate actively'; CBRC, 2006a). But because other banks will implement Basel II standards from 2007 onwards, the CBRC demanded that Chinese banks slowly edge towards the new rules and start to prepare (Ba S., 2005a). Pillar 2 on supervisory review and pillar 3 on market discipline of the new Accord were to be implemented more quickly in China. The CBRC has received the BIS approval for proceeding in this way.

For regulators, the implementation of Basel II can potentially increase information and bank-level data availability for a better and more accurate view and understanding of banks' risks and potential losses. This in turn will enable them to react in a more timely manner. The new Accord is unlikely to protect the finance industry from system-wide collapse or to reduce the amount of money authorities would need to spend if a bailout is again deemed necessary.

For banks, implementation will certainly initially bring higher costs, but pressure to comply comes from the regulators, the competitors and the investors. A risk-sensitive approach to business can help draw a competitive advantage, and smooth entry in other foreign markets (although ironically Chinese financial institutions were hailed as safe havens during the financial turmoil in 2008–09, even though their practices are still behind best practices). A better risk management can help increase investors' confidence.

Some authors (for example, Mrak, 2003; Ward, 2002) argue that emerging market economies need to meet various preconditions before going ahead with implementation. Unmet requirements (Table 13.7) could put a whole industry or country at risk (given the large influence and role that banks play in financing emerging markets enterprises).

Although Basel II is complex, costly, requires a substantial amount of historical data, gives a large degree of autonomy to banks and is calibrated to G10 countries (Balzarotti et al., 2004), implementing only the standardised approach (SA) across the Chinese banking industry makes little difference to the (relatively) risk-insensitive Basel I. Most conditions required for the full implementation of the SA in China are not yet fully realised: credit rating agencies are under-developed, externally rated borrowers are few and are unlikely to turn to banks for financing,

Table 13.7 Current situation in China in terms of Basel II implementation

Area: macro level	Current situation in China
Baseline supervisory system	Broadly in line with the requirements of Basel II, but lack of regulators independence.
Legal-regulatory infrastructure	Issues include: embryonic development of the external rating industry, lack of recognition of creditors' rights and absence of bankruptcy proceedings.
Human resources	Modelling experience is building up.
Disclosure regime	Broadly in line with the standards of Basel II.
Corporate governance	In place, are not (sufficiently) used.
Accounting/provisioning practices	Most obstacles have been removed.
Availability of loss data	Banks are still collecting the data and will need at least up until 2013 – or experience a full economic cycle.

Source: Based on BCBS (2004c) and own research.

the data on corporate bonds data are poor, and, finally, credit bureaus are under-developed.

While the SA does not seem feasible, there are definite challenges with IRB approaches. Apart from the availability of data which is a challenge for all banks, the fact that banks have yet to experience a full economic cycle adds a layer of difficulty. This, in turn, makes stress testing and calibration difficult.

As a result, the CBRC has chosen a phased approach to implement the new Basel accord. 'New Accord Banks' (that is, those with international operations, probably including ICBC, BOC, CCB, ABC, BoComm, China Development Bank (CDB), Merchants and SPDB) are to implement the accord from 2010, with the other commercial banks to adopt it from 2011 onwards. In the mean time, CBRC produced a number of relevant documents and conducted surveys and reviews on the potential impact. The IRB advanced approach is to be preferred. In May 2008 it established a specialised task force. The phasing of the implementation applies not only to the industry, but also to each individual bank. Those applying for IRB status need to be approved by CBRC and comply with minimum requirements. The coverage of assets weighted according to Basel II must be increased slowly from a starting point of 50% to 80% and higher. Internal models are required to calculate market risk. There should also be a review of the risks not covered by the Accord. The banks need to collect the data, establish rating systems and risk measurement models with the appropriate processes and procedures (References for laws 52).

For the aforementioned New Accord Banks, the CBRC wrote in its annual report in 2009 that six of them had already established obligor rating systems and four were developing transaction ratings, and three were working on ratings for retail business.

13.4 Basel II-compliant regulations in China

In October 2008, the CBRC issued the first notice concerning Basel II implementation in China (References for laws 53). The notice considers five parts in respect of the measurement of regulatory capital and the regulatory and technical requirements for classification of risk exposures, internal ratings systems, specialised lending ratings, credit risk mitigation and operational risk management. The notice was followed, two months later, by a further pack of eight notices (first for comment, coming into law as of 2011) concerning market risk measurement with the advanced approach, interest rate risk management on the banking book, liquidity risk management, information disclosure on the CAR, validation of the approach for operational risk, calculation of the CAR, securitisation exposures, and supervisory review of the CAR (References for laws 54).

The risk exposures in the banking book are to be divided into sovereign, financial institutions, corporates, retail, equity and other on- and off-balance exposures. Internal rating systems should cover the first three classes as well as retail but in the form of pools. The constituents of internal rating systems are their governance structure to ensure objectivity and reliability, technical standards to ensure the same treatment to similar exposures, workflows which ensure independence and fairness, risk parameters measurement reflecting characteristics into PD and LGD factors, and, finally, MIS and IT systems. Banks are required to conduct at least yearly reviews of their internal rating systems which are the responsibility of the BoD. Ratings shall cover both the borrower and the facility, should have at least seven non-default and one default grades, and can be through-the-cycle or point-in-time. Where information is scarce, ratings should be lower. Internal ratings are the judgement of the bank solely and external ratings shall be considered for information only. Models underlying the rating systems should also be reviewed and reassessed regularly so as to reduce model risk. Such systems must have been in use for at least three years before being approved by the regulators. The ratings produced should constitute the basis for setting risk management policies, loan approval, capital allocation and governance.

Capital disclosure should reflect the bank's disclosure policies. The content should include the components of the capital base, disclosure on the banks' individual asset portfolios (divided in the above risk classes at least), comments on the policies and objectives of risk management in each risk type (interest rate, market, liquidity, and so on), credit risk measurement and provisioning as well as concentration in industries, areas, products, borrowers and so on, risk-mitigating factors such as securitisation, collateral, and their respective calculations. For disclosure about capital, instruments and adequacy, the information should be disclosed every quarter, for exposures by risk types and various other relevant details half-yearly disclosure is sufficient.

Capital adequacy ratio calculations should cover all subsidiaries owned in which the institution has more than a 50% stake. The rules also detail how to treat other subsidiaries. The capital adequacy calculations will reflect internal ratings that cover at least 50% of all assets (80% after three years – but 90% within one single entity in the bank). A capital definition is provided again and some deductions to it are required for CAR calculations. The capital adequacy calculations are the same as put forward in the Basel II document.

As can be seen from the above, the majority of the requirements and content from the original Basel II Accord are found in Chinese regulations. In some aspects the regulators have adapted the regulations to fit more closely the Chinese situation and environment (for example, reducing the number of risk exposures classes in the banking book). Its regulations are more detailed in so far as they require more build up of structures and processes to achieve Basel II standards (this should come as no surprise since Chinese banks have more to catch up and CBRC has a more hands-on approach).

13.5 'Basel III'[6] in China

With the onset of the financial crisis, there was criticism of the reliance on banks' own systems and models to derive appropriate capital levels and the BIS proposed additional indicators and measures for regulators to manage other risks which featured prominently during the crisis (that is, apart from credit risk – especially liquidity risks). The BIS has proposed a new liquidity coverage ratio as well as a stable funding ratio (BCBS, 2009a, b and c). These measures should assess the likely standing of the banks under stress.

For Chinese banks, the lack of detailed data[7] from the annual reports means that calculating these ratios for the main Chinese commercial banks is not possible. However, if one calculates a simplified liquidity ratio (Table 13.8), it appears that liquidity could be – in case of emergency – freed from PBOC reserve accounts.

Table 13.8 Liquidity in Chinese banks, 2009

	ICBC	ABC	BOC	CCB	BoComm	Merchants	CITIC	SPDB	Minsheng	Industrial	Everbright	Huaxia	SDB	Zheshang	Bohai	GDB	Hengfeng	Total *Average*
Liquidity (%)	17.33	20.24	16.25	18.23	18.34	13.44	16.69	15.84	20.04	19.08	17.18	15.66	11.93	17.09	25.13	15.19	19.48	17.31

Note: Liquidity ratio = cash and equivalents (which for all banks entail a large portion of central bank reserves)/customer deposits (without differencing between maturities and types of deposits). Customer deposits make up 65% to 85% of the banks' total assets and are thus the main liabilities and source of funding for the banks.
Source: Banks' annual reports, own calculations.

A further document (BCBS, 2009c) highlights the quality of capital, calls for a strengthening of capital requirements, adds leverage ratios to the supervisory tools and advocates a counter-cyclical approach.

CBRC has acknowledged the BIS publications and published a Chinese version, but did not make any detailed public comments about the proposals (PBOC net, 2009). For Chinese banks, the quality of capital should be in line with the new BIS proposals (there was no tier 3 previously, tier 1 and 2 definitions are similar – albeit not as detailed as in the BIS proposals). Moreover the CBRC has insisted many times on banks reviewed their risk concentrations – something that is in line as well with the content of the document. However no new calculations of capital adequacy or of forward looking provisioning have been published (CBRC required higher CAR and LLP levels for now).

13.6 Current state of risk management systems in Chinese banks

Chinese banks started to establish risk management structures and rating systems only at the beginning of the new century. This late start was the consequence of years of policy lending, of capped interest rates, of historical burdens and of poor incentives to create sound banks. The newly established risk management units are separated from sales departments. Banks have changed the incentive structures of relationship managers, started off-loading NPLs and finally have been able to share data through the PBOC credit information platform. Despite the high hurdles that Chinese banks face, more and more are moving into risk management especially that of credit risk.

The first incursions into risk management were made at the turn of the century in SOCBs (Qian X., 2004). First, a link was created between exposure to a client and its rating and a mechanism was created for the analysis of borrowers. Different authorities needed to be consulted in respect of specific loan amounts and types of loans (for example, working capital loans and mortgage loans can be approved at branch level, while loans for investment in fixed assets required the head office approval at ICBC). The various lending authorities were adjusted subsequently to reflect the local economic conditions as well as the performance of individual branches, or the availability of collateral. Zhang Ran and Hou Guangming (2005) report that as early as 2000, Chinese banks were experimenting with rating grades. However, these were rudimentary, unstable, and lacking a mature methodology (most had only five or six grades, which were recently increased to 10–13 grades – for example, ICBC's system has 12 grades (as has ABC's),

Industrial's has nine and Bocomm's has ten). Rating scales are being unified internally, and now different rating modules are being designed to cater to different products (project finance, corporates, retail, and so on).

In many institutions, however, the reform process has been slowed down as a result of the resistance of managers. The challenge is that banks' branches are often independent and managed as mini-banks. Under the old lending processes, branches were responsible for all lending, and authorisation was given by the branch manager (Marshall et al., 2005a). ABC has reduced the number of loans approved at that level and all larger loans are approved at headquarters (Hu C. and Zhang M., 2010). In addition, technology and staff training have all helped to further strengthen the internal processes. But even the regulator, Liu Mingkang, asserts that it is no easy task for dozens of people to oversee over 400,000 staff (Zhang M., 2010d).

In 2005, ICBC and BoC announced they were using new internal rating systems and until 2011 at least all Basel II banks in China will at least have such more complex systems. By and large the other larger banks have already followed suit to get new Basel II-compliant credit rating systems together with the appropriate documentation as well as reforming their internal organisational structure to conform to international best practices.

Large banks have established centralised and vertical hierarchies for the management of risks (mainly credit, liquidity, market and operational). Yet the structures are not fully centralised: while the systems are common to all entities and levels of decisions within one group, the branches still retain a say in decisions through their local risk management units. These units sit awkwardly between two lines of responsibility, the first to their risk management counterparts at headquarters and the other to their local branch manager – as described in some of the largest banks' annual reports for 2009. Influence by local managers is thus still a reality and there is still no reporting lines separation between those managing risks and those doing business – thus the incentivisation of credit officers is challenged.

Other banks have chosen to centralise credit decisions with just a few separate centres: for example, Industrial has centres in Beijing, Shanghai, Guangzhou and Fujian. In those cases, the branches have to submit credit applications to these centres. To ensure that its officers are made responsible for their decisions (often as or within a committee), Industrial has also established a special committee investigating responsibilities. Its credit policies describe, among other things, which industries should be focused on (along the lines of government policies). Other large banks, such as Minsheng, still have to implement risk management systems to cover all of their activities, products, borrowers and risk types. Minsheng has also drawn three lines of defence: business department, risk management and audit department.

Moreover the bank's boards of directors (BoD) are now to be responsible for the design and implementation of a risk management strategy. To this end they can use a number of committees, including a risk management committee. It is interesting to note, however, that in a number of banks, there is not one single risk management committee: there is one for the BoD and chairman, another under the president, and possibly a third based at the headquarters. Observers might rightly question if such arrangements are efficient and can really increase the level of barriers to ensure good and independent risk management. Additionally, no bank has until now implemented a separation between business and credit reporting lines (all report finally to the president of the bank).

As an outside observer it is difficult to assess to what extent these credit rating systems are being used, how adequate they are and if they are being circumvented more than integrated into daily decisions. Furthermore while the professionalism of risk management departments will increase over time, it remains to be seen if the same also happens in respect of their independence and their responsibilities. Further to these, they also see more challenges. Credit and loss data are insufficient because a full economic cycle has yet to be experienced. A methodology measuring credit risk to support decision-making is lacking (still often based on collateral availability, and so on) and needs to be fully validated.

In line with the regulatory requirements, the banks are – while perfecting and strengthening their internal controls, credit monitoring and credit assessment systems – now establishing stress-testing capabilities and taking steps to manage their capital actively (using economic capital, RORAC and EVA, for example, to allocate capital to different industries, borrowers, sub-portfolios, geographic areas and so on). ICBC, for example, is using an internal capital adequacy assessment process[8] to allocate economic capital.

But that does not take into account the fact that most Chinese banks are much smaller with much lower capacities and capabilities. They are unlikely to implement the Basel II requirements and will stand on the sidelines for now.

13.7 Impact of the Basel II Accord

Researchers and surveys (BCBS, 2003; EU, 2003; PwC, 2004b) have shown that for most types of banks and for more complex approaches, the capital requirements should be lower than they are at present. The more complex approaches, all other things being equal, are said to have a positive impact on reduction of capital charges. The amount by which capital could be reduced following the implementation of any of the Basel II approaches is closely correlated to the structure and composition of a bank's loan portfolio, with its operating environment (bankruptcy codes impact recovery rates: Davydenko and Franks, 2005), its internal structure and strategy and so on.

Results from the QIS3 for Chinese banks (five banks representing 48% of the banking assets) have shown that the impact of Basel II in China would broadly be in line with the impact on banks worldwide (CBRC, 2003; Fan S., 2003). The five participating Chinese banks showed RWA increasing by 9.02% (credit risk by 5.19% and operational risk by 3.83%).

CBRC has conducted preliminary assessments similar to QIS exercises abroad to gauge the potential impact of Basel II implementation on capital adequacy levels (Dong Y., 2010a). The assessment concentrated on credit and operational risks and was finalised in the first half of 2010. Prior to the assessments, CBRC thought that capital adequacy levels would rise, but the contrary appears to have occurred. Results for ICBC, for example, appear to show that the bank could actually lend more than under Basel I because it was more than adequately capitalised. These results are based, however, on the bank's own calculations which have yet to be approved by CBRC (not only the models but also the data basis has to reflect the requirements).

Not only is there going to be an increase in the amount of available capital, but costs are also rising: the costs of implementation[9] are certainly high, but the costs of refinancing for banks will also increase, especially for those with poor standing and ratings. But, more importantly, the question is less quantitative and should be more qualitative: banks should refrain from exchanging credit risk against model risk.

In addition to the quantitative impact as analysed above, the implementation of the Basel II accord will also have a qualitative impact on Chinese banks. Implementation will certainly refocus the rewards and incentives of officers and managers and delimit their responsibilities more clearly. Internal organisational structures are likely to be remodelled to comply more closely with a separation of reporting lines between risk management and operational departments. Information disclosure and transparency will encourage more stakeholders to review the banks' activities and publications. The banks and the regulators will hold a wealth of data from which they can not only gauge risks but also increase the level of financial intermediation. All of these are likely to lead to a stronger credit culture and more proactive and dynamic risk management.

The impact of Basel II is likely to be felt at the level of the banking system in terms of systemic safety and soundness. Stephanou and Mendoza (2005) find that the last two pillars of the Basel II accord will contribute to establishing a well-functioning and stable financial system, something that is often missing from emerging markets. However, they also note that the impact on the domestic banking system is not fully understood (redistribution of capital requirements within and across banks, competitive disadvantages, refocus exposures to some products), and that in emerging markets, pillar 3 could be seen as inefficient (creditors have few incentives to monitor banks – because of the central and supportive role of the state, the inadequacy of the bankruptcy laws, and other factors).

For Chinese banks as for other emerging markets, the Basel II capital requirements are likely to require capital charges that are linked closely to economic cycles. Such swings will depend on the economy's ability to withstand crises (Segoviano and Lowe, 2002; Griffith-Jones et al., 2002), and also on the ability of markets and of regulators to discipline banks. At the same time it will also depend on asset correlations in emerging markets: usually assets that are more dependent on idiosyncratic factors than to systemic ones, thus an economic downturn would not spread equally among a portfolio.

The financial intermediation function of banks is likely to improve. The improved capacity to understand the risks incurred will also have an impact on the use of interbank lending by the Chinese banks themselves. This will increase the level of exchange with foreign and international banks and also the level of integration of the Chinese banking system. Credit infrastructure and the lending environment will be pushed to reform. Already signs appear that banks are pressuring authorities into adopting more lending-friendly measures (creditors' rights reforms, use of other collateral in coastal areas).

But capital adequacy might give a false sense of security – reforms must run deeper and in the minds of bankers and regulators: higher leverage or the optimisation of balance sheets should not be the answer to higher risks.

14
Corporate Governance

14.1 General remarks

Corporate governance is hailed as the 'first line of defence in managing bank risk' by McKinsey analysts (Bekier et al., 2005) and one of the most crucial reform areas in China (OECD, 2004 and 2005). Corporate governance is the most important issue as well for Liu Mingkang (Zhang M., 2010d). Corporate governance structures have the potential to reduce the number of corruption cases and to improve internal controls and risk management, as well as ultimately to improve the financial intermediation capacity of banks.

Improving corporate governance structures is crucial to the operation of all banks in China. It is an inescapable part of banking reforms and will help reduce banks' riskiness (Du Y. and Xu C., 2005). Reforms have already taken place; however, how much change has there been in the governance structures of Chinese banks?

Corporate governance mechanisms or 'checks and balances' can improve a firm's performance. Research has shown that (Denis and McConnell, 2003) Boards of Directors (BoDs) are more effective when they employ more independent directors, when the board's size is small and when turnover on the board is low. However, it could not be conclusively shown whether the board should be chaired by somebody who is not the CEO at the same time. Pay and incentives for managers should be aligned with those of shareholders, this leads to higher firm performance.

Ownership structure plays a key role in the development of sound corporate governance: the identity of the shareholders and the percentage of capital they hold will ultimately influence any conflicts of interests that may arise between managers and shareholders. Overall, ownership

Table 14.1 Profitability and major shareholding of Chinese banks, 2009

Bank name	Equity share (%)	ROE (%)	ROA (%)
SDB	17	24.6	0.9
Industrial	21	22.3	1.0
Merchants	18	19.7	0.9
SPDB	21	19.4	0.8
ICBC	35	19.1	1.1
CCB	57	19.1	1.1
ABC	48	19.0	0.7
BoComm	26	18.4	0.9
Everbright	60	15.9	0.6
BOC	68	15.6	1.0
CITIC	62	13.6	0.8
Minsheng	15	13.6	0.8
GDB	20	12.9	0.4
Huaxia	14	12.4	0.4
Hengfeng	26	11.8	0.6
Zheshang	14	10.0	0.5
Bohai	25	4.9	0.2

Definitions: ROE = net profit for the year/total equity; ROA = net profit for the year/total assets at year end; Equity share is the percentage share of the bank's capital held by the largest individual shareholder (regardless of its background).
Source: Own calculations based on data from banks' annual reports.

concentration (provided it is not in the hands of the state) appears to act positively on firm performance. Privatisation also has a positive impact on the performance and efficiency of firms. When the largest shareholder is the state and privatisation is incomplete, then performance is negatively affected (Clarke, 2003; Xu L. C. et al., 2002). This is also true in the case of banks. Zheng Lujun and Cao Yanqiu (2005) show that in China, the efficiency of commercial banks is determined largely by the concentration of capital ownership and by the liveliness of shareholders (and by the size of the bank but not by the type of bank itself, such as JSCBs or CCBs). The higher concentration of ownership stakes in one or a few hands can improve efficiency up to a point: a too high or too low concentration negatively influences efficiency (Table 14.1).

Finally, the external environment in which enterprises evolve is also crucial to the establishment of corporate governance structures (Figure 14.1). Ewing (2005) also describes further institutions required for corporate governance to take root: a functioning legal-regulatory environment,[1] sound accounting standards, shareholders with an oversight capacity,

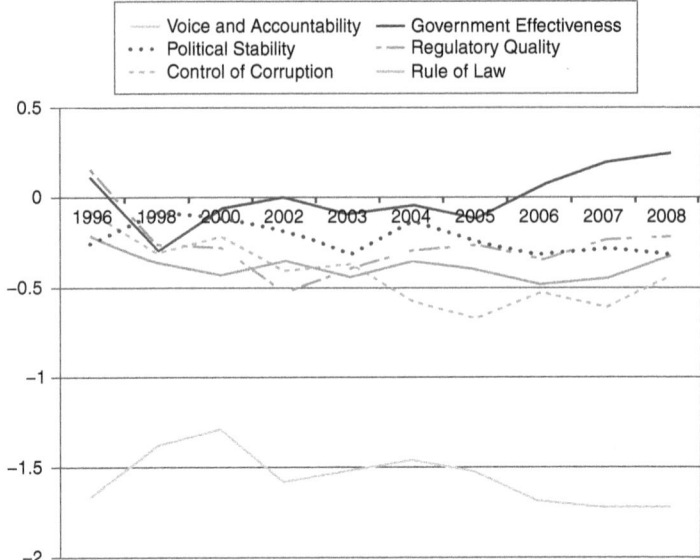

Figure 14.1   Governance in China
Source: Governance matters (World Bank), accessed on 23 July 2010 (http://info.worldbank. org/governance/wgi/sc_chart.asp#). The governance indicators range from −2.5 and 2.5 with the higher values showing better governance. These indicators are based on interviews with third parties. For a definition of each indicator: http://info.worldbank.org/governance/wgi/ index.asp.

efficient financial markets as well as institutional investors.[2] All these preliminary conditions are in the process of being built up or are being established in China, but remain weak for now.

14.2   Corruption

Another recurring challenge to the Chinese banking system is the system-wide corruption (Table 14.2). This should not be too surprising considering the low remuneration of bank officers and managers as well as the lack of effective internal controls, and checks and balances.

Dong and Torgler (2010) analyse series of regional data from 1998 to 2007 to find out in which environment corruption is more prevalent. Regulatory and discretionary power combined with economic rents (through strong weight of bureaucracies, decentralisation, lack of competition) meant that corruption is a worthy exercise since the costs of penalties are relatively low (likelihood of being caught decreases with fewer checks and balances such as investigative journalism, civil society

Table 14.2 Corruption in China

	2005	2009
Country rank	78	76
Corruption perception index (CPI) score	3.2	3.6
Bribe payers index (BPI)		6.5*

Note: CPI Score and BPI on a 10 to 0 scale, 10 being the highest. *BPI for 2008.
Source: Based on Transparency International 2005 and 2009 www. transparency.org.

Table 14.3 Corruption investigations

	2003–06 (avg.)	2007	2008	2009
Number of FI branches investigated	68,538	79,168	46,100	58,831
Amount of graft (bln CNY)	636	856	1,288	1,151
Number of FI branches with graft	1,506	1,360	873	4,212
Number of subsequently removed senior managers	267	177	78	86
Investigation coverage of FI branches (%)	33	42	24	31

Source: CBRC (2009c).

organisations and so on). The more regulatory power one holds, the more likely he is to be corrupt. Local governments tend to be less corrupt with higher degrees of fiscal decentralisation (the contrary holds with administrative decentralisation). An abundance of resources and of SOEs breeds further corruption. Anti-corruption drives by authorities depress the incidence of corruption. Controls by the press and higher bureaucrats' wages can also be effective.

The on-site investigation of unlawful activities has become a central focus of CBRC's work (Table 14.3). Irregularities are not solely an issue for Chinese commercial banks; even foreign banks are on the lists. Irregularities include not only graft, fraud and embezzlement of funds, but also lending for wrongful purposes or in contradiction of bank rules (illegal disbursements, weak lending practices and controls). The CBRC holds branch managers personally responsible for offences (involving more than CNY5 mln) under their watch. In addition to the work done by CBRC, the China National Audit Office (CNAO) also conducts investigations into the banks. Regulators often take a close look at loan uses and purposes to ensure that loan funds do not prop up the stock markets.

Last but not least, the banks' managers – as in any other enterprises staffed by Communist Party members – can be investigated by the Central Discipline Inspection Commission (CDIC). The organ[3] is responsible for any investigation on whether that individual has lived by the Party's rules and this is done prior to the initiation of legal proceedings. This is, however, far from being a useful check and balance in all cases: the investigation must first be cleared by the senior member under which that individual to be investigated is ranked and the CDIC bureaucrats report to the party secretary of that institution or enterprise (McGregor, 2010).

Corruption is not limited to the highly visible cases of branch managers and senior managers embezzling millions of Yuan. A survey ordered by the central government on real interest rates for loans in China shows the importance of informal payments in order to obtain a loan in certain geographical areas (Xie P. and Lei L., 2005). Some 45.5% of the respondents stated that to get a loan it is necessary to bring forward some advantages to the bank officer. Of all respondents, 46% believe that people are not held responsible for loans that turn bad. Enterprises have stated that, depending on their location, they have to pay an application fee for a CNY1 mln loan ranging from CNY14,000 in Eastern China to CNY63,000 in Northern China. On average, Chinese companies have to pay an application fee amounting to 3.8% of the loan amount. To keep a good banking relationship, surveyed Chinese enterprises estimate that they have to pay an interest rate of 4.9% on their loans.

The number of publicised corruption cases has started a process of change at these banks. Many are now starting to review their internal controls and channels to control business processes (Ling H. and Zhang X., 2005). Research suggests that corruption is anchored in the habit of cultivating separate and independent decision centres within one organisation.

14.3 The corporate governance regulatory framework in China

While corporate governance is viewed as a high priority by Chinese regulators and authorities, with much power remaining in the hands of the authorities, acting as shareholders, such mechanisms serve their own purposes rather than those of other stakeholders.

The corporate governance model chosen in China is one using a BoD staffed among others with independent directors supervising senior management combined with a supervisory board (SB) which supervises the Board. However, the scope of its functions is much more restrained and in practice it has a 'rubber stamp' function (IIF, 2006). The main responsibilities are with the BoD as in Anglo-Saxon countries although the two-tier structure is more akin to a German model.

In China, corporate governance requirements are described in the *Company Law*. The internal structure is composed of the general shareholders' meeting, the BoD, the SB and the senior managers. The general shareholders' meeting is composed of all shareholders and represents the highest authority in a company. It should make decisions in relation to the business policies and investments, elect and choose directors, approve reports submitted by the two boards, approve budgets and financial accounts, decide on the registered capital, on the issuance of bonds, on the distribution of profits and losses, on the organisation of the company and its articles of association as well as on any merger, dissolution and so on (Wei W., 2005). In practice, however, the business steering rights are on the side of the BoD and not with the shareholders' meeting which has less insight into the daily business operations and thus has to rely heavily on the proposals submitted by the BoD. This role is given further importance because other means of external supervision are often weak (Yang J., 2005).

The BoD is appointed by and reports to the general shareholders' meeting (as does the SB). It is often composed of some ten members. It controls the senior management of the company on behalf of the shareholders.[4] Its chairman is also the legal representative of the company and the party secretary[5] (Table 8.5). The SB supervises the BoD and senior management and brings any issues to the attention of the shareholders (it is composed of fewer members than the BoD, but should give appropriate representation to other stakeholders).

In the case of China, Liu Qian (2006) defines the corporate governance system as 'control-based', rather than market-oriented. This is due to the fact that Chinese regulators and authorities still make much use of administrative measures to control developments in the economy.

Nevertheless, the relationships with minority shareholders have improved as protection has been anchored legally (CFA Institute, 2007). Instruments such as proxy voting, cumulative voting, easier suit on directors, rights to check books and transactions, and the right to petition have all improved the framework. The reforms seem to have led to some positive results (Lin H., 2008). Large shareholders tend to appropriate less resources through related parties transactions since the strengthening of minority holdings. These can now earn larger gains and there has been an improvement in the efficiency of firms.

Zhou Xiaochuan (2004c), PBOC's governor, outlined a number of issues that remain to be resolved in China. The most important of these are: the clarification of ownership structures and role of senior managers; the role of the authorities and of the Communist Party; and the protection of investors' and creditors' rights.

As an improvement, it might be useful to increase 'bonding', that is requiring managers to spend time to reassure their shareholders – including minority ones – that resources will be spent wisely so as not to harm the value of their investments (Cai H., 2007).

14.4   Corporate governance in Chinese banks

Because principal–agent relations in banks are more complex and involve more stakeholders, corporate governance in banks is a special case compared with governance in other companies. Moreover, the impact of bank failure on the economy can be potentially devastating, so that control mechanisms including public scrutiny, supervisory committees, and staff incentives need to be adapted to the challenges (Cao X. and Zhao X., 2004; Wang X. and Huang Y., 2004). Finally, information asymmetry issues run deeper (Wei W., 2005).

Chinese authorities have chosen the following reform model for Chinese banks in terms of corporate governance (Thompson, 2005):

- ownership structure reform (through recapitalisation, the introduction of new operational and business practices, the diversification of shareholders, of foreign strategic investors albeit with capped stakes);
- the higher capacity and specialisation of regulators (the creation of CBRC, the definition of responsibilities of CBRC and PBOC, an emphasis on improving banks' governance, but regulators are still lacking independence);
- strengthened the legal regulatory environment (rules-based supervision, tackling enforcement issues);
- increased information disclosure and market discipline mechanisms (capital markets development, the raising of different types of capital and of debt, higher disclosure and transparency requirements which all tend to improve firms' performance and earnings; Lu T., Zhong J. and Kong J., 2009); and
- increased foreign entry and shareholdings (end of transition period to WTO entry, equal treatment and foreign strategic investors).

For commercial banks, CBRC has issued specific corporate governance guidelines (References for laws 7, 34 and 49). These require them to establish well-defined rules and procedures, responsibilities and reporting lines, disclosure and remuneration schemes. They also make it compulsory for banks to appoint independent directors (banks with a net worth of more than CNY1 bln should have at least three independent directors). Further to the requirements of the *Company Law*, the guidelines also introduces higher requirements for protecting minority shareholders and restricting related-parties transactions. The nomination and appointment of senior managers cannot be the activity of a sole shareholder, so that majority shareholders cannot control the board (nominations for SB and BoD are separated). Furthermore independent directors are required to sit on the Board, and committees[6] should be established. Related-parties transactions are regulated with more detail and ensure the independence of the listed entity. In the case of commercial banks the SB has wider and deeper powers: supervision of managers' performance and activities, responsible for mandating an external auditor and should report activities to the regulatory authorities.

CBRC also acts as an observer at initial BoD and SB meetings. Furthermore it requires two or three executive directors to sit on the BoD in order to achieve more efficiency and a stronger link to operations (Zhang M., 2010d).

Nicholas Howson (2009: 129, 131) writes: 'In theory then, corporatisation [...] was promoted as an instant panacea for the lack of operational or allocative efficiency at China's banks, not to mention the sturdy defence against manipulation of these firms by "insiders".' Yet, after analysing the new shareholding structures of the banks (Table 8.3), he concludes: '[...] after the bank's resoundingly successful [...] dual listing IPO, the capital structure remained heavily weighted in favour of China's state actors or proxies ... '. This sentence describes ICBC, but the same is true for most other banks in China.

The ownership structures of SOCBs have changed, but the state nevertheless continues to play its multiple roles: investor, manager and supervisor. Rights and responsibilities are all in one body. At the same time, listings for the SOCBs require them to comply with higher corporate governance and risk management standards (as required by the stock markets on which they are listed and by the new international investors). Improvements in information disclosure are useful to all stakeholders but above all to the authorities themselves.

Not only did owners stay the same, but essentially the staff and managers did not change either. On the surface banks and authorities were separated but below the surface the same arrangement prevails as before – just in a formalised and legally more stable way.

Most executives at Chinese banks are also members of the party committee – the exceptions largely being those recruited from abroad or from foreign firms (Huang and Orr, 2007). The Party Committee is the most important and crucial decision-making organ within any commercial bank (its secretary is the chairman of the bank): the BoD rubber-stamps the decisions of the Party (McGregor, 2010). Howson cites an interview with then Bocomm's chairman who states that the Party Committee's decisions can be vetoed by the BoD. It should actually work the other way round (Howson, 2009). The Party Committee is subordinated and staffed by the Party and can investigate party members through the CDIC (Howson, 2009). The Party Committee is in charge of strategy, personnel appointments and corporate social responsibility. Nonetheless, the Party – through its board appointments – tries to play an increasingly active and positive role within these institutions. It now takes more frequently into account other outside constituencies (Huang and Orr, 2007).

The obligatory independent directors which must make up one-third of the BoD are also mainly vetted and named by the Party or the Organisation Department. Furthermore their task is to act in the bank's interests (probably very close to those of the majority shareholder) and they do not have a right to veto (Howson, 2009). Thus all directors are answerable to the Party rather than the shareholders (although with the state as main shareholder, this would not make any difference anyway).

Board committees (Table 14.4) are very important as many BoDs just conduct simple votes based on succinct information prepared through lengthy discussions and analyses (Huang and Orr, 2007). Decisions can be more easily influenced at that level, while the BoD does change little to previously formed opinions.

Most banks base their employees' reward on market share in the local banking industry achieved for each period (Wen X., Zhang M. and Fang H., 2009). This often drives lending towards the end of the reporting period.[7]

Chinese researchers (Du Y. and Xu C., 2005; Wang X. and Huang Y., 2004) identify a number of areas in which the corporate governance of Chinese banks is still deficient which include:

- strong control from insiders 内部人控制 (the strategic development of banks is often decided by senior managers, decisions regarding the operations and distribution of benefits are influenced by personal interests and short-term incentives);
- rigid incentives (oriented towards bureaucratic requirements rather than operations, no separation between operational and risk management departments) and lack of trust between different parties;

Table 14.4 Corporate governance in banks, 2009

Bank name	Committees under BoD	BoD composition and attendance	SB composition
ICBC	Strategy, risk management, nomination, compensation, related parties transaction control, auditing	15 (3, 6, 6), 100%	5 (2, 2, 2)
BOC	Strategic development, risk policy, HR & compensation, related parties transaction control, auditing	15 (3, 7, 4), 100%	5 (3, 0, 2)
CCB	Strategic development, risk policy, nomination & compensation, related parties transaction control, audit	17 (4, 7, 6), 100%	8 (3, 2, 3)
ABC	Strategic planning, 'sannong' finance development, nomination and compensation, audit, risk management, related parties transaction control	13 (4, 6, 3), n.a.	5 (2, 0, 3)
BoComm	Strategy, audit, risk management, HR compensation, social responsibility	18 (4, 8, 6), 100%	11 (5, 1, 3)
Merchants	Strategy, risk management, nomination, compensation and examination, related parties transaction control, audit	18 (3, 9, 6), 95%	9 (4, 2, 3)
CITIC	Strategic development, audit and related parties transactions control, risk management, nomination and compensation	15 (2, 8, 5), 100%	8 (3, 2, 3)
SPDB	Strategy, nomination, risk controls and related parties transactions, nomination and examination, audit, capital and operations	19 (5, 7, 7), 100%	9 (3, 2, 3)
Minsheng	Strategic development and investment management, risk management, related parties transaction control, nomination, compensation, audit	18 (3, 9, 6), 100%	8 (3, 2, 3)

(*Continued*)

Table 14.4   Continued

Bank name	Committees under BoD	BoD composition and attendance	SB composition
Industrial	Executive, risk management, audit & related parties transactions, nomination, compensation and examination	14 (3, 6, 5), 100%	9 (4, 2, 3)
Everbright	Strategy, nomination and compensation, risk management, audit, related parties transactions control	15 (4, 6, 5), over 2/3	11 (5, 2, 4)
Huaxia	Strategy, audit, risk management, nomination, compensation and examination, related parties transactions	15 (X, X, 6), 100%	11 (X, 2, 4)
SDB	Audit, risk management, nomination, compensation and examination, related parties transactions	15 (8, 2, 5), 100%	7 (2, 2, 3)
Zheshang	Strategy, risk management and related parties transactions control, nomination and compensation, audit	15 (X, X, 3), n.a.	10 (4, 2, 4)
Bohai	n.a.	14 (X, X, 3), n.a.	5 (1, 2, 2)
GDB	Strategy, nomination, risk management and related parties transactions control, nomination and examination, audit	17 (4, 10, 3), n.a.	8 (3, 1, 4)
Hengfeng	Related parties transactions control, nomination, audit	12 (X, X, 1), n.a.	5 (n.a.)

Note: Attendance is given in % (at least four meetings are required per year), the composition of the BoD and SB members is given in parentheses as executive, non-executive and independent members (BoD) and as representing the general shareholders' meeting, outside stakeholders and employees (SB). X means that no number is stated in the annual report.
Source: Based on information from annual reports 2009 for the stated banks.

- endogenous supervision (both banks and supervisors are under the aegis of the central government); and
- inefficient organisational structure (strong power at the branch managers' level,[8] too many hierarchical levels, duplication of function at different hierarchical levels).

Chinese bankers themselves judge that there could still be improvements in the corporate governance mechanisms of banks. Nearly 40% of respondents to the PwC survey thought that the responsibilities of the different boards and internal institutions were not sufficiently well defined (PwC, 2009c).

For the authorities the already implemented corporate governance mechanisms enable a higher return in form of dividends and tax revenues to the state coffers. As long as they guarantee a steady stream of resources without endangering the carefully drawn balance between social and economic goals, the above mentioned deficiencies can still be regarded as side-effects to be reckoned with.

14.5　State ownership and corporate governance

Ewing (2005) finds that one of the strongest impediments to the sustainable establishment of corporate governance structures in Chinese enterprises is the overwhelming state ownership. With high levels of state ownership or block ownership, performance is hampered (Gunasekarage, Hess and Hu, 2007; Wei G., 2007). One fundamental requirement of corporate governance structures is the arm's-length relationship between enterprises and the state, even when it is the main controlling shareholder. However, the state still allocates to enterprises it owns a social and welfare role (generating employment, engendering economic growth, and so on).

For state-owned companies, the state acts simultaneously as both a principal and an agent. In China, the state draws no line between being an owner and a manager. With such large ownership stakes, the state can appoint and withdraw managers. Through the loyalty of managers to the Party, it takes influence on daily operations and on strategic decisions. Furthermore with the strong involvement of shareholders required by Chinese regulations, the state is assured to be able to control management and operations at all times. The state is outsider and insider at the same time (Lu M., 2004). Thus the principal does not become the control entity it should become and interest conflicts arise between bank and state. With control in the hands of insiders, moral hazard can flourish.

Chinese authorities stand to win from sounder corporate governance practices (as well as privatisation) because these can lead to stronger enterprise performance, which should in turn generate higher returns to the state in form of taxes as well as employment. Improved bank performance can benefit economic development in the long term. Conflicts of interests between state and enterprises are short term in nature but can be aligned in the long term.

Box 9 Compensation of bank executives in China

During the financial turmoil executive pay became a sensitive topic not only in western countries but also in the Middle Kingdom – even though salaries remain a fraction of those paid in the West. Bank executives' compensation fell by between one-half and one-third between 2008 and 2009 (SinoCast Banking Beat, 2010c). The Ministry of Finance failed to define an upper limit but managed to halt plans on stock appreciation rights and to require financial institutions to link pay to performance.

Linking pay to performance has long been an outstanding issue for Chinese banks but regulators and authorities have been more interested in reducing frictions in public opinion over that matter. For now banks' managers receive an annual package including a basic salary in the range of CNY50–700,000, an achievement bonus of up to three times the basic salary, welfare payments and a long-term incentivisation mechanism (which is actually seldom used). In addition, the Ministry of Finance released in early 2009 *Provisional rules for performance assessment at finance and state-owned companies* – which also apply to most banks. For example, the rules call for a point system where points can be deducted for large losses or performance worse than for peers.

The rules were then supported in September 2009 by the *Guiding opinion on further standardising the salary management of central enterprise executives* issued by six government departments (Wen X. and Lan F., 2009 and Yu N., Wen X., Fang H. and Zhang Y., 2009). Newspapers reported that no upper ceiling was introduced and it recognises the need to link pay and incentive structures. Additionally, from July 2010, senior officials – among which can be counted bank executives – are required to report – but unfortunately not to publicly disclose – their revenues and assets as well as those of their close relatives. CBRC also published its own guidelines (References for laws 43) which require remuneration to be linked to long-term capitalisation and financial viability.

The rules apply to all banks incorporated in China. The remuneration packages shall be the responsibility of the compensation committee under the BoD and each bank should show a remuneration policy. Base salary should not exceed more than one-third of total compensation. The achievement bonus is to be paid in part through the base salary and in part as a lump sum at the end of the year. That does not preclude the use of long-term incentivisation to be paid after a three-year lock-up period. Depending upon the level of responsibility, managers and executives shall receive part of their achievement bonus in a deferred manner (40–60%). If paid at all bonus guarantees should be limited to the first year of employment. The policy shall also introduce the details of achievement indicators. When a manager is unable to reach these, no increase in bonus and basic pay is mandatory (repayment is also required for departed executives). CBRC will conduct examinations and requires public disclosure in annual reports.

15
Chinese Banks and the Wider World

入世 is the Chinese abbreviation for China's accession to the World Trade Organization or WTO (the expression in full being 加入世界贸易组织). Taken to the individual meaning of each character, this abbreviation could also mean 'enter the world'. What will be the impact of Chinese banks entering the world? Or is the world finding access to Chinese markets through its accession to the WTO?

In the Chinese economy the finance sector was one of the last to open up and the pace at which it has done so has been relatively slow. This certainly reflects the fact that it represents the most crucial component for generating the necessary state resources. The full entry to the WTO in 2007 increases the pressure on Chinese banks to become more competitive in the face of foreign competition. Will this push Chinese banks to improve their performance and integrate further into the international banking system? Will the competitiveness and intermediation capacity of the Chinese banking system increase? Will it become safer and be induced to use sounder banking practices?

China is currently witnessing the internationalisation of its banking industry (Liu L., 2006a). First, the system is moving from a national monopolistic market to a more competitive one. Second, in terms of the internationalisation of supervisors their professional scope has changed from a focus on protection to anti-monopolistic supervisory activities. Third, in terms of spreading the risks incurred by Chinese banks in diverse international markets.

This final point is also illustrated by the entry of Chinese banks to the wider world. They have taken steps to increase their foreign exposures, through branches, acquisitions, business operations – chasing profits outside China and following their customers abroad.

15.1 Entry to the World Trade Organization

Chinese commitments

After some 15 years of negotiation, in December 2001, China finally became a member of the WTO. Part of the obligations to WTO entry includes commitments in the area of financial services and specifically banking. Since 2007, at the end of the transition period to accession, China's banking sector is almost fully open to foreign competition. The removal of restrictions gives the same business conditions to foreign and domestic banks.

Foreign banks are not new to the Chinese banking industry. As shown earlier, they started entering the Chinese banking markets directly in the 1990s, albeit in a limited manner (through representative offices, branches). At the beginning of this century they also started to participate indirectly in Chinese banking as shareholders.

The technical insolvency of the Chinese banks in the late 1990s required the Chinese authorities to make their banks more resilient to the international financial and economic system before a full opening up (*Agence France Presse*, 2005).

For China, the decision to enter the WTO challenged by itself the way it treats foreign entities. With the accession, national treatment should be granted to all entities (Table 15.1), regardless of their origin. The legal framework, the business restrictions as well as the strong administrative and unpredictable handling of these issues by the Chinese authorities placed foreign entities in China at a strong disadvantage (Jing X., 2005).

In an effort to close the gap between foreign and Chinese banks, the Chinese authorities allowed themselves to have a transition period of five years (between 2002 and 2007), before fully opening up the country's banking sector. The restrictions in force against foreign banks in terms of target customers, scope of business and geographical presence were phased out progressively. New licensing requirements were also introduced to ensure equality among foreign and Chinese financial institutions.

During the transition period, China scrapped the regulation that stated that the State Council could decide where foreign banks would be allowed to locate. It also scrapped the entry requirements for those foreign banks that wanted to access the CNY currency market (although limits in terms of currency amounts remained in place). The requirements for foreign banks willing to form a joint-venture were eased by a removal of the constraint of choosing a Chinese bank as a partner (Jing X., 2005). The restrictions on geographical presence were removed as progressively as originally committed. Restrictions on local currency business and on customer segments were also removed in full.

Table 15.1   China's WTO commitments for the banking sector

Scope of banking services: • Deposit taking; • All lending activities; • Financial leasing; • Payment and money transfer services; • Guarantees and commitments; • Trading in foreign exchange.	1. Excluded are the provision and transfer of financial information; and advisory, intermediation and other auxiliary financial services in cross-border supply and international consumption. But can be provided by Chinese branches of foreign banks. 2. No consumption abroad for these services. 3. Geographical and client coverage of commercial presence: restrictions will be removed for foreign currency businesses upon accession, and will be progressively phased out during the five-year transition period for all other terms. In 2007, there will be no geographical restrictions at all (foreign banks will also be able to provide services to clients located out of the geographical presence of that bank) on the provision of local currency business.* No limitations on national treatment.
Licensing	After the end of the transition period licensing criteria should be only prudential. Non-prudential ones such as ownership, operational and juridical ones will be removed. Exceptions: 1. Foreign financial institutions with total assets of at least USD10 bln can establish a subsidiary or finance company. 2. Foreign financial institutions with total assets of at least USD20 bln can establish a bank branch. 3. Foreign financial institutions with total assets of at least USD10 bln can establish a Sino-foreign bank or finance company. No limitations on national treatment.
Automobile finance by NBFIs	Scope of services is limited in the same way as above (see first line).

Notes: *To this there is only one limitation: for the provision of local currency services, foreign banks must have been profitable in the last two consecutive years and have operated at least three years in China prior to their application for a local currency business licence.
Source: Based on WTO (2001c) and Jing X. (2005).

Since December 2001, foreign banks were allowed to conduct foreign currency business with all kinds of customers (Chinese and foreign enterprises and individuals) in all of China. For local currency business, the opening was more gradual[1] and started in 1996.

In terms of licensing requirements, the minimum capital requirements for both foreign and Chinese banks are now identical. Apart from

Table 15.2 Comparison between licensing requirements

Institution type	Minimum registered capital	Minimum operating capital for branches
JSCBs	CNY1 bln	CNY100 mln (and SOCBs)
CCBs	CNY100 mln	
Foreign invested bank	CNY300 mln	CNY100 mln
Sino-foreign bank	CNY300 mln	CNY100 mln
Foreign finance company	CNY200 mln	
Sino-foreign finance company	CNY200 mln	
Foreign banks' branches		CNY100 mln
Further outlets in same city		CNY10 mln

Source: Based on References for laws 14.

the exceptions that were granted at the time of entry (requirement for foreign entities to have total assets amounting to either USD10–20 bln, depending on whether they establish a subsidiary or a branch), the other requirements are solely prudential 审慎性条件 (such as sound banking practices, risk management, corporate governance). These are, when considering the same licensing areas (that is licensing for same new products or establishment of same legal entities), the same for both Chinese and foreign banks (Table 15.2). It must also be acknowledged that in addition Chinese banks have to apply for a license for each new location and outlet.

Compliance has been positive, but does this amount to a full opening? Constraints and barriers still remain, making the establishment and development of foreign competition difficult (Metcalfe, 2005). Such barriers were not part of the banking sector commitments or were argued by the CBRC as being prudential in nature (Crosby, 2007).

In terms of equity participation in Chinese banks, the entry of foreign banks is still strongly constrained. These were actually no part of any specific agreement under the WTO (WTO commitments concentrated on shares in joint-ventures of at least 25%). At the moment the equity share foreign banks can buy of the Chinese banks' capital are limited to 20% (individually, or 25% together). Regulators have even added further conditions that need to be fulfilled by foreign investors to make their strategic investment in China (Box 1; Crosby, 2007).

Barriers still exist in terms of the provision of financial services by foreign banks. Foreign banks' scope of financial services was defined in the WTO agreement and these are allowed, but for any other types of services or activities foreign banks still face restrictions. In the case of investments in securities, the QFII regulations still apply. For the issuance of forex credit cards, foreign banks are, for example, required to have five years of operations in CNY-denominated cards before they can make an application. The issuance of bonds is becoming a reality with the first such exercise in 2009 by a foreign bank.

Cultural barriers, an underdeveloped interbank market, a weak credit culture, the shortage of experienced human resources, as well as the preferential treatment of the Chinese state towards large Chinese banks (in terms of financial support and implicit guarantee) also influence the standpoint of foreign banks trying to take hold of market share in China.

Regulations are seen as being one of the most crucial and most difficult issues in respect of banking in China (PwC, 2010b). While progress has been made in some aspects, the Chinese banking system is still over-regulated. Legal risk is often perceived by foreign banks as being a major risk for foreign banks (Metcalfe, 2005).

Finally, while conditions for operating a foreign bank have become more equal over time, historical legacies still create disparities in the system and make foreign bank activity in China still rather cumbersome, restricted and costly.

WTO entry commitments are not only working in one way: they have also removed the preferential treatment that foreign banks enjoyed in some limited areas. The first such advantage was regarding the corporate tax rate which increased for foreign entities from 15% to 33% and the business tax of 5% which foreign banks now have to pay in common with other banks.

Some constraints are established on commercial banks' activities and now apply to all banks regardless of origin (EIU, 2010a):

- Liquid assets must make up more than 25% of liquid liabilities.
- Assets of a branch by currency should amount to more than the liabilities in the corresponding currency.
- 60% of the bank's operating capital shall be invested as follows: half in forex deposits and the other held in local currency government bonds or times deposits maturing in less than six months.
- SAFE requires a foreign off-shore debt quota of 40%.
- Interbank market loans can make up max. 150% of the branch's capital.
- A loan to deposit ratio of 75% must be complied with (up to 2011; potentially the most difficult issue in compliance).

Finally, foreign banks (when established as under prior-WTO rules) can provide investment-banking services (including the sale and purchase of securities, and government and corporate bonds), whereas these types of services are off-limits for Chinese banks and must be conducted through securities firms (Tang H., 2004). Here regulators have liberalised the rules for Chinese banks and foreign banks have also chosen to keep the pre-2006 business entities working as before to enjoy both sides of the advantages.

Regulatory risk remains the main risk in the eyes of foreign banks (PwC, 2010b). But competition from Chinese banks is also becoming a prominent issue for foreign executives.

The impact of foreign entry on China

Foreign banks have a strong degree of expertise, and in some limited areas and services have clear leadership. The competitive advantages of foreign banks lie in the provision of good services (by putting the customer at the centre of their reflections), their expertise (by encouraging innovation and new products) and experienced management (by ensuring sound systems and procedures in managing liabilities and assets, risks, internal controls) as well as diverse products and an international presence (most foreign banks are linked in one way or another to an internationally active bank; Li Z., 2004). To add to these strengths, foreign banks now enjoy a larger scope of business: they are able to expand from foreign to local currency, from wholesale to retail services, from foreign to Chinese customers, as well as into other products and geographical areas. Nonetheless their space for expansion remains narrow and the level playing field has yet to be achieved (PwC, 2010b).

Chinese banks have a strong customer and branch base, with high visibility. They also remain implicitly guaranteed by the state. Thus the mass of Chinese customers is unlikely to move away from such secure institutions. In addition, foreign banks are starting from such a small base that their share of banking assets is unlikely to grow to substantial levels in the next few years.

Some researchers (Leung M. K. and Chan R., 2006) think that foreign banks in China can choose between two strategies depending upon their asset base and expertise: a niche strategy or a market-challenging strategy. The former is basically available to all banks that have branches in China and they can choose the niche depending on their expertise. For those few with a strong *force de frappe*, in terms of both financial resources and local knowledge, the latter can also be an option by competing with domestic banks in all mainstream banking areas.

Traditional Chinese banking markets (such as lending) are already only marginally profitable for foreign banks, and it is therefore unlikely that they will expand in these areas (Metcalfe, 2005). Foreign banks are unlikely to provide all types of services, as Chinese banks do. Rather they are likely to target only those customers or business areas that promise sufficient returns to cover the expenses. Only profitable channels are going to be pursued. Thus these will only include a small number out of a wide range of possible activities.

More rapid growth for foreign banks could be achieved through the establishment of a strategic partnership with a commercial bank in China (although more likely are those with smaller banks). Joint-ventures are no longer preferred options because of the challenges resulting from the lack of clear ownership and control structures (Metcalfe, 2005) – organic growth remains the best choice. A range of products interesting to foreign banks can also be dealt with through strategic partnerships (for example, credit cards), to enhance market participation of the foreign bank.

Faster lending growth did not lead to higher market traction for foreign banks however. The lending surge in 2009 was a feature of Chinese banks.

The expectation is that overall WTO membership will lead to greater efficiency in the provision of financial services in Chinese banks. This is because the technology level will be raised and the quality of services at domestic banks will also improve. This should spur financial innovation, increase the role of technology and information systems, and promote the use of sound risk management systems and the disposal of bad assets. It will also require the nurturing of human resources and expertise. This in turn will ensure a more effective use of funds and of capital, thus raising the overall level of efficiency.

The WTO entry increased the internationalisation and integration of the Chinese banks into the world financial system. In order to be able to withstand the challenges, they have to greatly increase the depth and breadth of their intermediation capacity, in terms of both product strength and customer focus. In this sense the impact of the WTO entry is more in the nature of a wakeup call than an earthquake or a tsunami.

15.2 Entry of Chinese banks into the world

In the run up to the end of the WTO transition period and in the following few years there were a large number of foreign investments (Table B.1). But that was not the only impressive development in Chinese banking: from 2007 onwards, Chinese banks ventured abroad at a growing pace (BCG, 2008). From then on, the days when Chinese banks faced a wall of poor results and even poorer governance and standards were over.

First, CCB took over Bank of America's Hong Kong branch, and then ICBC purchased 20% of the South African Standard Bank for USD5.5 bln.

Emerging markets appealed to Chinese investors because of lower entry requirements and the already existing links with Chinese firms doing business there (Hansakul, Duck and Kern, 2009).

The investment scope grew enormously in 2007, with the clout and confidence of Chinese investors reaching previously unknown levels. In just the first ten months of 2007, the deals signed by Chinese banks abroad amounted to half the amount that foreign banks had invested in China for the same period of time.

The banks were accompanied by other securities companies, insurers and the sovereign wealth fund. Their expansion encountered growing criticism which floundered in the financial crisis that followed.

The search for profitable investments and experienced management are not the only reasons for going overseas. The banks follow their customers (funding infrastructure projects in Africa, for example) but also broaden their revenues and diversify their assets (geographically and currency-wise). Establishing a bank's name in foreign lands can also be a time-consuming practice – as a result the banks have each their own individual strategy: ICBC is venturing into new strategic investments, while CCB and BOC are working on organic growth. CCB is wary of developed markets because of the relatively low levels of potential seen there (Anderlini and Tucker, 2009).

Where deposits seem a perpetual resource and where loan growth is limited only by the caution of regulators, but combined with high savings and feverish equity investment, all deals highlight the need for Chinese banks to invest their large pools of funds wisely, to diversify their income streams and risks, and to find a more natural hedge to a growing exposure to foreign exchange (especially for those Huijin-invested banks). But such concerns are not the sole reason for entering the wider world. Chinese financial institutions often lack an understanding of finance management standards; they often crave more experience and deeper knowledge.

With the unfolding financial turmoil, the banks have had to ask themselves if they went down the right path and if diversification did bring higher returns to their shareholders. Indeed, losses were also common (Minsheng in the US and Merchants in Hong Kong took home losses: SinoCast Banking Beat 2009c) but in other circumstances there were also opportunities to assume control (Anderlini and Cookson, 2009 and Bo W., 2009). Increased integration and linkages with the world will make Chinese institutions more resilient, visible and – at some point – more transparent. But the string of acquisitions and new loans (Goff, 2009) must be managed while institutions are growing in size – Chinese finance investors will have to prove their integration capabilities in the near future to digest all these diverse activities under one umbrella (the areas of management and control are recognised by Chinese banks as the main learning focus for making overseas investments: PWC, 2009c). They will need to prove themselves to new regulators and new customers.

Regulators have appreciated acquisitions where the target company was of higher standing, where partnering was felt to add real value and where the international standing of China could be enhanced. Authorities are even writing investment manuals for Chinese venturing abroad and SAFE has scrapped its approval process for investing abroad but authorities did not formulate any explicit strategy to that effect – that remains the responsibility of the banks themselves. As such, these goals can be fulfilled without taking controlling stakes – something that Chinese investors were often reluctant to do for fear of increasingly critical foreign public opinion (most controlling stakes purchased were with institutions in emerging markets). Last but not least, entering the world is also about finding recognition on the world stage and an opportunity to form national champions. Chinese officials can be proud. But it will take much more to make Chinese finance brands global ones.

This also raises the question of reciprocity – as long as Chinese banks are happy to take minority stakes in banks in developed markets, foreign banks in China can expect little change in terms of the limits in resepect of the foreign ownerships of Chinese banks. For now the restrictive stance of US regulators over Chinese banks establishing their branches in the US does not pressure CBRC into relaxing its own restrictions.

China no longer requires to be lectured about banking and investment best practices. Chinese banks are showing their ability to integrate the practices deemed most suitable to their environment and conditions and to do without the remaining ones. Advice is welcome as long as it does not disturb the potential future champions.

15.3 Lessons from the crisis

China was able to gain both influence and clout from the worldwide financial crisis that unfolded between 2007 and 2009. Chinese banks appeared largely unscathed – although a conclusion can only by drawn in 2013 at the earliest. Where a few years ago foreign bankers would have laughed, they came now asking for funds and favours. Most importantly, the industry maintained a strong stability throughout the crisis – but additional capital was required in order to sustain further lending growth (Table 15.3).

The crisis and its resolution highlighted the need for strong governments and authorities – giving the Chinese regulators and other authorities a reliable basis for their interference in markets. The authorities – in the form of the NDRC – crafted a plan for a CNY4 trn fiscal stimulus (Pearson, 2010). With its raison d'être as an authority dealing with industry policy and economic development, the NDRC pushed for a strong and decisive plan. Other regulatory agencies – despite holding ministerial rank – needed time to counter such initiatives which could potentially annihilate their reform efforts in the banking system.

After enacting the fiscal stimulus, the NDRC continued to review single large projects that the banks would finance under CBRC supervision. This was also especially true for projects launched by local authorities. The financial crisis and the response of the Chinese authorities did not strengthen the independence of the regulators. At the beginning they seem even to have been bypassed in order to enact the stimulus plan. They appeared to have regained a stronger foothold when the growth in lending was too fast and could be the harbinger of more risks than thought (see the chapter on regulators and their administrative measures). It was difficult for banks to maintain the balance between economic development and risk management. More than anything the crisis gave the authorities further reasons to intervene and interfere. The crisis seemed to point to the need for a regulatory state in China rather than the free hand of the markets.

The central and technocratic faction needed to be omnipresent. It could even show and remind markets and players alike that the presence of the state is meaningful and should, if anything, be bolstered. The crisis has not eroded any of the powers that the central government had already acquired. It has given it another raison d'être and not simply as a frame- and standard-setter. This increased capacity is derived not from a more credible power over resolving failed institutions but rather derived from the financial resources available and the previous experience – both issues that resurfaced during the financial crisis.

If moral hazard and lack of proper regulation were at the centre of the financial turmoil, the Chinese regulators reacted with more hands-on supervision, moving further than ever before from any principles-based supervision.

The financial crisis posed the further question: are many regulators better than one? The issue is being discussed internationally, and to date Chinese regulators have been unable to agree on more than a coordinating mechanism where they exchange data. Competition between the different regulators has reduced the chance of a unified supervision (see chapter on regulators under 'multiplicity of regulators').

Before the crisis the administrative measures to steer the economy and the country's resources were widely criticised by observers for being inefficient and backward. In 2009 the same administrative instruments

Table 15.3 Capital buffers and resulting potential asset growth (CNY bln, 2009)

	ICBC	ABC	BOC	CCB	BoComm	Merchants	CITIC	SPDB	Minsheng	Industrial	Everbright	Huaxia	SDB	Zheshang	Bohai	GDB	Hengfeng
Difference actual to target CAR (%)	1.36	-0.93	0.14	0.70	1.00	0.45	0.14	0.34	0.83	0.75	0.39	0.20	-1.12	1.06	0.21	-1.02	1.00
Free capital (missing capital to target CAR)	75.57	-24.29	7.00	36.50	18.86	5.22	12.26	2.49	8.28	5.68	2.88	0.09	-3.72	1.25	0.15	-3.91	0.10
Support new asset volume up to	630.04	-243.41	62.66	306.29	152.60	49.85	120.86	24.07	75.92	52.55	27.71	0.87	-41.42	11.21	1.47	-43.05	0.82
equivalent to a % increase	*10.6*	*-5.6*	*1.2*	*5.9*	*8.1*	*4.3*	*11.8*	*2.6*	*7.6*	*7.4*	*4.1*	*2.0*	*-11.5*	*11.0*	*2.1*	*-11.3*	*8.1*

Note: Based on assuming an 11% CAR for SOCBs and BoComm and 10% for all others (as currently required by CBRC: 'target CAR').

Source: Banks' annual reports 2009, author's own calculations.

proved their worth with the authorities taking the banks on a lending spree and then with the regulators requiring them to be prudent and thoughtful about where and to whom to lend to. The tools proved to be fully appropriate to the Chinese context.

Blanket guarantees are implicit in the Chinese banking industry and the fiscal strength of the government also reassures any outsiders of sufficient resources – if need be. If the Chinese authorities had a prepared blueprint for crisis resolution as advocated as best practices by Demirgüç-Kunt and Serven (2009), then the plans certainly do not entail a list of institutions that are solvent and thus should be saved (in fact, all deemed of systemic importance would probably be supported, regardless of their actual financial standing). The high costs to the government are certainly also a reality in China – but the authorities prefer to bear the costs rather than tackling social instability instead. The latter would amount to a complete loss of confidence because the rescue is expected by all stakeholders. The cost of future rescues is borne by the banks and the taxpayers in the form of policy lending which they have to comply with and which weight down their revenues and long-term development.

Nevertheless the Chinese banking industry is now feeling the pinch of the financial crisis as the problems it is now addressing resemble those over which western banks are chewing: capital adequacy, information disclosure and the globalisation of banking supervision. In contrast to their western counterparts, Chinese banks do not need to go back to the basics since they never left them, but they will need to be careful with financial innovation.

Even the notoriously bubble-prone real estate markets cannot worry the authorities as much as could those markets in the US and the UK: most lending takes place with urban dwellers with prior savings. Most urban dwellers have benefited from the housing reforms to acquire an apartment of their own and thus the financing of new homes remains limited to a small percentage of the population. Furthermore the rapid urbanisation and the high savings rates underline the reasons behind such growth. Local governments will be able to rely on land sales a little longer to fund their spending on infrastructure and public welfare.

Being asked for funds and investments abroad also gave both the authorities and the banks a new sense of pride and confidence and of integration with the rest of the world. Given its financial clout, China might well become the next superpower (Tan, 2010). China no longer felt itself to be behind developed markets because the West's banking industry was now technically insolvent. However, this should not be mistaken as signalling the establishment of a new Chinese Model for banks.

16
The Crisis-withstanding Ability of the Chinese Banks

Since the financial crisis, which started in 2007, research into the failure of banks and even that very possibility has found a wide audience of regulators, journalists and readers. With considerable interest, researchers have delved into the available data to measure the fragility of banking systems around the world. The same exercise would also be useful for China.[1] Furthermore, researchers have argued that the vulnerability of the banking system is high following financial liberalisation – something that is now happening in China (Demirgüc-Kunt and Detragiache, 1998).

16.1 Macroeconomic environment

As highlighted above, the Chinese banks are a central instrument for finance within the country and their healthy figures have yet to reflect improved banking practices rather than simple restructuring exercises. The focus of the following chapter is much more on understanding the ability of the Chinese banking system to withstand a crisis rather than predicting an upcoming banking crisis. The central question to be answered is how fragile Chinese banks and the banking system as a whole are. The answer to this question entails a simplified stress test based on a macroeconomic scenario applied on the major banks as a whole and on an individual basis.

As can be seen from Table 16.1, the environment remained benign and did not suffer any dramatic change over the ten-year period. Moreover if anything the position of the state, with its extremely large exchange reserves, has improved, thus giving it an even greater capacity to handle a crisis.

Nevertheless, the growth of credit has been very high in 2009 – perhaps hinting at a possible worsening of credit quality and a loosening

Table 16.1 Macroeconomic statistics, 2000–2009

	Real GDP growth*	Loan volume growth**	Consumer prices***	Real loan interest rate	M2/ foreign exchange reserves	Exchange rate****
Mean	9.8%	17.0%	1.97	4.0%	587.9%	7.88
Median	10.0%	15.2%	1.50	4.6%	480.7%	8.28
Standard deviation	0.02	0.07	2.53	0.02	2.22	0.57
Minimum	6.1%	6.0%	−1.40	−0.6%	348.5%	6.82
Maximum	13.4%	33.0%	8.10	6.4%	968.8%	8.28

Notes:
*Year to date % change, including adjustments by National Bureau of Statistics in 2006–07.
** % change compared to same quarter of the previous year. ***% change, year on year.
****CNY to USD at quarter end.
Source: Dragonomics, PBOC, EIU, NBS.

of standards at banks. At the same time, the Chinese economy appeared to bounce back. But combining commercial goals with Party loyalty remains a challenge. These are counter-balanced by a relative shelter from international funds (as a result of capital controls), the improved financial disclosure of banks to the public, the introduction of consistent reporting and accounting standards for all players as well as further private but limited oversight mechanisms such as international rating agencies and foreign minority shareholders.

The short time series for macroeconomic data above mask any relation to the late 1990s – a time when the banking system was technically insolvent. After years of policy lending where proof of creditworthiness was not a necessary requirement for borrowing and funds were allocated and flowed freely to state projects and enterprises, the banks (re-)established two decades earlier had amassed an alleged 30–50% NPL ratios in their balance sheet. By any standard, Chinese banks were insolvent and that was not the result of a recession.[2] China was able to sustain high levels of NPLs for years without triggering widespread bank runs because it has the financial resources to answer any qusetions about the solvency of the system as a whole (at the same time it maintains tight controls over capital movements, thus ensuring that liquidity is not exported towards better returns). As a result, one cannot take the 1990s as basis for a 'normal' banking crisis.

16.2 Current bank-level data

Further to these findings (Cole and Wu, 2009; Arena, 2005), one should also bear in mind that researchers to date have concluded that explanatory factors for bank failures are best found in idiosyncratic factors – that is, factors that pertain to the bank individually. Macroeconomic indicators or exogenous factors can amplify or worsen an already precarious situation but show poor explanatory power to predict a bank failure. Looking at the bank factors, researchers have found that – although these become quickly obsolete (within six months) – the following indicators are good predictors of upcoming fragility:

- capital adequacy,
- liquidity,
- asset quality, and
- volatility of returns.

As shown above, the main Chinese banks exhibit healthy profiles (Table 16.2). None of them is in a precarious situation. While such a healthy stance was not always the case, the banks' indicators have largely improved over the years. Therefore it remains worthwhile to consider how much stress these banks can bear.

The following stress test will focus on credit risk. In most of the world's financial systems, the major risk is related to lending for banks (Kuritzkes and Schuermann, 2008). This is also true in the case of China. Other risks are also present in Chinese banks but these are considered to be of lesser importance in terms of the survival. Due to the restrictions on the trading of securities other than bonds, banks tend to hold small trading books. Other types of risks are only emerging as banks are slowly able to enter insurance, leasing and so on. Interest rate risk is very limited as lending and deposit rates are set by the central bank and banks tend to remain in a narrow band around these. Finally, operational risks are potentially large, but due to lack of information and data as well as the low understanding of those, these cannot be quantified.

Other risks cannot be included either. Because there are no data publicly available on bank-to-bank exposures, contagion risk cannot be included into the present stress test exercise – although it would certainly be meaningful because the interbank market and the payment system[3] show deep vulnerabilities. This also holds for liquidity risk. It is also important to note that the major exposures of Chinese banks are not to other banks but rather to large corporates. Risk transfers, for example securitisations remain in their infancy for now, so that these

Table 16.2 Bank-level core indicators (%, 2009)

	ICBC	ABC	BOC	CCB	BoComm	Merchants	CITIC	SPDB	Minsheng	Industrial	Everbright	Huaxia	SDB	Zheshang	Bohai	GDB	Hengfeng	Total
Tier 1 capital/ assets	5.0	3.8	5.7	5.1	4.7	4.3	5.6	4.0	6.2	4.3	3.9	0.3	3.4	5.3	4.5	3.2	0.5	4.3
Cash and central bank reserves/ customer deposits	17.33	20.24	16.25	18.23	18.34	13.44	16.69	15.84	20.04	19.08	17.18	15.66	11.93	17.09	25.13	15.19	19.48	17.31
NPL ratio (overdue more than 90 days)	1.54	2.91	1.52	1.50	1.36	0.79	0.95	0.80	0.84	0.54	1.25	1.50	0.68	0.01	0.10	2.40	0.38	0.89
Net income/assets	2.09	2.04	1.82	2.20	2.01	1.95	2.03	2.07	2.26	2.04	1.64	1.87	2.21	1.90	1.54	1.97	1.34	1.99

Source: Banks' annual reports 2009, own calculations.

Table 16.3 Combined balance sheet and P&L for main Chinese commercial banks, 2009

	SOCBs	JSCBs
Total assets	39,043	15,326
Net loan portfolio	19,085	8,506
Loan loss reserves	512	167
Non-performing loans	356	90
Customer deposits	31,955	11,382
Capital	2,126	726
Subordinated debt	279	175
Net loan portfolio	19,085	8,506
NPL ratio (%)	*1.87*	*0.89*
Basel I ratio (total capital in %)	*11.73*	*10.48*
Net interest income	798	305
Fee & commission income	185	41
Operating profit before provisions	595	205
Net profit	387	123
Return on equity (%)	*18.19*	*15.34*
Return on assets (%)	0.98	0.69

Note: Figures in italic show unweighted averages, the others are sums (bln CNY).
Source: Banks' annual reports 2009, own calculations.

do not appear to represent strong vulnerabilities for now but rather loan transfers need to be considered (Boxes 6 to 8). As a consequence, the assumption is that capital will be set aside for credit risks only.

The portfolio(s) to be looked at will consist of the four state-owned commercial banks as well as the 13 joint-stock commercial banks. Together these form the mainstay of the banking system. Furthermore, they have a nationwide presence and are those most capable of introducing new practices. As a group they are of systemic importance to the banking system (Table 16.3).

All of their actions have repercussions on the macro-economy and on the business cycle – and vice versa. Finally, the data on their assets and management are more widely available – thus making a stress test more meaningful.[4] Because the banking system dominates the financial system (other sources of finance such as equity markets and bond financing play only a subordinate role in China), the analysis will concentrate on the banking system and will not include the financial system as a whole. The present chapter will not only confine itself to a top-down approach but will also add a bottom-up approach – but relying on publicly available data in both cases. The following table (Table 16.4) summarises the

Table 16.4 Financial sector indicators (%)

	2007	2008	2009
Regulatory capital to risk-weighted assets	10.57	11.9	11.3
Regulatory Tier 1 capital to risk-weighted assets	8.57	9.6	8.9
Non-performing loans net of provisions to capital	−2.32	−2.8	−8.2
Non-performing loans to total gross loans	5.69	2.4	1.6
Return on assets	0.93	1.0	0.9
Return on equity	12.53	18.1	18.0
Interest margin to gross income	1.51	1.4	1.4
Non-interest expenses to gross income	43.10	42.1	44.5
Cash and reserves to total assets	17.00	20.4	17.7
Capital to assets	3.25	5.7	5.2
Large exposures to capital	13.50	18.4	24.3
Distribution of loans to total loans	0.00	0.0	0.0
construction	2.19	2.2	2.3
real estate	7.36	7.0	8.6
mortgages	13.59	13.2	16.6
unsecured or guaranteed	39.65	39.6	48.2
trust loans	8.31	0.1	5.1
restructured loans	0.68	0.0	0.2
coastal areas	69.83	64.2	64.3
Interest income to total income	87.48	83.8	79.1
Customer deposits to total (non-interbank) loans	1.65	1.7	1.6
Net forex open position/capital	n.a.	0.21	0.21
Nominal derivatives amount/total assets	n.a.	0.10	0.09
Government exposure/total assets	n.a.	0.17	0.31
3m liquidity gap (in Bln CNY)	n.a.	−50	−526

Notes: The 2007 averages do not include ABC and Everbright for capital adequacy. In 2007 and 2008 CITIC and ABC did not publish breakdowns of their portfolios by industry. All FIs are considered by themselves on a group and consolidated basis. All financial statements are based on local GAAP. Definitions are in many cases as given by the regulators (NPLs, CAR, LLR). Interbank transactions are not netted and no valuation adjustments were made.
Sources: Banks' annual reports, author's own calculations based on financial sector indicators as proposed by the IMF (weighted averages).

financial sector indicators in the format of the IMF – but adapted to the Chinese environment.[5]

16.3 Scenarios for stress testing

The scenarios for a stress test should be relevant to the Chinese environment, realistic but extreme and informative and therefore based on the risks described above:

1. Policy lending which would directly increase the volume of non-performing loans because loans would be distributed without taking

into account borrower capacity or their willingness to repay. Under this scenario, the NPL ratio of banks would increase to previously experienced levels of 10%, 20% and 30% (this is a good reflection of the situation at the end of the 1990s). This is the most realistic scenario as lending is mostly influenced by political indicators and its resolution will depend upon the resources available.

2. A slowdown in economic development as highlighted through a lower growth of GDP (that is, lower than the current average or even negative: 30% and 80% lower than previous year GDP growth) which would lead to higher default rates among banks' borrowers (both retail and corporate clients).[6] A third case stresses particularly weak segments of the portfolio: the trust loans become non-performing and banks are affected by the risk transfer which did not take place. The same can be said of loans that are overdue for less than 90 days, for loans that have already been restructured and for loans that are categorised as special mention. These are recognised as being the first to default in the case of a worsening environment. Finally, interest rates would remain at sustainable levels, because these are fully in the hands of the central bank – which has always kept the banks with sufficient margins.

3. Crash in the real estate market[7] as it makes up a large proportion of the portfolio of large banks and has been advocated in stress tests by the CBRC.[8] Under this scenario, the real estate prices would fall by 10%, 20% and 30%[9] – as required by the CBRC.

4. Failure to repay by the ten largest borrowers of each bank. Under this scenario, the exposure to the ten largest borrowers becomes non-performing and the recovery volume depends largely on loss given default estimates. Impact is also felt on the earnings side.

5. Lending to local government financing platforms increasing to high levels. Under this scenario, loan portfolio exposure to local governments is assumed to reach 10% of each loan portfolio (which is approximately that level nationwide) and 30% of that exposure becomes non-performing. Impact is also felt on the earnings side.

Under all scenarios, the loan loss need to be provisioned for in full and capital set aside for expected losses need uniformly to reach the required 8%. The NPL ratio is taken for simplicity as the average probability of default in that portfolio. Expected losses equal to the probability of default multiplied by the loss given default estimate and the loan portfolio volume at the end of the previous year. The loss given default is based on the recovery rate – which is set at 22% (across all types of loans and independently of the collateralisation). This figure reflects the latest available cash recovery rate achieved on average by all four asset management companies (Box 6). This figure is realistic because it reflects the Chinese environment and the difficulties of financial institutions to realise their securities if any.[10]

The stress test did not take into account the following issues:

- Herding behaviour or flawed incentives of bank managers.
- The scenarios are only simple point scenarios.
- Risk-mitigating techniques that individual institutions may make use of to reduce credit risk inherent to their activities. Loan portfolios are assumed to remain unchanged.
- Diversification benefits, dependencies between counterparties and any other adverse correlations between risk factors.
- Rating goal of an individual financial institution that will also be related to its risk appetite and its risk management strategies derived thereof.
- Multi-year developments and as such any feedback or second-round effects. Outside the scope of the scenario definition are any actions that regulators or authorities may take in response to a changed environment.
- Rural economy and rural financial services are not considered explicitly.
- Some over- or underestimation in the scenarios might occur as lending has never really experienced a full economic cycle (that is lending in its present form since the reforms of banking practices). This is even truer for retail lending which came into being with a relatively benign macroeconomic environment.
- The different scenarios are not assigned a probability of occurrence, as this remains a question of judgement by a single analyst.
- The scenarios consider only the effect on capital buffers, but nonetheless the effect on earnings should not be taken lightly: banks' earnings will drop possibly sharply in the event of a downturn (of a segment or of the economy as a whole) and could create losses that reduce capital available even further (this is especially true for Chinese banks which rely heavily – around 80% of their total net income before non-financial expenses, provisioning and taxation – on interest income for their business).
- The scenarios did not consider the possibility of large loan growth as already experienced in 2009 prior to the scenarios above taking place. The effect on the capital buffer would be even worse.

- Correlations between different risk factors are not considered. Each is considered independently.
- Does not account for financial intermediaries other than banks in China (for example trust companies which may hoard significant risks – albeit small compared to banks).

16.4 Stress test results

The results of the above stress test scenarios are as follows (Table 16.5).

This simple exercise shows that the banks can sustain modest loan losses with their capital buffers. NPL ratios above 5–7% of the loan portfolio are those that become unsustainable. This is not a large buffer if banks face widespread worsening asset quality (following a strong loan growth). This is especially the case when credit standards are looser and local authorities' influence is widespread. As predicted, some individual banks would suffer more than others because their financial indicators are poorer than others (and JSCBs more than SOCBs).

What is the individual risk-bearing capacity of the banking system and of the largest banks? If such scenarios occur, then the banks would

Table 16.5 Effect on the core capital ratio of the main Chinese commercial banks (2009, %)

	SOCBs	JSCBs
Original core capital ratio	6.68	2.21
Scenario 1		
– NPL ratio = 10%	1.34	−1.30
– NPL ratio = 20%	−3.99	−4.81
– NPL ratio = 30%	−9.33	−8.33
Scenario 2		
– GDP drops by 30%	5.86	1.64
– GDP drops by 80%	5.00	1.08
– GDP drop is such that trust loans, restructured loans, special mention loans and yuqi[11] loans become non-performing	0.34	−0.74
Scenario 3		
– Real estate prices drop by 10%	5.67	1.76
– Real estate prices drop by 20%	5.26	1.55
– Real estate prices drop by 30%	4.58	1.21
Scenario 4	4.26	1.12
Scenario 5	5.08	1.16

Note: The table shows the new core capital ratio for that bank under the particular scenario.
Source: Banks' annual reports 2009, own calculations.

Table 16.6 Cost of recapitalisation under the respective scenarios (in CNY bln)

	SOCBs	JSCBs	Total
Scenario 1			
– NPL ratio = 10%	1,529	677	2,205
– NPL ratio = 20%	3,057	1,353	4,410
– NPL ratio = 30%	4,586	2,030	6,615
Scenario 2			
– GDP drops by 30%	234	105	339
– GDP drops by 80%	479	212	691
– GDP drop is such that trust loans, restructured loans, special mention loans and yuqi loans become non-performing	1,797	600	2,397
Scenario 3			
– Real estate prices drop by 10%	285	86	371
– Real estate prices drop by 20%	403	134	537
– Real estate prices drop by 30%	600	214	814
Scenario 4	692	274	966
Scenario 5	459	203	662

Note: This is the cost to recapitalise the banks so that their core capital ratio again reaches the 2009 core capital ratio. It does not take into account any growth in the portfolio (risk-weighted assets are assumed to remain unchanged).
Source: Author's own calculations based on banks' annual reports 2009.

need to be recapitalised again – by their main shareholders the Chinese state (Table 16.6).

The costs of a renewed recapitalisation of the main Chinese commercial banks would be high.[12] Compared to a real GDP amounting to CNY30,686 bln, the costs remain bearable – as long as policy lending is not assumed. Otherwise the costs could still be lower than what has already been paid during the last restructuring exercise in the late 1990s.

Conclusion of Part V

Since the majority of the banking system's assets, financial intermediation and the regulatory authorities are in the hands of the state, market forces have had little chance to penetrate the banking system – but that is not the goal. The state has allocated to itself the main role in finance. Such a situation is supported by the argument that markets would not allocate resources fairly and that, culturally, the government has a responsibility in controlling the financial system if it is to advance rapid and orderly economic development.[1] Put simply, the state still finds it necessary to intervene in the allocation of financial resources to ensure that its economic and social goals are reached.

One issue is that the role taken over by the state is not under the control of any other independent institution. This inefficiency results in distorted financial intermediation, poor service quality and a widespread short-term orientation.

The state attempts to take advantage of its dominant situation by promoting its own policies and projects through the provision of financial services by influencing the lending process at many points (choice of managers, support of banks, influence of lending decisions, and so on) with a number of methods (such as loyalty, corruption, co-opting, rent seeking). This is actually a rational choice of the state: who would cut the tree on which it is sitting?

The state is not committed to relinquishing any of its power and control. Reforms that may reduce its power or control are compensated by an increase of influence in one way or another, mostly with an indirect or more subtle influence elsewhere. This results in influence and control becoming less visible, through channels that are less easy to monitor and measure. Thus, targeting changes in these areas is even more challenging. The basic assumptions underlying the role of the state in the banking system has not changed much over recent years, and the state does not seem to be too willing to change.

Annexes

List of the main players in the Chinese banking industry

Regulatory authorities

People's Bank of China (PBOC)
China Banking Regulatory Commission (CBRC)
China Securities Regulatory Commission (CSRC)
China Insurance Regulatory Commission (CIRC)
Ministry of Finance (MOF)
Communist Party of China (CPC)

State-owned commercial banks (SOCBs), ranked by assets as of end-2009

Industrial and Commercial Bank of China (ICBC)
China Construction Bank (CCB)
Agricultural Bank of China (ABC)
Bank of China (BoC)

Joint-stock commercial banks (JSCBs), ranked by assets as of end-2009:

Bank of Communications (BoComm)
China Merchants Bank (Merchants)
China CITIC Bank (CITIC)
Shanghai Pudong Development Bank (SPDB)
China Minsheng Banking Corp. (Minsheng)
Industrial Bank, formerly Fujian Industrial Bank (Industrial)
China Everbright Bank (Everbright)
Huaxia Bank (Huaxia)
Guangdong Development Bank (GDB)
Shenzhen Development Bank (SDB)
Evergrowing Bank (Hengfeng)
China Zheshang Bank (Zheshang)
China Bohai Bank (Bohai)

Asset Management Companies (AMCs)

Huarong Asset Management Company (Huarong AMC) /ICBC
Orient Asset Management Company (Orient AMC) /BOC
Great Wall Asset Management Company (Great Wall AMC) /ABC

Cinda Asset Management Company (Cinda AMC) /CCB
Huida Asset Management Company (Huida AMC)

Policy-lending banks

Export–Import Bank of China (EximBank)
China Development Bank, formerly State Development Bank (CDB)
Agricultural Development Bank of China (ADBC)

Table A.1   CAMELS bank assessment system

Factor		Pts	Indicator & comments	Pts
Capital adequacy	Quant.	60	CAR	30
			Tier 1 CAR	30
	Qual.	40	Components and quality of bank capital: stability, fully paid in or not	6
			Overall financial status of the bank and its impact on capital: profitability, competitive position, adverse factors	8
			Asset quality and its influence on capital (comparing trends in NPLs / provisions)	8
			Ability of banks to raise capital in markets or other channels	8
			Management of capital: plans, strategy, forecasting, profits distribution	10
Asset Safety	Quant.	60	NPL ratio	15
			Estimated loan loss ratio	10
			Lending ratio of the biggest single customer or group customer	10
			Reserve coverage ratio	20
			Non-credit asset loss ratio	5
	Qual.*	40	Tendency of NPLs changes and other non-performing assets and their influences on the bank's asset safety situation	5
			Loan industry concentration and its impact on bank's asset safety	5
			Procedure and effectiveness of credit risk management	10
			Completeness and effectiveness of loan risk classification system	10
			Management of guaranteed loans and mortgages (pledges)	5
			Risk management status of non-credit assets	5

(Continued)

Table A.1 Continued

Factor		Pts	Indicator & comments	Pts
Management Administration	Bank management	50	Fundamental structure of the bank's management: structure, institutions in place and responsibilities	10
			Decision making system of banking corporate governance: shareholders, directors qualifications	10
			Execution system of the bank's corporate governance	10
			Supervision system of the bank's corporate governance	10
			Encouragement, restriction and responsibility specification system of the bank's corporate governance	10
	Internal Controls	50	Internal control environment and culture (mechanisms, structures, culture)	10
			Risk identification and assessment: risk management procedures and systems	10
			Controlling behaviour and responsibilities (business policies, responsibilities, control mechanisms, emergency systems)	10
			Information communications: information sharing, integrity of information	10
			Supervision and Correction	10
Profitability	Quant.	60	ROA	15
			ROE	15
			Interest Income Recovery Rate	15
			Asset Expense Ratio	15
	Qual.	40	Cost and income status as well as profitability level and development tendency	15
			Quality of the bank's profitability and its influences on the bank's business development and asset loss provisions	15
			Financial budget and settlement system, completeness and effectiveness of its financial management	10
Liquidity	Quant.	60	Liquidity Ratio	20
			RMB Excessive Reserve Ratio: RMB Excessive reserves means RMB reserves after deduction of required reserves	10
			Foreign Currency Excessive Reserve Ratio	5
			Loans Deposits Ratio: Combination of RMB and Foreign Currency	10
			Loans Deposits Ratio: Foreign Currency	5
			Net Interbank Borrowing Ratio	10

(Continued)

238

Table A.1   Continued

Factor	Pts	Indicator & comments	Pts
Qual.	40	Composites, development tendency and stability of the bank's capital sources	5
		Assets and liabilities management policy and the capital distribution situation	5
		Management over liquidity	20
		Ability of the bank to meet its liquidity demands through methods of voluntary liabilities	5

Market Risk

Ability of the bank's Board of Directors and senior management to identify, measure, supervise and control its market risk exposure

Character and complexity of interest rate risk exposure originated from (non-)trade position No market risk assessment for now due to the lack of capacity and expertise in Chinese banks in using relevant products

Definitions: NPLs defined as last three categories. Estimated loan loss ratio = (normal loans × 1% + precautionary loans × 2% + substandard loans × 20% + doubtful loans × 40% + loss loans × 100%)/ total loans. Reserve coverage ratio = (general reserves + specific reserves + special reserves)/ (substandard loans + doubtful loans + loss loans). Non-credit asset loss ratio = Non-credit asset losses / Total non-credit assets. Asset Expense Ratio = Operation Expense/Total Assets. Net interbank borrowing ratio = interbank borrowing ratio − interbank lending ratio.
* Each type of procedure will be marked with a set number of points.
Source: based on References for laws 29.

Table A.2 Banking regulations in China, 2008

	Topic	Comment	Source	Quantification
1. Entry into Banking				
1.1	What body/agency grants commercial banking licenses?	China Banking Regulatory Commission	Art. 16 Law of Banking Regulation	
1.1.1	Is there more than one body/agency that grants licenses to banks?	No	Art. 19 Law of Banking Regulation	
1.1.2	Is more than one license required (e.g., one for each banking activity, such as commercial banking, securities operations, insurance, etc.)?	Yes	Art. 18 Law of Banking Regulation	
1.2	How many commercial banks were there at year-end 2008?	462	CBRC Annual report	
1.2.1	What are the total assets of all commercial banks at year-end 2008?	CNY 50 trn	CBRC Annual report	
1.2.2	What are the total deposits of all commercial banks at year-end 2008?	CNY 48 trn	CBRC Annual report	
1.3	What is the minimum capital entry requirement? (in US$ and/or domestic currency, state which)	CNY 1 mln for rural entities and up to CNY 1 bln for large banks	Art. 13 Commercial Banking Law	
1.3.1	Is this minimum capital entry requirement the same for a foreign branch and subsidiary?	Yes, compared to large commercial banks	Art. 13 Commercial Banking Law	
1.4	Is it legally required that applicants submit information on the source of funds to be used as capital?	not actually mentioned in the regulations	–	

(Continued)

Table A.2 Continued

	Topic	Comment	Source	Quantification
1.5	Are the sources of funds to be used as capital verified by the regulatory/supervisory authorities?	not actually mentioned in the regulations	–	1
1.6	Can the initial disbursement or subsequent injections of capital be done with assets other than cash or government securities?	not actually mentioned in the regulations	–	1
1.7	Can initial disbursement of capital be done with borrowed funds?	not actually mentioned in the regulations	–	1
1.8.1	1.8 Which of the following are legally required to be submitted before issuance of the banking license? Draft by-laws?	not actually mentioned in the regulations	–	0
1.8.2	Intended organization chart?	Yes	Art. 15 Commercial Banking Law	1
1.8.3	Financial projections for first three years?	Yes	Art. 15 Commercial Banking Law	1
1.8.4	Financial information on main potential shareholders?	Yes	Art. 15 Commercial Banking Law	1
1.8.5	Background/experience of future directors?	Yes	Art. 20 Law of Banking Regulation	1
1.8.6	Background/experience of future managers?	Yes	Art. 20 Law of Banking Regulation	1

1.8.7	Sources of funds to be disbursed in the capitalization of new bank?	Yes	Art. 15 Commercial Banking Law	1
1.8.8	Market differentiation intended for the new bank?	Yes	Art. 20 Law of Banking Regulation	1
1.9	In the past five years, how many applications for commercial banking licenses have been received from domestic entities?	4-5 successful ones	–	not available
1.9.1	How many of those applications have been denied?	unknown	–	not available
1.10	In the past five years, how many applications for commercial banking licenses have been received from foreign entities?	32 successful ones	–	not available
	How many of those applications have been denied?	unknown	–	not available
1.10.1	Number of applications from foreign entities to enter through the acquisition of domestic bank? Received	not allowed	Art. 9-10 Administrative Rules Governing the Equity Investment in Chinese Financial Institutions by Overseas Financial Institutions	not available

Table A.2 Continued

Topic		Comment	Source	Quantification
	Denied	not allowed	Art. 9-10 Administrative Rules Governing the Equity Investment in Chinese Financial Institutions by Overseas Financial Institutions	not available
1.10.2	Number of applications from foreign entities to enter through new, capitalized subsidiary?			
	Received	32	CBRC Annual report	not available
	Denied	not disclosed	–	not available
1.10.3	Number of applications from foreign entities to enter through opening a branch?			
	Received	N/A	CBRC Annual report	not available
	Denied	not disclosed	–	not available
1.10.4	Number of applications from foreign entities to enter through some other means?			
	Received	not allowed	–	not available
	Denied	not allowed	–	not available
1.11.1	What were the primary reasons for denial of the applications in 1.9.1 and 1.10.1?	Capital amount or quality?	not disclosed	–
1.11.2		Banking skills?	not disclosed	–

1.11.3	Reputation?	not disclosed	—	
1.11.4	Incomplete application?	not disclosed	—	
1.11.5	Other reason(s). Please list.	not disclosed	—	
1.12.1	1.12 Are foreign entities prohibited from entering through — Acquisition	Yes	Art. 9-10 Administrative Rules Governing the Equity Investment in Chinese Financial Institutions by Overseas Financial Institutions	0
1.12.2	Subsidiary	No	Regulations of the People's Republic of China on Administration of Foreign-funded Banks	1
1.12.3	Branch	No	Regulations of the People's Republic of China on Administration of Foreign-funded Banks	1

(Continued)

Table A.2 Continued

Topic	Comment	Source	Quantification
2. Ownership			
2.1 Is there a maximum percentage of bank capital that can be owned by a single owner?	depends on the bank type (no limits on JSCBs, but on rural entities for example)	regulations concerning rural financial institutions	
2.1.1 If yes, what is the percentage?	0.5% on individuals	regulations concerning rural financial institutions	
2.2 Can related parties own capital in a bank?	not explicitly prohibited	–	
2.2.1 If yes, what are the maximum percentages associated with the total ownership by a related party group (e.g., family, business associates, etc.)?	no maximum on enterprises but on local governments (CCBs e.g. 20%)	–	
2.2.2 Are there penalties for violating this rule?	N/A	–	
2.3 Can nonfinancial firms own shares in commercial banks?	Yes	Banks annual reports	
2.4 What fraction of capital in the largest 10 banks is owned by commercial/industrial and/or financial conglomerates? If there are fewer than 10 banks, use that number in your answer.	Controlling shareholders in three JSCBs	Banks annual reports	3

2.5	Can non-bank financial firms (e.g. insurance companies, finance companies, etc.) own commercial banks?	Yes, but limited on a case by case basis	Banks annual reports	3
2.6.1	Of commercial banks in your country, what fraction of: Deposits are held by the five (5) largest banks at year-end 2008?	58	Banks annual reports	
2.6.2	Assets are held by the five (5) largest banks at year-end 2008?	68	Banks annual reports	
2.7	Of all deposit-taking institutions in your country, what fraction of their assets is held by just commercial banks?	N/A	Banks annual reports	
3. Capital				
3.1	What is the minimum capital–asset ratio requirement?	10–11%	Art. 7 Management Rule on Commercial Banks' Capital Adequacy	
3.1.1	Is this ratio risk weighted in line with the Basle guidelines?	Yes	Art. 11 Management Rule on Commercial Banks' Capital Adequacy	1
3.2	Does the minimum ratio vary as a function of an individual bank's credit risk?	No	Management Rule on Commercial Banks' Capital Adequacy	0

(Continued)

Table A.2 Continued

	Topic	Comment	Source	Quantification
3.3	Does the minimum ratio vary as a function of market risk?	No	Management Rule on Commercial Banks' Capital Adequacy	0
3.4	What is the actual risk-adjusted capital ratio in banks as of year-end 2008, using the 1988 Basle Accord definitions?	99.9% of all assets reach min. 8%	CBRC Annual report	
3.4.1	What is the actual capital ratio (i.e., not risk-adjusted) of banks as of year-end 2008?	6	CBRC Annual report	
3.5	Is subordinated debt allowable as part of capital?	Yes	Art. 14 Rules on the Issuance of Subordinated Bonds by Commercial Banks	1
3.6	Is subordinated debt required as part of capital?	No	Rules on the Issuance of Subordinated Bonds by Commercial Banks	0
3.7	What fraction of revaluation gains is allowed as part of capital?	Max. 70%	Management Rule on Commercial Banks' Capital Adequacy - Appendix 1	1

3.8.1	What fraction of the banking system's assets is in banks that are:	50% or more government owned as of year-end 2008?	47% (directly owned)	Banks annual reports
3.8.2		50% or more foreign owned as of year-end 2008?	0	Banks annual reports
3.9.1	Before minimum capital adequacy is determined, which of the following are deducted from the book value of capital?	Market value of loan losses not realized in accounting books?	No	Management Rule on Commercial Banks' Capital Adequacy - Appendix 1
3.9.2		Unrealized losses in securities portfolios?	No	Management Rule on Commercial Banks' Capital Adequacy - Appendix 1
3.9.3		Unrealized foreign exchange losses?	No	Management Rule on Commercial Banks' Capital Adequacy - Appendix 1
3.10	Are accounting practices for banks in accordance with International Accounting Standards (IAS)?		Yes	Banks annual reports
3.11	Are accounting practices for banks in accordance with U.S. Generally Accepted Accounting Standards (GAAS)?		No	–

	0
	0
	0
	1
	0

(Continued)

Table A.2 Continued

Topic		Comment	Source	Quantification
4. Activities				
4.1	Securities	Prohibited	Art. 3 Commercial Banking Law	4
4.2	Insurance	Limited	Art. 3 Commercial Banking Law	3
4.3	Real Estate	Prohibited	Art. 3 Commercial Banking Law	4
4.4	Bank Owning Nonfinancial Firms	Limited	Art. 3 Commercial Banking Law	3
5. External Auditing Requirements				
5.1	Is an external audit a compulsory obligation for banks?	Yes, unless assets of RCCs below CNY 1 bln	Art. 6 Rules on Information Disclosure of Commercial Banks	1
5.2	Are specific requirements for the extent or nature of the audit spelled out?	Yes	Auditing Law of the PRC	1
5.3	Are auditors licensed or certified?	Yes	Auditing Law of the PRC	1
5.4	Do supervisors get a copy of the auditor's report?	Yes	Art. 17 Rules on Information Disclosure of Commercial Banks	1

No.	Question	Answer	Reference	Score
5.5	Does the supervisory agency have the right to meet with external auditors to discuss their report without the approval of the bank?	No, mentioned are only three-parties meetings	Art. 17 Rules on Information Disclosure of Commercial Banks	0
5.6	Are auditors required by law to communicate directly to the supervisory agency any presumed involvement of bank directors or senior managers in illicit activities, fraud, or insider abuse?	Yes	Art. 29 Rules on Information Disclosure of Commercial Banks	1
5.7	Can supervisors take legal action against external auditors for negligence?	unknown	–	0
5.8	Has legal action been taken against an auditor in the last 5 years?	Not known	–	
6. Internal Management/Organizational Requirements				
6.1	Can the supervisory authority force a bank to change its internal organizational structure?	No	not actually mentioned	0
6.2	Has this power been utilized in the last 5 years?	N/A	–	
7. Liquidity & Diversification Requirements				
7.1	Are there explicit, verifiable, and quantifiable guidelines regarding asset diversification? (For example, are banks required to have some minimum diversification of loans among sectors, or are their sectoral concentration limits)?	No	not actually mentioned	0
7.2	Are banks prohibited from making loans abroad?	No	–	
7.3	Are banks required to hold either liquidity reserves or any deposits at the Central Bank?	Yes	PBOC website	0

(Continued)

Table A.2 Continued

	Topic	Comment	Source	Quantification
7.3.1	If so, what are these requirements?	varies with monetary policy and size of the bank (e.g. 15.5% for large banks by end-2008)	PBOC website	
7.4	Do these reserves earn any interest?	Yes	PBOC website	
7.4.1	What interest is paid on these reserves?	1.62%, and 0.72% when above the minimum deposit requirement	PBOC website	
7.5	Are banks allowed to hold reserves in foreign denominated currencies or other foreign denominated instruments?	Yes	Commercial Banking Law	
	If yes, please state the ratio	Max. 20% of capital as forex exposure	Commercial Banking Law	
7.6	Are banks required to hold reserves in foreign denominated currencies or other foreign denominated instruments?	No	Commercial Banking Law	
	If yes, please state the ratio		PBOC website	
7.7	What percent of the financial institutions' loans is foreign-currency denominated?	0.76%	PBOC website	
7.8	What percent of the financial institutions' deposits is foreign-currency denominated?	0.37%	PBOC website	

7.9	What percent of the commercial banking system's assets is in central government bonds?	n.a.		
7.10	What percent of the commercial banking system's assets is funded with deposits?	96	PBOC website	
7.10.1	What percent of the commercial banking system's assets is funded with insured deposits?	0% since 2004	–	0%
8. Depositor (Savings) Protection Schemes				
8.1	Is there an explicit deposit insurance protection system? If no, you may skip to question 8.2. If yes:	No, protection only up to Sept. 2004	only implicited in Opinion on purchasing personal creditor's rights and client securities transaction liquidation funds	0
8.1.1	Is it funded by (check one): the government, the banks, or both?	funded by the (central and local) government - ex-ante	Opinion on purchasing personal creditor's rights and client securities transaction liquidation funds	0

(Continued)

Table A.2 Continued

	Topic	Comment	Source	Quantification
8.1.2	Are premia collected	no	–	
8.1.3	Do deposit insurance fees charged to banks vary based on some assessment of risk?	no	–	0
8.1.4	If pre-funded, what is the ratio of accumulated funds to total bank assets?	no	–	0%
8.1.5.1	What is the deposit insurance limit per account (in US$ and local currency)?	US$: equivalent	Opinion on purchasing personal creditor's rights and client securities transaction liquidation funds	
8.1.5.2		Domestic currency: CNY 100,000 (above that to 90%)	Opinion on purchasing personal creditor's rights and client securities transaction liquidation funds	0
8.1.6	Is there a limit per person?	CNY 100,000 (above that to 90%)	Opinion on purchasing personal	0

			creditor's rights and client securities transaction liquidation funds	0
8.1.6.1	If yes, what is that limit (in domestic currency)?	CNY 100,000 (above that to 90%)	Opinion on purchasing personal creditor's rights and client securities transaction liquidation funds	0
8.1.7	Is there formal co-insurance, that is, are depositors only insured for some percentage of their deposits, either absolutely or above some floor and/or up to some limit?	N/A	–	0
8.1.8	Does the deposit insurance scheme also cover foreign currency deposits?	No, the Opinion does not establish an entity	–	
8.1.9	Are interbank deposits covered?	No	–	
8.1.10	Does the deposit insurance authority make the decision to intervene a bank?	N/A	–	0
8.1.10.1	If no, who does?	N/A	–	

(Continued)

Table A.2 Continued

	Topic	Comment	Source	Quantification
8.1.11	Does the deposit insurance authority have the legal power to cancel or revoke deposit insurance for any participating bank?	N/A	–	0
8.2	As a share of total assets, what is the value of large denominated debt liabilities of banks-subordinated debt, bonds, etc.-that are definitely not covered by any explicit or implicit savings protection scheme?	100%	Opinion on purchasing personal creditor's rights and client securities transacction liquidation funds	
8.3	As part of failure resolution, how many banks closed or merged in the last 5 years?	N/A	–	
8.4	Were depositors wholly compensated (to the extent of legal protection) the last time a bank failed?	Yes	diverse research/ literature	1
8.4.1	On average, how long does it take to pay depositors in full?	N/A	–	
8.4.2	What was the longest that depositors had to wait in the last 5 years?	N/A	–	
8.5	Were any deposits not explicitly covered by deposit insurance at the time of the failure compensated when the bank failed (excluding funds later paid out in liquidation procedures)?	Yes	–	
8.6	Can the deposit insurance agency/fund take legal action against bank directors or other bank officials?	N/A	–	0

#		Answer		
8.7	Has the deposit insurance agency/fund ever taken legal action against bank directors or other bank officials?	N/A	—	0
8.8	Are non-residents treated differently than residents with respect to deposit insurance scheme coverage?	No	—	
8.9	Who manages the insurance fund? Is it managed:			
	(a) solely by the private sector	N/A	—	
	(b) jointly by private-public officials	N/A	—	
	(c) solely by public sector	N/A	—	
8.10	Is participation in the deposit insurance system compulsory for all banks?	N/A	—	

9. Provisioning Requirements

#		Answer		
9.1	Is there a formal definition of a "non-performing loan"?	Yes	Opinion on categories of loan risks	
9.1.1	The primary system for loan classification is based on (please pick one):	the number of days a loan is in arrears	Yes	Opinion on categories of loan risks
		a forward looking estimate of the probability of default	—	Opinion on categories of loan risks
		Other	—	Opinion on categories of loan risks
9.2.1	After how many days is a loan in arrears classified as:	Sub-standard?	—	Opinion on categories of loan risks

(Continued)

Table A.2 Continued

	Topic	Comment	Source	Quantification
9.2.2	Doubtful?	–	Opinion on categories of loan risks	0
9.2.3	Loss?	situational (recovery is unlikely after all means have been tried out)	Opinion on categories of loan risks	0
9.3.1	What is the minimum provisioning required as loans become: Sub-standard?	25%	Opinion on raising loan loss provisions	25
9.3.2	Doubtful?	50%	Opinion on raising loan loss provisions	50
9.3.3	Loss?	100%	Opinion on raising loan loss provisions	100
9.4	What is the ratio of non-performing loans to total assets as of year-end 2008?	2.42	CBRC Annual report	
9.5	If a customer has multiple loans and one loan is classified as non-performing, are the other loans automatically classified as non-performing?	Yes	Opinion on categories of loan risks	
9.6	What is the aggregate net interest margin-to-asset ratio as of year-end 2001?	2.7	Banks annual reports	
9.7	What is the aggregate overhead costs-to-asset ratio as of year-end 2001?	n.a.	–	

9.8	What is the tax deductibility of provisions: 9.8.1 Specific provisions can be deducted 9.8.2 General provisions can be deducted 9.8.3 Provisions cannot be deducted	all can be deducted	Notice on Issues concerning the deduction of loan loss provisions before corporate taxes	

10. Accounting/Information Disclosure Requirements

10.1	Does accrued, though unpaid, interest/principal enter the income statement while the loan is still performing?	Yes	China accounting standards	1
10.1.1	Does accrued, though unpaid, interest/principal enter the income statement while the loan is still non-performing?	Yes	China accounting standards	1
10.2	After how many days in arrears must interest income accrual cease?	180 days	China accounting standards	1
10.3	Are financial institutions required to produce consolidated accounts covering all bank and any non-bank financial subsidiaries?	Yes	Art. 25 Law on Banking Regulation	1
10.4	Are off-balance sheet items disclosed to supervisors?	Yes	Art. 36 Law on Banking Regulation	1
10.4.1	Are off-balance sheet items disclosed to the public?	Yes	Art. 36 Law on Banking Regulation	1
10.5	Must banks disclose their risk management procedures to the public?	Yes	Art. 36 Law on Banking Regulation	1

(Continued)

Table A.2 Continued

	Topic	Comment	Source	Quantification
10.6	Are bank directors legally liable if information disclosed is erroneous or misleading?	Yes	Art. 43-47 Law on Banking Regulation	1
10.6.1	What are the penalties, if applicable?	Fines depending on the related illegal gains	Art. 43-47 Law on Banking Regulation	
10.6.2	Have they been enforced?	unknown	–	
10.7	Do regulations require credit ratings for commercial banks?	No	–	0
10.7.1	How many of the top ten banks are rated by international credit rating agencies (e.g. Moody's, Standard and Poor)?	10	International rating agencies	100%
10.7.2	How many of the top ten banks are rated by domestic credit rating agencies?	unknown	–	–
10.7.3.1	Which bank activities are rated? Bonds issuance?	Yes	Rules on the Issuance of Subordinated Bonds by Commercial Banks	
10.7.3.2	Commercial paper issuance?	No	–	
10.7.3.3	Other activity (e.g., issuance of bank certificates of deposit, pension and mutual funds, insurance companies, financial guarantees, etc.)?	No	–	

11. Discipline/Problem Institutions/Exit

11.1	Are there any mechanisms of cease and desist-type orders, whose infraction leads to the automatic imposition of civil and penal sanctions on the banks directors and managers?	Yes	Art. 37–42 Law on Banking Regulation	1
11.1.1	Are bank regulators/supervisors required to make public formal enforcement actions, which include cease-and desist orders and written agreements between a bank regulatory/supervisory body and a banking organization?	No	Art. 37 Law on Banking Regulation	0
11.2	Can the supervisory agency order the bank's directors or management to constitute provisions to cover actual or potential losses?	unknown	—	0
11.3.1	Can the supervisory agency suspend the directors' decision to distribute: Dividends?	Yes	Art. 37 Law on Banking Regulation	1
11.3.2	Bonuses?	No	not actually mentioned	0
11.3.3	Management fees?	No	not actually mentioned	0
11.4	Have any such actions been taken in the last 5 years?	unknown	—	0
11.5	Which laws address bank insolvency?	Rule on Dissolution of Banks, Law on Banking Regulation	—	0

(Continued)

Table A.2 Continued

Topic		Comment	Source	Quantification
11.6.1	Who can legally declare – such that this declaration supersedes some of the rights of shareholders – that a bank is insolvent:	Bank supervisor	Yes	Art. 38 Law on Banking Regulation	1
11.6.2		Court	No	–	
11.6.3		Deposit insurance agency	No	–	
11.6.4		Bank restructuring or Asset Management Agency	No	–	
11.6.5		Other (please specify)	Central Bank	–	
11.7.1	According to the Banking Law, who has authority to intervene – that is, suspend some or all ownership rights – a problem bank?	Bank supervisor	Yes	Art. 38 Law on Banking Regulation	1
11.7.2		Court	No	–	
11.7.3		Deposit insurance agency	No	–	
11.7.4		Bank restructuring or Asset Management Agency	No	–	
11.7.5		Other (please specify)	No		
11.8	Does the Law establish pre-determined levels of solvency deterioration which forces automatic actions (like intervention)?		Yes	based on prudential ratio requirements and Art. 37 of Law on Banking Regulation	1

11.9.1.1	Regarding bank restructuring and reorganization, can the supervisory agency or any other government agency do the following:	Bank supervisor	Yes	Art. 37 Law on Banking Regulation	1
11.9.1.2		Court	No	–	
11.9.1.3		Deposit insurance agency	No	–	
11.9.1.4	11.9.1 Supersede shareholder rights?	Bank restructuring or Asset Management Agency	No	–	
11.9.1.5		Other (please specify)	No		
11.9.2.1	11.9.2 Remove and replace management?	Bank supervisor	Yes	Art. 37 Law on Banking Regulation	1
11.9.2.2		Court	No	–	
11.9.2.3		Deposit insurance agency	No	–	
11.9.2.4		Bank restructuring or Asset Management Agency	No	–	
11.9.2.5		Other (please specify)	No		
11.9.3.1	11.9.3 Remove and replace directors?	Bank supervisor	Yes	Art. 37 Law on Banking Regulation	1
11.9.3.2		Court	No	–	
11.9.3.3		Deposit insurance agency	No	–	
11.9.3.4		Bank restructuring or Asset Management Agency	No	–	
11.9.3.5		Other (please specify)	No	–	

(Continued)

Table A.2 Continued

	Topic	Comment	Source	Quantification
11.9.4.1	11.9.4 Forbear certain prudential regulations? Bank supervisor	Yes	Art. 37 Law on Banking Regulation	1
11.9.4.2	Court	No	–	
11.9.4.3	Deposit insurance agency	No	–	
11.9.4.4	Bank restructuring or Asset Management Agency	No	–	
11.9.4.5	Other (please specify)	No	–	
11.9.5.1	11.9.5. Insure liabilities beyond any explicit deposit insurance scheme? Bank supervisor	No	–	0
11.9.5.2	Court	No	–	
11.9.5.3	Deposit insurance agency	No	–	
11.9.5.4	Bank restructuring or Asset Management Agency	No	–	
11.9.5.5	Other (please specify)	State Council?	–	
11.10.1	During the last five years, how many banks have been resolved in the following way, and what was the percentage of assets of the banking system accounted for by each — Closure and liquidation: Number	unknown	–	
	Closure and liquidation: Percentage of banking system assets	unknown	–	
	Intervention and open bank assistance: Number	unknown	–	
	Intervention and open bank assistance: Percentage of banking system assets	unknown	–	

		unknown	–
	Transfer of assets and liabilities (incl. purchase and assumption) or merger and acquisition: Number	unknown	–
	Transfer of assets and liabilities (incl. purchase and assumption) or merger and acquisition: Percentage of banking system assets	unknown	–
	Other (please specify)	unknown	–
11.10.2.1	What percentage of total bank assets did each of these resolution methods account for?		
11.10.2.2	Closure and liquidation	unknown	–
	Intervention and open bank assistance	unknown	–
11.10.2.3	Transfer of assets and liabilities (incl. purchase and assumption) or merger and acquisition	unknown	–
11.10.2.4	Other	unknown	–
11.10.3	How many months did each of these resolution techniques take on average, from the moment of intervention by the responsible authority to the moment of resolution?	unknown	–

(Continued)

Table A.2 Continued

	Topic		Comment	Source	Quantification
11.11.1	Who is responsible for appointing and supervising a bank liquidator/receiver:	Bank supervisor	The CBRC is self-appointed	Art. 37 Law on Banking Regulation	
11.11.2		Court	No	–	
11.11.3		Deposit insurance agency		–	
11.11.4		Bank restructuring or Asset Management Agency	No	–	
11.11.5		Other (Please Specify)	No	–	
11.12	Is court approval required for supervisory actions, such as superceding shareholder rights, removing and replacing management, removing and replacing director, or license revocation?		No	not actually mentioned	0
11.13	Is court order required to appoint a receiver/liquidator in the event of liquidation?		No	not actually mentioned	0
11.14	Can the bank shareholders appeal to the court against a decision of the bank supervisor?		N/A	not actually mentioned	0
12. Supervision				PBOC law and Law on Banking Regulation	
12.1	What body/agency supervises banks?		CSRC	Art. 2 & 16 Law of Banking Regulation	
12.1.1	Is there more than one supervisory body?		Yes, also PBOC (in some cases MOF, CSRC)	PBOC Law	1

12.1.2	Is there a single financial supervisory agency for the financial sector?		No, at least routinely four	Laws governing CSRC and CIRC as well	0
12.2	To whom are the supervisory bodies responsible or accountable?	(a) the Prime Minister	No	–	0
		(b) the Finance Minister or other cabinet level official	No	–	
		(c) a legislative body, such as Parliament or Congress	No	–	
		(d) other	State Council	Art. 2 & 14 Law of Banking Regulation	
12.2.1	How is the head of the supervisory agency (and other directors) appointed?	(a) the decision of the head of government (e.g. President, Prime Minister)	not actually mentioned in the regulations	–	
		(b) the decision of the Finance Minister or other cabinet level authority	not actually mentioned in the regulations	–	
		(c) a simple majority of a legislative body (Parliament or Congress)	not actually mentioned in the regulations	–	
		d) a supermajority (for example, 60%, 75%) of a legislative body	not actually mentioned in the regulations	–	

(Continued)

Table A.2 Continued

	Topic	Comment	Source	Quantification
	(e) other (Please specify)	presumably the State Council	–	0
12.2.2	Does the head of the supervisory agency (and other directors) have a fixed term? If yes, how long is the term?	No	not actually mentioned	
12.2.3	The head of the supervisory agency can be removed by:	–	–	
	(a) the decision of the head of government (e.g. President, Prime Minister)	not actually mentioned in the regulations	–	
	(b) the decision of the Finance Minister or other cabinet level authority	not actually mentioned in the regulations	–	
	(c) a simple majority of a legislative body (Parliament or Congress)	not actually mentioned in the regulations	–	
	(d) a supermajority (for example, 60%, 75%) of a legislative body	not actually mentioned in the regulations	–	
	(e) other	presumably the State Council	not actually mentioned	
12.3	Are there important differences between what the supervisory agency is expected to do and what is mandated by law?	No	–	
12.4	How many professional bank supervisors are there in total?	23000	CBRC Annual report	

12.5	How many onsite examinations per bank were performed in the last five years? (average)	5	CBRC Annual report	
12.6	What is the total budget for supervision in local currency or dollars (please specify) in 2002?	undisclosed	–	
12.7	How frequently are onsite inspections conducted in large and medium size banks?	Annually	CBRC Annual report	
12.8	How many of the total bank supervisors have more than 10 years of experience in bank supervision?	undisclosed	–	
12.8.1	What is the average tenure of current supervisors i.e. (what is the average number of years current supervisors have been supervisors)	undisclosed	–	
12.9	If an infraction of any prudential regulation is found by a supervisor, must it be reported?	not actually mentioned in the regulations	Art. 43 Law on Banking Regulation	0
12.9.1	Are there mandatory actions in these cases?	not actually mentioned in the regulations	Art. 43 Law on Banking Regulation	0
12.9.2	Who authorizes exceptions to such actions?	not actually mentioned in the regulations	not actually mentioned	0
12.9.3	How many exceptions were granted last year?	not actually mentioned in the regulations	not actually mentioned	0
12.10	Are supervisors legally liable for their actions (e.g., if a supervisor takes action against a bank can he/she be sued)?	not actually mentioned in the regulations	Art. 43 Law on Banking Regulation	0

Source: based on Caprio, Barth and Levine, 2006, author's own assessment and calculations.

Main licensing requirements for establishing rural financial institutions

General requirements

Have professional and qualified board and senior management, at least a director and a vice-director, at least 80% of employees have 1 year of relevant finance experience, sound organisational structure and management system, business premises and security system, sound risk management and internal controls, effective HR management system, mechanism for replenishing capital, local government does not hold any capital.

Table A.3   Licensing requirements for rural financial institutions

Rural financial institutions	Minimum number of issuers	Capital required (CNY mln)	Further requirements
RCCs* 农村信用合作社	500 people	1	Natural persons cannot hold more than 2% alone. Local governments cannot invest.
Union of RCCs 农村信用合作社 联合社	8 RCCs	1	Employees cannot hold more than 25% together or 2% alone of the capital, other unions cannot invest, issuers should be local RCCs with equity investments should not be more than 50% of net assets. An individual RCC shall not hold more than 50,000 shares or 20% of the capital.
Rural credit unions (RCUs) 农村信用合作联社	1000 people	10	Natural persons cannot hold more than 0.5% alone; other credit unions or RCCs cannot invest. Core capital no less than 2%. Min. capital may be adjusted by CBRC but no less than CNY 5 mln. Local governments cannot invest.

(Continued)

Table A.3 (*Continued*)

Rural financial institutions	Minimum number of issuers	Capital required (CNY mln)	Further requirements
Union of RCUs 农村信用社联合社	–	5	Issuer can be local rural FIs. Issuer must have no more than 50% of its capital invested in equity, hold no more than 10% of shares or 30% of capital.
Rural Commercial Bank*, ** 农村合作银行	1000 people	20	Established on the basis of RCUs or RCCs. Natural persons cannot hold more than 0.5% alone of the capital. Unions cannot invest. Local governments cannot invest.
Rural Commercial Bank*, ** 农村商业银行	–	50	Natural persons cannot hold more than 0.5% alone of the capital. Unions cannot invest. Local governments cannot invest.

* Requirements for issuers: Issuers can be natural persons, non-FIs and FIs (also foreign). *Natural persons* must have good records and be living in area at least for 3 years. All employees together cannot hold more than 25%. *Non-FIs* must have also good records and reputation, at least profitable in last 2 years, have strong profitability ability, net assets of no less than 30% of total assets, equity investments should not be more than 50% of enterprise capital, registered in local area of RCC, should not hold alone more than 10% of the RCC capital. *FIs* (excluding unions) should have CAR of 8% at least (NBFI 10%), equity investments should not be more than 50% of net assets, at least profitable in last 2 years, sound corporate governance and structures, should not hold alone more than 20% of the RCC capital (for foreign financial institutions additionally: total assets no less than USD 1 bln, 2 years of good international rating, together do not hold more than 25% of the capital).
** Higher merger requirements: Merger should be made on own will of participating entities, have a strong management ability, consolidated accounts, NPLs no more than 15% (five-tier), core capital no less than 4%, CAR 8%, investment shares no less than 60% of all shares, set percentage of agricultural lending set by shareholders meeting.
Source: Based on References for laws 23, 24 and 25.

Requirements for branches and other outlets: Respond to a service need in area, strong internal controls (no unlawful activities in last 2 years), good asset quality, at least 80% of employees have 1 year of relevant finance experience, business premises and security system, professional and qualified directors board and senior management, at least a director and a vice-director.

Table A.4 Licensing requirements for branches of rural financial institutions

	Operating capital* (CNY mln)	Further requirements for the applicant
RCCs	0.3	CAR no less than 2%
RCUs	1	CAR no less than 4%, min. capital can be adjusted by CBRC to CNY 0.5 mln
Rural cooperative or commercial bank branch	1	CAR no less than 4%, NPLs less than 15%
Rural cooperative or commercial bank outlet	0.5	CAR no less than 4%, NPLs less than 15
Cooperative FIs' savings branch	none	none

* making up no more than 60% of HQ capital.
Source: Based on References for laws 14.

Table A.5 Licensing requirements for new rural financial institutions

	Operating capital* (CNY mln)	Further requirements for the applicant
Village and township banks	3 (county level) or 1 (township level)	Financial institutions=>20% and other single shareholder =<10%, established by financial institutions
Loan companies	0.5	Established by commercial banks or rural SMEs only
Rural mutual aid group	0.3 (township level) or 0.1 (village level)	Only voluntarily established by farmers or rural SMEs. single shareholder =<10%
Small loan companies	5 (limited co.) or 10 (shareholding co.)	single shareholder =<10%

Source: Based on References for laws 14.

Notes

1 Introduction

1. The State Council is the highest executive organ in the state administration. Under the State Council are ministries, commissions and bureaus. It is further represented through government authorities at the provincial and local levels. The National People's Congress (NPC) represents the legislative. It is represented at national, regional and local levels. Current affairs are dealt with by their respective standing committees. The judicial power is represented by People's Courts. Preliminary administrative rules may be issued by the State Council, but the NPC must enact a proper law after a period of time (Wei W., 2005). Running in parallel is the party hierarchy: above all sits the Politburo standing committee with nine members. Below that is the Politburo itself with the Central Discipline Inspection Commission (CDIC) and the Central Military Commission. The third level consists of the Central Committee of the Communist Party of China (CPC). This is reported to by a number of leading groups (economics, finance, agriculture, and so on) and departments (Organisation Department (OD), propaganda and so on) as well as local committees (provincial, city, county and so on) (McGregor, 2010).
2. At the end of the references part, the reader will find a list of legal texts.
3. The China Banking Regulatory Commission (CBRC) counts 12 joint-stock commercial banks because it now considers Bank of Communication a large commercial bank – similar to the other four state-owned commercial banks. It has done so since 2006–2007.
4. Other leasing companies exist in China – these are registered with the Ministry of Commerce and do not fall under the regulatory realm of the CBRC.
5. The stock and bond markets are respectively erratically volatile and highly fragmented. They do not yet play the role that these markets usually play in other developed markets. The choice of investments is very small as regulators proceed cautiously in opening the markets. Market players are often restricted to certain investments or markets. Fundamental improvements have yet to take place and thus transaction risks and costs are much higher for all firms seeking funds.
6. Testing for competition levels with the H-statistic is difficult in China: the banks have few means to price correctly their loans and deposits rates are restricted. (Gutierrez de Rozas L., 2007).
7. No changes in terms of domestic power sharing and in terms of regulatory arrangements should be witnessed as a result from further international convergence and integration at the thematic level.
8. The issues presented here that have not yet been discussed will be analysed in depth at a later stage in the book.

Part II Overview

1. In the present book, the author uses 'state' as a collection of central and local authorities, encompassing all levels of administration and all kinds of ministries and agencies of the state (and therefore of the Communist Party). The terms 'local authorities' and 'local governments' are used interchangeably and this encompasses authorities in the townships, provinces, municipalities – in fact, the antithesis to the central authority or central government.

2 The State as Regulator

1. The PBOC was still authorising loans until 1998 and was therefore vulnerable to interference by local governments. To curb the interference channels and the derived additional risks to the financial sector, in 1998 the PBOC embarked on a restructuring programme which led to the creation of regional branches and operational offices in larger cities which are totally independent of the local government hierarchy.
2. For example, the controversial discussion about the setting of the exchange rate for the Chinese currency will be finally decided by the State Council – based on research and proposals made by the PBOC among others (to that effect in 2008–09 it has established an exchange rate policy department and a currency research department).
3. Financial institutions under its supervision include commercial banks, credit cooperatives and policy banks, as well as asset management companies, trust institutions, finance companies and leasing institutions (*Law on Banking Supervision and Administration*, art. 2 §§2–3). In 2009 the CBRC oversaw 3,857 institutions and some 2.8 million staff at these financial institutions.
4. Laws are those rules enacted by the National People's Congress and its Standing Committee; regulations are also called administrative regulations and are formulated by the State Council. They are used for the implementation of the laws. Local regulations are formulated and enacted at the local level. Administrative regulations may also be formulated by departments and ministries below the State Council.
5. The notice does not deal, however, with regulatory agencies' powers. It only requires banks to disclose certain information on intra-group transactions and liabilities, on the calculation of capital and also gives a definition of control.
6. A recent paper (Caprio, 2010) looked at the experience of counter-cyclical regulations in the wake of the financial crisis, since it was argued, for example, that it had played a major positive role in regulating Spanish banks. Nonetheless Caprio found that overall higher provisioning does not reduce risk taking because regulatory arbitrage continues to take place in such environments. Counter-cyclical measures make sense only when combined with higher transparency and with the correct incentives. It would thus appear more useful to focus on stronger regulatory requirements on those institutions that pose a larger threat to the stability of the system. He finally pointed to the fact that risk taking decreases with less concentrated ownership structures in banks (which would mean that the highly concentrated state ownership in

the state-owned commercial banks could potentially have an adverse effect on their risk appetite and risk management).

7. The size of each bank's contribution reflects the depth and breadth of supervisory work, depending upon some ten ratios (including size, operations, results, net assets, market share and level of riskiness). The fees are divided into institution-based fees and business fees. The first are based on the previous year's capital multiplied by 0.05% and a risk-adjusted index (ranging from 0.9 and 1.1, in five steps). The second are based on total assets (minus the capital) multiplied by the risk-adjusted index and a further fee multiplicator ranging between 0.014% to nil (depending on business size) – as prescribed by the Notice of the National Development and Reform Commission (NDRC) and the Ministry of Finance on issues regarding the fee structure for supervisory fees of banking institutions (CBRC, 2009c) from December 2007. The rules apply from 2004 until end-2010.

8. According to Miller (2008), the Leading Group for Finance and Economy (中共中央经济小组) is one of the most important decision groups within the state apparatus. It was reinstated in March 1980 and was chaired then by Zhao Ziyang. Currently Wen Jiabao is the chairman. It is staffed with high-level chairmen from the relevant ministries and regulatory bodies.

9. The Organisation Department is a highly secretive and massive organisation which is in charge of human resources on behalf of the Communist Party. It penetrates every state entity within the country – regardless of it being private or not. It acts behind closed doors: it conducts candidates' interviews and investigations, and removes and changes the positions of senior managers and bureaucrats. As a result it is also the place of strong political battles meaning that posts can be bought and sold. Appointments depend upon experience, education, and so on. Indicators inform about the executive's performance. Its professional head-hunter practices operate only up to a certain official rank, however. Promising officials are rotated between enterprises, industries, departments and regions.

10. For example, in June 2007, Tang Shuangning, previously vice-chairman of the CBRC, was appointed chairman of the board of China Everbright Bank. Similarly, Xu Feng, former director of CBRC, became president of the Shanghai Pudong Development Bank and Xiang Junbo, a deputy director at PBOC, was named president of the Agricultural Bank of China (Anderlini, 2007).

11. Further rules detail what requirements are to be fulfilled when extending certain types of loans such as mergers and acquisitions, working capital, real estate, project finance, or fixed assets.

12. At the end of 2009, without the issuing of a new rule the CBRC required banks to set aside 10% and 11% of their capital for risk assets (for smaller and larger banks respectively).

13. Central bank re-lending is an important tool of the state to adjust the timing and direction of financial flows in China (including disaster relief and any other policy lending objective), especially in rural China (Park and Sehrt, 2001). The funds can also be directed to certain areas and to specific rural activities. Up to 2005, the central bank had issued CNY1.02 trillion in re-lending, with more than CNY14 bln issued each year on average. At the end of 2005, there were CNY59.7 bln of such outstanding loans. Around 90% of

these funds are designated for rural farmers and transferred through RCCs (China Economic News Net, 2006).

14. Rural financial institutions are excluded from these new rules. For credit cooperatives, the upper cap has been widened to 2.3 times, and deposit rates are uncapped.

15. Although the final word would be by Wang Qishan the current vice-premier for the finance industry but someone who rarely makes public speeches (The Economist, 2010a).

3   The State and the Banking Safety Net

1. A safety net is composed of a lender of last resort, a deposit insurance mechanism and finally a framework for a government bailout (Barth, Caprio and Levine, 2006).

2. This case took four years to resolve and had an average recovery rate of 12.54 cents to the dollar (Wormuth, 2004).

3. The institutions targeted for closure are urban credit cooperatives, whose names are not known (for fear of bank runs).

4. CBRC has classified CCBs according to their riskiness and profitability into six groups in order to increase specialisation in supervision.

4   Further Roles of the State

1. The Communist Party delegates its appointment functions to the Organisation Department (which oversees all state personnel appointments within China) and to the CDIC.

2. In November 2004, the previously required party membership for middle management has been removed at both BoC and CCB (Zhang X., 2004b).

3. Some of its activities and responsibilities were then transferred to CBRC. The commission prepared appointments by the Organisation Department but did not interfere in banks' internal management decisions. It also staffed supervisory boards.

4. Senior appointments at large banks and at regulatory authorities also require the approval of the Communist Party, through its Central Leading Group for Finance and Economics (EIU, 2006b). Party members must fill a minimum of four seats on the Board of Directors in banks.

5. 'Open' means, however, that the positions are open for competition, but applicants need to be from the head quarters, the PBOC Shanghai office and units directly under the head quarters.

6. 'Even highly insulated bureaucrats in a professional bureaucracy have an interest in getting promoted, and financial resources constitute a powerful policy tool that can quickly bolster one's administrative accomplishments and thus speed up promotion' (Shih, 2009: 8).

5   State Interference

1. A faction is a 'personal network of reciprocity that seeks to preserve and expand the power of the patron', which is formed based 'on personal relationships

between the patron and its clients' and which 'exists as a channel to exchange goods and influence'. Generalist factions have the highest power, while the technocratic factions arrange themselves around specialised mandates such as in the financial sector (Shih, 2009). A member of a faction gets promoted either because he/she brought additional investments and resources to his/ her home province (mainly through loan allocation because they can form the largest fund volumes) if he/she is part of a generalist faction, or because he/she shows sufficient authority to have the resources to be spent in case of need or financial problems if he/she is part of a technocratic faction. All are rent-seekers nonetheless.

2. Alternative views to explain the country's reform path also include one which contrasts modernist and conservative factions and another one which puts centralisation vs decentralisation efforts at the centre of the explanations. The latter concentrates on the fact that political and fiscal decentralisation allowed local authorities to use resources as they pleased and to test different policies locally to innovate. Authors, however, found that this did not provide a full explanation of China's economic miracle (Cai, Treisman, 2006). The former is superficial and fails to recognise the fact that loyalty is to the Party and/or to a person (or a faction) and not to an idea and that the centre–periphery relationship is of paramount importance in Chinese governance: 'the dominance of the centre is the precondition to guarantee the unity of the state' (Weigelin-Schwriedzik 2004). At the same time the periphery – through local authorities – ensures the enforcement and implementation of decisions of the central authorities which also devolve a number of other duties and responsibilities to the peripheries. The relative independence of local authorities or the periphery allows for a larger unified state while expending less effort on controlling it. The means to ensure that the relationship remains stable (apart from guaranteeing unity) include control over human resources and the bureaucracy, the armed forces and the propaganda (McGregor 2010). These three pillars ensure that all are loyal to the Party and speak in one voice. The bureaucracy embodies the complementary link between centre and periphery. This arrangement has endured throughout the long Chinese history. A failure to balance out power and control between the centre and the periphery may lead to a change of regime.

3. As noted by Shih (2009), the first introduction of such limits and ratios came only after the Asian Financial Crisis which provided the technocratic faction with a powerful rationale and narrative to restrict the power of the generalist faction.

4. Private sector monitoring is understood here as a range of institutions in the largest sense of the word, including, for example, international accounting standards enforced by independent auditors, international rating agencies, foreign (thereby external to the state) shareholders or accession to the FATF to fight money laundering (as it adds reporting requirements to the banks under the guidance of the PBOC; References for laws 44). Any type of international standards reflecting best practice is a tool of private sector monitoring. Standards have the advantage that they can be implemented selectively, as the state sees fit. Specific to China, it is not possible to consider industry associations, legislature or payment system institutions as independent from the state. They do not constitute private monitoring mechanisms.

5. Actually to a lesser extent because the recruitment of all lower levels of hierarchy are now open – however their superiors and the goals they set are in accordance with those principles.

Box 1 The Role of Peripheral Private and Independent Arrangements: Foreign Investors

1. Limits on foreign ownership are intended only for companies that are not listed (South China Morning Post 2005b) and stakes are calculated on a consolidated basis, meaning that foreign banks cannot use their own subsidiaries to entry into Chinese banks' capital. Since then, press articles repeatedly reported that the CBRC was thinking about a further increase of the ceiling for failed banks, but any hopes came to a halt as regulators refused to let foreign investors take a majority stake in the ailing Guangdong Development Bank.
2. Shares in listed companies in China take mainly two forms: A-shares are CNY-denominated locally listed shares that can only be traded by Chinese entities and QFII; B-shares are those USD or HKD-denominated shares which can be traded by both foreign and Chinese investors. Chinese state enterprises have large chunks of up to recently non-tradable shares which often also represent state stakes (so-called 'legal person shares'). Finally H-shares pertain to those Chinese enterprises which are listed in Hong Kong and red-chips to Hong Kong listed companies with high levels of revenues from China.
3. Cornerstone investors compared to strategic ones have the advantage of being able to take relatively small stakes in the capital with the intention of cementing a co-operation or an exchange but not taking a board seat or influence the decision making of the invested banks (Hu C. and Zhang M., 2010). This appeared to be a preferred arrangement after the relative failure of foreign strategic investments into SOCBs.

Part III Demand

1. This is supported by the practice of the central authorities to issue rather general and at times even vague regulations and laws which are then filled with meaning by local authorities. Needless to say, the latter use much of this latitude to ensure their own strong economic development.

6 Financial Intermediation

1. Basically, the remaining administrative measures or policies would only correct market imperfections or failures – so the liberal market view.
2. From 1988 to 1995 the credit quotas were designed to control financial flows from banks to enterprises. The banks included the four SOCBs as well as the Bank of Communications, CITIC and China Everbright Bank. Other banks were required to keep a loan-to-deposit ratio of 75%. The credit quotas were prepared by the NDRC, the Ministry of Finance and the PBOC. It was based on GDP, investments and inflation indicators and local industry financing needs. The plan was never really enforced: if the banks surpassed

the limits, they would receive further funds from the central bank. After its abolition, the plan was replaced by window guidance for selected industries or enterprises. The plan created massive credit creation (Girardin, 1997), and encouraged expansion, disregarding viability and sustainability. Banks were simply transfer machines with no risk management or internal controls (Montes-Negret, 1995). Finally, it created a channel for interference by local and central governments alike as well as a channel for funds transfer between the central government and the provinces.

3. This is only a rather general view of the sector and does not account for the large discrepancies that might arise between the best-in-class enterprises nurtured by the central government and the smaller enterprises which are only active at local level for example.

4. Indeed, most of them are responsible for the sizeable amounts of non-performing loans sitting in Chinese banks (Jiang J., 2005) as ICBC's president acknowledged in late 2005 that 81% of its NPLs came from SOEs.

5. Nevertheless it should be noted that large discrepancies exist between the figures provided by different researchers about the private sector (McGregor, 2010). In fact, the size and impact of private enterprises is very difficult to assess correctly: many have to wear a 'red hat' (that is, to take on a collective or state ownership while being private in fact to circumvent the bias towards private entrepreneurs) and others use round-tripping to register as foreign companies to benefit from preferential treatment.

6. The information opacity issue is likely to be an issue for all borrowers – regardless of their ownership: Wu Min and Wang Xia (2009) found that listed companies often have to restate their financial statements which they have talked up when profitability is low. Even though SOEs use that tool more frequently, private ones also do this.

7. In China, land is owned by the state (rural land is owned by the collective). The state grants enterprises and individuals the right of use for a limited period (70 years for residential purposes, 40 years for commercial and recreational purposes and 50 years for industrial, science/educational and other purposes). Land use rights (with the exception of collectively owned rural land) can be collateralised (Chen X., 2009). Today PBOC is endorsing a pilot scheme where land used for farming could also be used as bank loan collateral (the rights to it) (Yang C., 2009, Qiu L., 2009, Ma S., Zou H. and Xiong C., 2009, Huei P., 2008, PBOC, 2008a).

8. The TVEs were created as collective enterprises (at a time where there was no legal room for private enterprises). De facto, they are mainly owned by managers and employees – in private hands (Huang, 2008).

9. Normally the large central SOEs are also the customers of the banks as both borrowers and issuers of debt instruments. The bargaining power of SOEs is very strong and they often end up dragging the prices down as far as below the banks' own costs or asking for fix interest rates for debt issuance (Zhang M., 2010a). In order to counter such issues the banks and investors have established a pricing joint conference (定价联席会议) to assess interest rates and enable the banks to ensure a downward limit. The banks appear to be victims of their own choice: losing a borrower puts them in a worse situation in terms of profits than losing a debt issuer. Debt issuance services are no more than bait for banks; they do not help them gain a competitive advantage. Finally,

the banks are fighting over a limited number of good corporate customers. Debt issuance services remain only a small portion of income for banks that suffer from loan to deposit restrictions among others.

10. The Ministry of Industry and Information Technology is especially active in this field. In December 2009 it signed a MoU with the four state-owned commercial banks to lend more to SMEs. All financial institutions in China had SME outstanding loans amounting to CNY14.1 trn by end-September 2009, of which 4.05% were non-performing – that is, about 36% of all CNY loans outstanding (SinoCast Banking Beat, 2009e and PBOC, 2009b and 2010a).

11. The informal financial sector meant here does not comprise illegal activities such as money laundering, fraud nor financial crimes, but rather the financial activities which are outside the mainstream but offer productive ways of financing and depositing money in the same way as formal finance, even though they may be curbed or forbidden in some cases (as with loan sharks or high-interest loans).

12. It is also worth noting, as Huang (2008) has shown, that the lending bias is a feature of the 1990s and that during the 1980s many private enterprises, especially in rural areas, thrived on the basis of financial liberalisation. During that period of time, the credit policies of banks (at that time all were state-owned) were favourable to them and informal lending proliferated and was even permitted, albeit tacitly. It is only in the 1990s that informal finance became more a substitute rather than a complement to formal bank finance.

13. Individuals can also make use of trust deposits and loans to finance a chosen target enterprise and the bank acts only as intermediary (Box 7).

14. Pawnbrokers are active since 1988 with the first house being established in Chengdu at that time. The Bureau for Industry and Commerce is in charge of their regulation. However, some regulations have also been issued by the PBOC. With its full recognition by the authorities, this is often considered to be 'grey' finance.

15. These refer to funds by individuals pooled together without being advertised. They frequently use trust contracts or invest through a joint-stock company which does not hold a licence to do so (Li and Hsu, 2007).

16. PBOC has issued a notice allowing lending up to four times the PBOC base rate – as defined by the Chinese Supreme Court (References for laws 62). When the Loan Principles (References for laws 15) are being revised and implemented it could be that enterprises lending no more than CNY1m or with interest income of more than 5% of their total sales would be required to register with the PBOC (Caijing Magazine, 2010b).

7 New Forms of Financial Intermediation

1. Most projects did not have follow-up financing arrangements nor did they produce sufficient profits to be reinvested. Finally, another drag on performance is certainly the fact that most government-sponsored projects face high delinquent loan rates (50–70%) while other institutions still have NPLs of 10%.

2. In 2004 the document encouraged the establishment of new forms of financial organisations, in 2005 the attention went to building a more competitive

rural financial market, in 2006 authorities again emphasised the need to create institutions with various forms of capital, subject to efficient supervision, in 2007 the document concentrated on the reform of RCCs, in 2008 asked for further market openings and reflected on access policies, and in 2009 the attention went to capacity building.

3. Rural areas are all those that are administratively at or below county level (below that are towns, townships and villages). This means that cities at the administrative levels of counties and townships will be counted as rural – sometimes leading to the impression that a much larger part of China is rural than is actually the case.

4. Surveys have found that savings branches reach only 16% of villages, that 10,000 farmers are served by just a little over one bank branch on average (less than half the figure for the urban population) (He G., Du X., Bai C. and Li Z., 2009).

5. The PBOC had published other regulations prior to this (Management Guidance on Microcredit Loans for Farmers of RCCs), but this was limited to the RCCs and did not give access to other institutions.

6. Most local authorities take a similarly conservative stance. In Zhejiang, for example, the first steps were made to enable a thriving microfinance industry. In July 2008 the authorities began to register the previously informal lenders into small loan companies (EIU, 2009c). Their numbers were initially limited to 16 companies and their registered capital needed to be CNY80 mln for a joint-stock company – just below the CNY100 mln required in Beijing. Further limitations also apply: a single client exposure shall not be higher than 5% of the lender's capital and 70% of the lender's capital shall be lent out to SMEs in loans of max. CNY500,000 (Cai, 2008).

7. China UnionPay, which manages the country's largest payment network, is setting the standards for a national infrastructure of ATMs and POS as well as the entire payment and settlement infrastructure. For smaller banks, UnionPay can even take over data processing – leaving little room for banks. UnionPay will probably keep its monopoly in future years. Competitors such as MasterCard and Visa can only issue dual currency cards for usage outside China – with member banks. In 2010 the foreign entrants clashed with CUP over its unfair competition: it is expanding freely abroad while foreign access in China remains highly restricted (Anderlini, 2010a). VISA required its merchants to process all payments through its own system only – this deals a challenge to CUP which needs more time to increase card use and transaction volumes abroad, to establish a flexible offering to partner banks and to repeal its bureaucratic structures (Hu J. and Dong Y., 2010). For now the central government is analysing the situation but still hopes to create a great and strong company with CUP while pushing aside concerns over its compliance with WTO pledges.

8. Overheating in itself remains a matter of analysis (The Economist, 2010c). In fact, while prices rise and fall at a quick pace, only a small part of the Chinese population has an outstanding mortgage because most of their apartments were transferred by the authorities in the 1998 reform and privatization process. Analysts think that possibly only a quarter of households have been active in the property market. Furthermore, the one child policy means that parents with the financial means will have no problem in supporting their

single offspring in purchasing a home. Thus the real estate lending market is solely a small part of the picture.

Box 2   Credit registry

1. The following paragraphs are based on: *China Consumer Net* (2005), *Xinhua Economic News* (2005), *SinoCast China Business Daily News* (2005), *Shanghai Securities Times* (2004), *Dow Jones International News* (2004), *Xinhua Net* (2003) and Kelleher and Dyer (2005), unless stated otherwise.
2. The issue should not be taken lightly – even in an authoritarian state. Publications of some individuals' details and ratings have raised the urgency of the relevant regulations (Shang B., 2010).

Box 3   Interbank Bond Market

1. Segmentation is not that easy to resolve because the trading systems, the settlement methods, regulators and depository agencies are all different. Thus no arbitrage takes place between the markets. Segmentation increases costs, reduces liquidity and efficiency and thus depth. Although the regulators and central authorities are working on unifying the bond markets, the unwillingness of regulators to let down their power and the fear of renewed market chaos means that the unification is far off.

Conclusion to Part III

1. The representation of the entrepreneurs' business interests also takes place through industry associations which were established in the first place by the Party to ensure its tight grip over the private sector – which it saw as a competitor for power. Increasingly, however, the associations also serve their members' interests (McGregor, 2010).

Part IV   Supply

1. These NPL figures include only SOCBs and JSCBs.

8   Large Commercial Banks

1. The CBRC considers Bank of Communications since 2007 in that group as well – although its structure and history is closer to that of JSCBs.
2. The names of the SOCBs and the JSCBs are all listed in the Annex.
3. The history of policy lending has also brought the banks close to insolvency. The central government agreed to recapitalise the four state-owned banks with CNY27 bln in August 1998 and again with USD45 bln in CCB and BoC in December 2003 as well as with USD15 bln in early 2005 in ICBC and USD30 bln for ABC (see chapter on non-performing loans).
4. The SOCBs' capital could therefore be negatively impacted by an appreciation of the Renminbi.

5. For example, at its branch in Loudi (Hunan province) the NPL ratio is as high as 55% (Zeng J. and Liang H., 2008). NPLs taken off the balance sheets amounted to CNY346 bln in 1999 and CNY816 bln in 2008 (Hu C. and Zhang M., 2010).

6. This assessment does not hold for China Everbright Bank, Shenzhen and Guangdong Development Bank which are just coming out of lengthy reform processes where they had to clean up their books extensively.

7. Central Huijin Investment Co. (Huijin) is also called SAFE Investment.

8. SDB is the only Shenzhen listed bank.

9. BoC Hong Kong's (July 2002), CCB's (October 2005, USD11 bln) and BoC's (May 2006, for USD8 bln) stock market listings in Hong Kong were followed in October 2006 by ICBC (raising USD21 bln). The ABC listing in July 2010 raised USD22.1 bln.

10. Until 2008, Hengfeng did not publish its financial statements on its website. Everbright did not publish during the four years before its restructuring was completed in 2008. GDB and ABC were also prone to poor transparency – reflecting their poor performance as well.

11. The state in the form of SOEs also influences IPO subscriptions and share prices as far as possible (South China Morning Post, 2010). It boosts its holdings' values, that of foreign investors and above all market confidence.

12. The major banks now have compensation committees which overview the payment of bonuses and salaries. For further details on the regulations, refer to the corporate governance part.

9 Smaller Local Banks

1. By way of a notice from the State Council in 1995, they were given their current designation of city commercial banks in 1998.

2. With the urban credit cooperatives money houses were allowed to be registered as collectives with the cooperative form being emptied of its meaning since control was exercised by only a few individuals. They started in Wenzhou in 1984 and it is only during the early 1990s that they were required to come under the PBOC's supervision (Li J. and Hsu S., 2009).

3. A survey of some CCBs in 2005 showed that local governments directly hold an overall 24.2% share in the capital of the surveyed banks (Eastern China 22.3%, Central China 21.9% and Western China 28.9%), and indirectly, through wholly owned subsidiaries, 73.6%. Only an average of 23.75% is held by private enterprises or investors (*Financial News*, 2005a as well as SCDRC, 2005).

Box 4 Public–Private Oversight Mechanism: Central Huijin Investments Co.

1. Huijin's board is composed of nine members: two are senior managers while the others come from the MOF, PBOC and SAFE. The same institutions also staff the supervisory board (Wang J., 2009) – thus there is a double representation and the original function of the SB is empty.

2. These include revising articles of association, rules of procedure, adjusting and improving functions and responsibilities of directors, clarifying rights and duties of shareholders and directors (Wang J., 2009).
3. Thus if it is run under the sovereign wealth fund, the State Council or SASAC or any other government agency for that matter, the strategy and goals will remain unchanged.

10   Foreign Banks

1. In 2009 it fell again to 1.7% from a previous rate of above 2%. This was probably due to the strong loan growth experienced especially by other Chinese commercial banks but which was less visible at foreign ones.
2. Registering only a branch as previously would result in facing the same restrictions as before, principally not being able to take deposits below CNY1 mln. This was explained by the CBRC as being necessary because of the upcoming deposit insurance scheme under which incorporated banks would all fall (but not branches of foreign registered banks). Registering a branch requires capital of CNY20 bln and for each additional branch operating capital of CNY200 mln.
3. 30% of the working capital must also be deposited with local banks.
4. Opening a representative office has become less advantageous with the reform of corporate taxes in China (EIU, 2010b).
5. This remains the main restrictions that foreign banks face in China: stakes are limited to 20% individually and 25% together.
6. Even though the expected potential in credit card lending failed to materialise because the banks first need to set up a data processing centre (see chapter on new forms of financial intermediation).

11   Rural Financial Institutions

1. The ADBC supports state-owned agricultural entities with purchasing grain, cotton and oil.
2. The RCCs were already established in the 1950 but lost their independence within the centralisation process of the banking system.
3. The RCFs were established in the early 1980s to manage the funds of dismantled rural communes (they can be characterised as fund cooperatives owned by collectives and households, Cheng E. et al., 2003). These were (quasi-)formal institutions: they were not regulated under the PBOC and operated without its approval, but had received permission in a 1986 central document, rules were set by the Ministry of Agriculture, complied with more or less the same prudential rules as other FIs (Cheng E. et al., 2003). These were operated by local authorities (by their respective local Agricultural Economic Management Station) at township level (Girardin, 1997). The RCFs showed strong growth until the mid-1990s. In 1997 total deposits amounted to CNY200 bln. Their operational model had the following characteristics: lending only to members depositing money and those within their local reach; employed agents to gather necessary information about borrowers; credit limits were a function of creditworthiness, enterprise size and manager character. The model resulted in lower costs than at RCCs, higher returns and better portfolio

quality, better financial intermediation than other rural FIs (Cheng E. et al., 2003). While not all of them were fully successful, the model showed its commercial viability. In 1999, the State Council decided to dissolve them because of mismanagement (authorities were losing control and NPLs were reaching unsustainable levels of 20%) and because they posed a competitive threat to the RCCs. RCFs were recuperated by RCCs and this meant losses amounting to 10% of the RCCs total assets (or CNY108.3 bln) in 2000.

4. Huang (2008) shows that this was not always the case: during the 1980s the RCCs and ABC were encouraged to innovate and to lend to the private sector. It is only in the 1990s where the state influenced and centralized decisions in order to favour state enterprises and direct funds towards their operations that the RCCs became completely insolvent. Preferential policies and state control combined with financial repression meant lower overall growth and productivity gains.

5. Initially, the capital was held by individual farmers from the area in which they operated. Li Changyu and Jie Shuqing (2004: 83) comment, 'Up to now, after 25 years of reforms towards marketisation, the 'cooperative' label of RCCs got lost somewhere early on, and the related cooperative principle has been almost entirely abandoned.'

6. Most RCCs are now branches organised around a county or township level RCC union. These unions normally do not undertake any business directly but rather undertake centralised management functions on behalf of the branches (such as financial accounting, senior management, training, relationship with regulators, human resources, cash management, settlement, and so on). The member RCC branches are ordered in a hierarchy reflecting the administrative level at which they are established (county, township, village) and depending on the type of entity (branch or deposit outlet). The network of RCCs controls the county-level RCC union. The transfer of control of RCCs to the unions has advantages (the interference capacity of local governments at the level below the county is reduced; economies of scales are possible by centralising certain activities; reducing administrative expenses and increasing management capabilities) as well as negative aspects (the concentration of power and of influence at union level away from the locality and the conflict of interests arising between union and individual RCC, Liu M. *et al.*, 2005).

7. Already some CNY166 bln in special bills and CNY18.7 bln in diverse subsidies have been spent.

8. The reform efforts yielded some fruits nonetheless and these were summarised in a preliminary investigation of 49 RCCs in eight provinces (Xie P. *et al.*, 2005b). RCCs from the first batch of reforms reduced the number of shareholders from 52,169 in 2002 to 27,898 by 2004. Meanwhile the average total capital of each cooperative increased from CNY26 mln in 2002 to CNY131 mln in 2004. RCCs in the second batch of reforms increased their average number of shareholders from 17,812 to 19,263 and increased their individual total capital from CNY7 mln to CNY12 mln. The percentage of shares in the hands of individuals is above 97. The dividend payout ratios for those paying dividends are around 6% on average. On the corporate governance side, efforts have not been as successful: 57% of RCCs managers responded that the power was in the hands of the provincial-level RCCs and not in the hands of shareholders.

12 Non-performing Loans

1. A very large number of NPLs was transferred to the asset management companies (see Box 6) to resolve the issue from its beginning in 1997 up to 2005, but the scheme was unsuccessful in shedding NPLs from the system.
2. All banks are required to report NPLs according to the five categories classification standards (for the largest since 2004 but for rural FIs for example 2007), so at least the figures are more comparable across banks but between years this is not yet the case.
3. One journalist mentioned recently that, for example, an unsecured loan with arrears of one month is counted as 'performing' at CCB, but as 'special mention' at Bank of Communications (Lu Y., 2005).
4. For sovereign risk, banks need to raise stated provisions depending on five risk categories with each provisions ranging from 0.5% to 50% (References for laws 39).
5. At some point regulators had asked banks to require new collateral for these loans, but in practice banks are unlikely to turn to their long-standing customers to ask for collateral for the first time (*China Business*, 2003b).
6. Reassuringly, a study (Miao, Tian and Bhati, 2009) found that loan contracts are increasingly adapted to the credit risk of the borrower: a higher credit risk results in shorter-termed loans and higher collateral requirements – at least for listed firms for which banks can share oversight with other shareholders and public opinion.
7. For example, according to Huaxia's annual report, the NPL ratios for manufacturing, wholesale and trade and real estate are 1.95%, 2.88% and 2.11% in 2009 respectively – although not worrying still above the overall NPL ratio of 1.57%.
8. This is based only on those large commercial banks that do publish such figures (Everbright, Zheshang, GDB and Hengfeng do not publish these). In the case of Everbright and GDB because of their poor loan portfolio quality record the lack of transparency could possibly be the result of yet to be resolved issues concerning NPLs.
9. Apparently, some banks have decisively halted the practice (Xinhua China Facts and Figures, 2010).
10. The CBRC required banks to conduct tests of their real estate loan portfolios. The results show that a slump of 30% in real estate prices is still bearable (Reuters News, 2010b).

Box 6 AMCs and NPL Sales

1. In August 2005 the authorities created a fifth AMC called Huida AMC. This entity deals with PBOC's bad loans stemming from the re-lending activities of PBOC, amounting to a total of CNY1.9 trn up to May 2005 (Chu *et al.*, 2006a and b).
2. The approval for participating in a debt–equity swap deal is given by the State Economic and Trade Commission (SETC), a government administration without any experience in restructuring or lending. The purpose of transferring the responsibilities to SETC was to avoid debt relief or debt amnesty to

be granted by local governments to their enterprises. However, this is exactly what happened (Steinfeld, 2005).

3. A CINDA report (CINDA Asset Management Company Research Center, 2010) interviewed a number of AMCs' managers and finds that most expect the speed of recovery and resolving bad assets to decrease. Most think that this is due to the market liveliness. At the opposite, investors believe that the reason for the market's travails comes from legal and policy environment issues.

4. They lack voting rights and rights for intervening in enterprises' restructurings (Li D., 2006). The AMCs did not take over their owner responsibilities, thus the ownership mechanism and pressure did not have any effect (owners were neither interested nor allowed to take any influence or control on management, on operations and on assets) (Steinfeld, 2005).

Box 8 Local Government Financing

1. The bonds were actually issued by the Ministry of Finance on their behalf. Their applications are reviewed and approved by NDRC and thus their riskiness is likely to be lower than the average financing platforms on the banks' books. The funds for repayment are then forwarded by the end-issuer to the MoF (Asia Pulse, 2009c).

2. They then went through a number of restructuring exercises which turned their operations around (they act now under the name of trust & investment companies or TICs and do not act as borrowing structures to local governments anymore). Foreign investors burnt their fingers here when they realised that local governments did not implicitly guarantee their debts and let them go bankrupt (the most famous case was Guangdong ITIC).

3. Shih even estimates an exposure by banks amounting to CNY11.4 trn – not including undrawn lines of credit (compared to CNY1 trn in fiscal deficit for China in 2009). The CNY7.7 trn estimate would be equivalent to roughly 250% of local governments' revenues – way beyond their capacity. In 2010, ABC revealed during the run up to its listing, that its exposure to such platforms amounted to CNY533 bln by end-2009 (15% of its loan portfolio).

13 Capital Adequacy and Risk Management

1. A news article recently quoted Liu Mingkang as stating in 2003 that the weighted average CAR of Chinese commercial banks was −2.98% (Xinhua Economic Focus, 2010).

2. Additionally, capital was not an issue in a socialist economy (Walter and Howie, 2006: 69–73).

3. CBRC's annual report in 2010 states that where commercial banks did not comply with the required capital adequacy, it issued a 'Warning letter on capital supervision' (《资本监管预警通知书》) which included measures to curb market entry, requirements to increase capital, to decrease risks, raise provisions, write off NPLs and reduce dividends and so on. Constraints are also on the table for incompliant RCCs.

4. Those banks will have two months to submit a plan to get their capital adequacy in line and they might suffer restrictions in terms of asset growth, and so on, as CBRC sees fit. Those significantly undercapitalised will see their senior management removed and other sanctions could follow.
5. Previously, CBRC had posted the notice for comments where all cross-held subordinated bonds would be deducted from the capital base (not only those issued after July 2009).
6. No such new capital accord has been published, but corrections and enhancements by BCBS to Basel II have been dubbed Basel III in the international press – thus such name will also be used here.
7. The annual reports, for example, separate interbank lending into foreign and domestic but do not give any information about large exposures. Information on cash in- and outflows is also not available publicly.
8. This is a process to determine the risk appetite of the bank, reflecting its business strategy and material risks (operational, market, credit, and so on), based on capital planning and stress testing to finally allocate efficiently capital. After identifying risks, capital availability and needs are assessed (taking into account possible future changes) to determine required economic capital.
9. Based on estimates from international researchers (Intrater and Garside, 2003a, b; PwC, 2004b), there is a wide variation in the ranges given for implementation costs: anything between 0.05% and 1% of a bank's assets or anything between USD50 mln and USD150 mln is possible. For China, two papers estimate that the costs of implementation could be USD50 mln per bank (Deloitte & Touche, 2005a; Zhao R., 2005).

14   Corporate Governance

1. Sheng et al. (2005) find that corporate governance structures cannot provide a fertile ground for their long-term establishment as long as the property rights issue is not resolved conclusively. Property rights on equity, land and assets must enjoy an infrastructure in which they can be effectively transferred, exchanged, recognised, and clearly defined. Institutions such as registries, accounting standards (for defining and valuing rights), trading places (auctions and stock markets, for example), intermediaries (to facilitate transactions), settlement systems, rules and regulations, transparent and independent judiciary, efficient and reliable enforcement system, mandatory disclosure requirements, and public entities (such as consumer groups) are all part of the infrastructure. These permit the more efficient flow of wealth.
2. The takeover threat and the protection of investor rights are mechanisms that put pressure on management to perform in the interests of shareholders. In a competitive environment, the threat of change of control acts for management as a motivation to perform. Such pressure is, however, only meaningful and effective as long as the takeover market is lively and competitive. The lower the protection of investor rights, the more likely ownership is to be concentrated in order to compensate for the lack of protection. The protection of shareholders, and especially of minority shareholders, is an important part of the effective corporate governance framework. In China both of the

above mechanisms are either nonexistent or too weak to act as meaningful mechanisms of corporate governance.

3. In an effort to tackle corruption in September 2007 China established the National Bureau of Corruption Prevention (following the UN Convention on Corruption). The CDIC further issued in May 2007 the *Strict prohibitions on the use of state official positions to gain improper benefits*. The regulation defines the concept of 'individuals with special relationships' as 'individuals with close familial relations, mistress/lover relations, or other relations of common interests with state officials.'

4. The BoD's responsibilities include the definition of the operational strategy, choosing and supervising the senior management of the bank, and proposing the allocation of resources, capital and earnings. In the case of banks, the BoD also defines risk management and internal controls policies (including monitoring, auditing, related-parties transactions) and takes responsibility for information disclosure.

5. The party secretary chairs the party committee of that bank and is the party's representative within the firm with the responsibility of exercising the party's power in daily decisions. Party secretaries are also senior executives (such as CEO or chairman of the BoD).

6. Some committees are mandatory: one for related transactions, one for internal audit and one for risk management. Banks with a net worth of more than CNY1 bln will also have further committees for remuneration, strategy and choosing managers.

7. CBRC has required that the banks stop including growth indicators in employees' performance and that they instead concentrate on quality (Xinhua Net Comprehensive, 2009).

8. As hierarchies in banks and in administrations run in parallel at local levels and because historically head offices were organized around small numbers of personnel, bank managers remain a force to reckon with in many banks. They often run their branch as a personal fiefdom – as has been highlighted by a number of scandals in recent years.

9. In each year between December 2001 and December 2006, increasing numbers of cities were added to the list of permitted and opened locations – until finally the whole of China was within reach.

15 Chinese Banks and the Wider World

1. In each year between December 2001 and December 2006, more and more cities were added to the list of permitted and opened locations – until finally all of China was within reach.

16 The Crisis-withstanding Ability of the Chinese Banks

1. Indeed, since 2008 the major banks in China and since 2009 smaller institutions are required to carry out their own internal stress tests (References for laws 65). The banking regulatory requires banks to quantify an adverse impact in credit, market, liquidity and operational risks. It even promulgates a series of concrete examples that should be modelled: recessions at home

and abroad, high volatility in real estate prices, a worsening of loan quality, payment difficulties at large borrowers and borrower concentrations, large changes in exchange rates and interest rates, and so on.

2. A number of researchers have designed models able to predict bank failures (see, inter alia, Demirgüc-Kunt and Detragiache, 1998, 200 and 2005; Kaminsky and Reinhart, 1999; Caprio and Klingebiel, 2003). The first paper identifies a banking crisis when one of the following conditions holds: (1) NPL/assets of the banking system >10%; (2) cost of the rescue operation >2% of GDP; (3) large-scale nationalisation of banks was required; or (4) extensive bank runs were observed. The second paper asserts that a crisis has occurred once all or most of the banks' capital has been depleted. Under both definitions the banking system in China was completely bankrupt in 1998. Unfortunately, the data basis for macroeconomic and bank-level data is very poor for that period, so that no conclusion can be inferred from that period about the establishment of a future early warning system in China. The experience from that time period, however, did show that policy lending had wrecked the banking system (the crisis was 'man-made' and did not intrinsically reflect a macroeconomic crisis) and the strong muscles of the state and its willingness and capacity to rescue the banking system as a whole.

3. The Chinese payment system is being overhauled and modernised, but it remains highly fragmented (see PBOC, 2010b; He and Sappideen, 2009). In 2009 it processed over 88 bln transactions with a volume of CNY1,208 trn but still shows a two-tier infrastructure (at the local level and duplicated at the central level) which is cumbersome, slow and at times inefficient in transferring funds (banks communicate horizontally with local-level PBOC branches which then transfer funds vertically). Regulations were drafted but there remains a lack of clarity over loopholes such as payments under bankruptcy conditions. A common platform is being designed and implemented since December 2009 which divides payments into large ones (over CNY500,000 based on real-time gross settlement with strict requirements on participants), small and bulk transactions (based on one-sided entries, daily netting) as well as clearing payments. All payments can be processed electronically, but they are yet to be managed centrally (although oversight is solely with PBOC).

4. Using publicly available data restricts the scope of the exercise, but that is not the main issue here. Some useful data which are available for other markets are not publicly available in China. This is true in the case of borrower leverage (it can only be inferred on the basis of household surveys), for credit registry information, as well as firm-level data (accounting or market based: since the equity markets have yet to play a similar role to that observed in western markets). Furthermore interest rates are poor estimates of the riskiness of borrowers since banks use very narrow bands around the central bank's rates, and since the interbank market rate (called SHIBOR) was created only a few years ago and does not yet serve as a tool in setting lending rates for retail and corporate borrowers. Finally, asset prices in stock markets are poor indicators of the banks' performance or value (short historical data, a small share of listed stocks, the strong influence of the state on the markets and on the banks and so on).

5. Therefore not all indicators have been calculated for lack of data (for example, sectoral distribution, geographical distribution on an international basis,

household debts, indicators for non-bank financial institutions) or lack of relevance (for example, forex exposure, derivatives exposure, trading income, foreign currency loans, and securities market exposure).

6. Although some analyses by Chinese researchers (Ren Y. et al., 2007; Song J., 2009; Feng J. and Zhu H., 2009) based on logit regressions suggest that the NPL ratios of local banks are correlated with local GDP, M2 and loan interest rates, the same at a nationwide level cannot be observed because the available data series are too short (quarterly data for all factors is publicly available only since 2004). Alternatively, this specific scenario will rely on estimates by the rating agency S&P with two cases of forecast GDP falling to 6.9% and 5% (respectively a 30% and 80% drop in GDP compared to the previous 9% GDP growth) and the related NPL rates for different segments of the loan portfolios (Jain et al., 2007).

7. With land prices being crucial to the financial health of local governments as a major part of their budget, the authorities are doing their utmost to ensure that real estate prices do not take a hit. A soft landing or a soft increase would be the only viable options. This would also protect the banks' loan portfolio quality. Consequently, the authorities are unlikely to act too harshly on the real estate market and will continue to use a series of administrative measures to control it (see also part on real estate lending).

8. The results of the stress tests required by CBRC at the individual banks were reported in the press as showing that the banks could withstand a 30% fall in house prices. For example, in Shanghai the NPL ratio would rise by 40 bp as a result (Reuters News, 2010b). Loans for land purchases make up only 1% of total lending.

9. The scenario assumes that prices dropping by 10%, 20% and 30% increase NPLs for that segment to 2%, 5% and 10% respectively.

10. Furthermore the reader should be aware that the recovery rate is lower in crises than in normal environments.

11. Yuqi loans are those underperforming loans under the previously used four categories.

12. This is especially true if as now the banks need to tap the securities markets for funds – this would definitely overburden the markets.

Conclusion of Part V

1. While foreign funds are welcomed for the capital and the expertise they bring into the Chinese banking system, the state is still seen widely (by itself and by the domestic institutions and economic players) as the entity that is ultimately responsible for stability, both economic and social, and thus this (in itself) continues to justify the predominant position of the state in the banking system.

Bibliography

Agence France Presse (2005) China says WTO deadline on banking to be met, no more bank bailouts, 5 December.

Allen, F., Qian, J. and Qian, M. (2004) *China's Financial System: Past, Present and Future* (Wharton School, University of Pennsylvania Working Paper).

Allen, F., Qian, J. and Qian, M. (2005) Law, finance and economic growth in China. *Journal of Financial Economics*, 77, pp. 57–116.

Anderlini, J. (2007) Concern at China banks' appointments. *Financial Times*, 22 June.

Anderlini, J. (2010a) Visa in China payments clash. *Financial Times*, 3 June.

Anderlini, J. (2010b) Chinese banks resigned to default. *Financial Times*, 27 July.

Anderlini, J. and Cookson, R. (2009) ICBC set to raise stake in Credit Suisse venture. *Financial Times*, 19 October.

Anderlini, J. and Tucker, S. (2009) CCB reveals aversion to western banks' stakes. *Financial Times*, 1 June.

Andrews, D., Prescott, C., Mah, S. and Dias, B. (2005) Fitch bank failures study 1990–2003. Available online at www.fitchratings.com.

Arena, M. (2005) Bank failures and bank fundamentals: a comparative analysis of Latin America and East Asia during the Nineties using bank-level data (Toronto: Bank of Canada working paper 2005-19).

Arnone, M., Laurens, B. J., Segalotto, J.-F. and Sommer, M. (2007) *Central Bank Autonomy: Lessons From Global Trends* (IMF Working papers WP/07/88).

Asia Pulse (2005a) Chinese banks adjusting risk management systems, 25 January.

Asia Pulse (2005b) Chinese banks seek to implement Basel II requirements, 21 February.

Asia Pulse (2009a) Analysis: improved controls lessen China banks' NPL risk, 11 March.

Asia Pulse (2009b) Bank of China: lending is determined by market not by govt leaders, 17 March.

Asia Pulse (2009c) China publishes admin measures on budget of local govt bonds, 23 March.

Asia Pulse (2009d) Analysis – Chinese banks start restructuring credit, 11 December.

Asia Pulse (2010) China's auto consumer credit takes up less than 10% of total, 13 January.

Ayyagari, M., Demirgüc-Kunt, A. and Maksimovic, V. (2010) *Formal versus Informal Finance: Evidence from China* (Washington, DC: World Bank), accessed under papers.ssrn.com/sol3/papers.cfm?abstract_id=1080690.

Ba, S. (2005a) Challenges confronting banking sector. *Business Weekly China*, 7 February.

[Ba, S.] 巴曙松 (2005b) 巴塞尔新资本协议对中国银行业的十大挑战 [The ten challenges brought by the new Basel capital accord to the Chinese banking industry]. *财经时报* *[Finance News]*. 16 January. Accessed online under www. finance.sina.com.cn [25 November 2005].

[Ba, S.] 巴曙松 (2005c) 金融改革: 国际化亟需解决五大新问题 [Financial reform: internationalisation can help resolve five big new questions]. *中国经济周刊* *[China Economic Weekly]*, 51.

[Bai, B.] 白冰 (2010) 管控万亿灰色信贷 [Bureaucrats control trillions in loans] *《财经》* *[Caijing Magazine]*, 4 January.

Bai, C., Liu, Q., Lu, J., Song, F. M. and Zhang, J. (2003) *Corporate Governance and Market Valuation in China*. William Davidson Institute Working Paper 564.

[Bai, X.] 白晓鸥 (2010) 大银行再融资悬念 [Big banks' refinancing suspense] *《财经》* *[Caijing Magazine]*, 28 February.

Balfour, F. and Roberts, D. (2004) The leak in China's Banking System: Frustrated with low returns Chinese savers are taking money out of state banks and lending it themselves. *Business Week*, 67(3908), 15 November.

Balzarotti, V., Castro, C. and Powell, A. (2004) *Reforming Capital Requirements in Emerging Countries: Calibrating Basel II using Historical Argentine Credit Bureau Data and CreditRisk*. Centro de Investigacion en Finanzas, 07.

Bank for International Settlements (BIS) (2004) *Implementation of the New Capital Adequacy Framework in Non-Basel Committee Member Countries – Summary of Responses to the Basel II Implementation Assistance Questionnaire*. Occasional paper (Basel: BIS).

Bank for International Settlements (BIS) (2005) *Studies on the Validation of Internal Rating Systems*. Working Paper 14 (Basel: BIS).

Bank for International Settlements (BIS) (2006) *Enhancing Corporate Governance for Banking Organisations* (Basel: BIS).

Barth, J., Caprio, G. and Levine, R. (2000) *Banking Systems Around the Globe: Do Regulation and Ownership Affect Performance and Stability?* Accessed online under www.auburn.edu/~barthjr/papers/Cheeca.pdf [5 March 2006].

Barth, J. R., Caprio, G. and Levine, R. (2006) *Rethinking Bank Regulation – Till Angels Govern* (New York: Cambridge University Press).

Barth, J. R., Koepp, R. and Zhou, Z. (2004) *Banking Reform in China: Catalyzing the Nation's Financial Future*. Milken Institute Working Paper.

Barth, J. R., Zhou, Z., Arner, D. W., Hsu, B. F. C. and Wang, W. (eds) (2007) *Financial Restructuring and Reform in Post-WTO China* (London: Kluwer Law International).

Basel Committee on Banking Supervision (BCBS) (1997) *Core Principles for Effective Banking Supervision* (Basel: BIS).

Basel Committee on Banking Supervision (BCBS) (2000a) *Principles for the Management of Credit Risk* (Basel: BIS).

Basel Committee on Banking Supervision (BCBS) (2000b) *Range of Practices in Banks' Internal Ratings Systems* (Basel: BIS).

Basel Committee on Banking Supervision (BCBS) (2003) *Quantitative Impact Study 3: Overview of Global Results* (Basel: BIS).

Basel Committee on Banking Supervision (BCBS) (2004a) *International Convergence of Capital Measurements and Capital Standards* (Basel: BIS).

Basel Committee on Banking Supervision (BCBS) (2004b) *Modifications to the Capital Treatment for Expected and Unexpected Credit Losses in the New Basel Accord* (Basel: BIS).

Basel Committee on Banking Supervision (BCBS) (2004c) *Implementation of Basel II: Practical Considerations* (Basel: BIS).

Basel Committee on Banking Supervision (2008) *Principles for Sound Liquidity Risk Management and Supervision* (Basel: Bank for International Settlements).

Basel Committee on Banking Supervision (BCBS) (2009a) *Enhancements to the Basel II Framework* (Basel: Bank for International Settlements).

Basel Committee on Banking Supervision (BCBS) (2009b) *International Framework for Liquidity Risk Measurement, Standards and Monitoring – Consultative Document* (Basel: Bank for International Settlements).

Basel Committee on Banking Supervision (BCBS) (2009c) *Strengthening the Resilience of the Banking Sector – Consultative Document* (Basel: Bank for International Settlements).

Basel Committee on Banking Supervision (2009d) *Range of Practices and Issues in Economic Capital Frameworks* (Basel: BIS).

Bekier, M. M. and Lam, K. (2005) What Chinese consumers want from banks? *McKinsey Quarterly*, June.

Bekier, M., Huang, R. and Wilson, G. (2005) How to fix China's banking system. *McKinsey Quarterly*, January.

Bepari, M. K. and Mollik, A. T. (2008) *Banking System in Bangladesh: Stable or Vulnerable? A Macro-Prudential Assessment*. Electronic copy available at: http://ssrn.com/abstract=1513822.

Bhattasali, D., Li, S. and Martin, W. (eds) (2005) *China and the WTO: Accession, Policy Reform and Poverty Reduction Strategies* (Washington, DC: World Bank).

Bi, X. and Shen, J. (2009) Both small and medium prove to be beautiful. *China Daily*, 25 August.

Bo, W. (2009) CCB to purchase AIG's Hong Kong financial unit. *China Daily*, 13 August.

Boston Consulting Group (BCG) (2005) *Banking on China: Where to Place the Chips?* (n.p.: BCG).

Boston Consulting Group (BCG) (2008) *Venturing Abroad – Chinese Banks and Cross-border M&A*, accessible online http://www.bcg.com.cn/en/files/publications/reports_pdf/China_MA_Sept_2008.pdf.

Boyreau-Debray, G. (2003) *Financial Intermediation and Growth: Chinese Style* (Washington, DC: World Bank). Accessed online under econ.worldbank.org/files/25828_wps3027.pdf [14 June 2004].

Boyreau-Debray, G. and Wei, S. (2005) *Pitfalls of a State-dominated Financial System: The Case of China* (n.p.: National Bureau of Economic Research).

Bradsher, K. (2004) China's informal lenders pose risks to its banks. *The New York Times*, 9 November.

Brandt, L. and Li, H. (2003) Bank discrimination in transition economies: Ideology, information, or incentives? *Journal of Comparative Economics*, 31, pp. 387–413.

Brandt, L., Li, H. and Roberts, J. (2005a) Banks and enterprise privatization in China. *Journal of Law, Economics, & Organization*, 21(2), pp. 524–46.

Brandt, L., Park, A. and Wang, S. (2005b) Are China's financial reforms leaving the poor behind? In Huang, Y., Saich, T. and Steinfeld, E. (eds), *Financial Sector Reform in China* (Cambridge, MA: Harvard University Press), pp. 204–30.

Brehm, S. and Macht, C. (2004) Banking supervision in China: Basel I, Basel II and the Basel core principles. *Zeitschrift für Chinesisches Recht*, pp. 316–27.

Brehm, S. and Macht, C. (2005) Is a new broom sweeping clean? The emergence of the China Banking Regulatory Commission. *Aussenwirtschaft*, 60(2) pp. 169–207.

Brown, C. O. and Dinc, I. S. (2005) *The Politics of Bank Failures: Evidence from Emerging Markets*. Electronically accessible at atpapers.ssrn.com/sol3/papers.cfm?abstract_id=905100.

Brunnermeier, M, Crockett, A., Goodhart, C., Persaud, A. D. and Shin, H. (2009) The fundamental principles of financial regulation. *Geneva Reports on the World Economy* – preliminary conference draft.

Buckley, C. (2005) Lax management at China's banks remains a concern of regulators and investors. *The New York Times*, 8 February.

Busch, A. (2003) *Staat und Globalisierung – das Politikfeld Bankenregulierung im internationalen Vergleich* [State and globalisation: an international comparison in banking regulation] (Wiesbaden: Westdeutscher Verlag).

Cai, E. (1999) Financial supervision in China: Framework, methods and current issues. In *Strengthening the Banking System in China: Issues and Experience*, Joint BIS/PBOC Conference proceedings, Beijing, 1–2 March 1999 (Basel: BIS), pp. 169–73.

Cai, H. (2007) Bonding, law enforcement and corporate governance in China. *Stanford Journal of Law, Business and Finance*, 13(1), 82–120.

Cai, H. and Treisman, D. (2006) *Did Government Decentralization Cause China's Economic Miracle?* Accessed under http://www.sscnet.ucla.edu/polisci/cpworkshop/papers/Treisman.pdf.

Cai, J. (2008) Underground banks in legal twilight zone Trial scheme to legitimise operations hits bumps, *South China Morning Post*, 16 December.

[Caijing Magazine]《财经》 (2009a) 地方政府：融资的狂欢 [Local authorities: financing craze], 8 June.

[Caijing Magazine]《财经》(2009b) 宏观审慎监管 "中国策" [Macro-prudential supervision 'China policy'], 28 September.

[Caijing Magazine]《财经》(2010a) 信贷潮再汹涌 [Loan tide re-surges], 18 Jan.

[Caijing Magazine]《财经》(2010b) 民间利率攀升 [Rising informal rates], 12 April.

Caijing (2010c) Qatar to Invest US$2.8 Bln in AgBank IPO, 21 June.

Caixin (2010) Can Banks Get a Grip on Wobbly Platform Loans? Accessed under http://english.caing.com/2010-05-06/100141699.html.

Calomiris, C. W. (2007) *China's Financial Transition at a Crossroads* (New York: Columbia University Press).

[Cao, X.] 曹幸仁 and [Zhao, X.] 赵新杰 (2004) 国有商业银行公司治理改革问题研究 [Research into issues of corporate governance in SOCBs]. 金融论坛 *[Finance Forum]* (01) pp. 3–8.

Caprio, G. (2010) *Safe and Sound Banking – A Role for Countercyclical Regulatory Requirements?* (Washington, DC: World Bank Policy Research working paper 5198).

Caprio, G. and Honohan, P. (2004) *Can the Unsophisticated Market Provide Discipline?* (Washington: World Bank Policy Research working paper 3364).

Caprio, G., Klingebiel, D. (2003) *Episodes of Systemic and Borderline Financial Crises.* Accessed online at http://econ.worldbank.org/WBSITE/EXTERNAL/EXTDEC/EXTRESEARCH 0,,contentMDK:20699588~pagePK:64214825~piPK:64214943~theSitePK:469382,00.html.

Caprio, G., Laeven, L. and Levine, R. (2004) *Governance and Bank Valuation* (Washington: World Bank Policy Research working paper 3202).

Carey, M. (2002) A guide to choosing absolute bank capital requirements. *Journal of Banking and Finance*, 26, pp. 929–51.

Carvajal, A., Dodd, R., Moore, M., Nier, E., Tower, I and Zanforlin, L. (2009) *The Perimeter of Financial Regulation* (Washington: IMF staff position note).

CFA Institute (2007) *China Corporate Governance Survey* (Hong Kong: CFA).

Chang, G. C. (2003) China and the WTO: Progress, perils and prospects. *Columbia Journal of Asian Law*, 17, pp. 6–11.

Chen, A. and Everling, O. (2002) Finanzsystem und Rating in China [Financial system and rating in China]. *Die Bank*, 11, pp. 727–31.

Chen, J. (2003) Capital adequacy of Chinese banks: Evaluation and enhancement. *Journal of International Banking Regulation*, June (4.4) pp. 320–27.

[Chen, J.] 陈军, [Cao, Y.] 曹远征 (2008) *农村金融深化发展评析 [Analysis of the deeper development of the rural finance]* (Beijing: 中国人民大学出版社 [Renmin University Press]).

Chen, J. P. (2004) *Non-performing Loan Securitization in the People's Republic of China* (n.p.: Stanford University).

Chen, X. (2005) *Problemkredite und die chinesische Bankenreform in Anbetracht von asymmetrischer Information und institutionellen Anreizen [Problem loans and Chinese banking reform while considering information asymmetry and institutional incentives]* Diss. (Frankfurt/Main: Johann Wolfgang Goethe Universität).

Chen, X. (2009) Agriculture financing in China: the difficult transition from a planned to a market system. In Zhu, M., Cai, J. and Avery, M. (eds) (2009) *China's Emerging Financial Markets – Challenges and Global Impact* (Singapore: John Wiley & Sons), pp. 181–202.

Chen, Y. (2004) Safety line nearing final stage. *Business Weekly*, 16 March.

Chen, Z., Li, D. and Moshirian, F. (2005) China's Financial Services Industry: The intra-industry effects of privatization of the Bank of China Hong Kong. *Journal of Banking and Finance*, 29, pp. 2291–324.

Cheng, E., Findlay, C. and Watson, A. (2003) Institutional innovation without regulation. In Findlay, C., Watson, A. and Cheng, E. (eds), *Rural Financial Markets in China* (Canberra: Asia Pacific Press), pp. 89–104.

China Banking Regulatory Commission (CBRC) (2003) *刘明康主席致巴塞尔银行监管委员会主席卡如纳先生的信：中国银行业监督管理委员会对巴塞尔新资本协议的意见和建议 [Letter from Liu Mingkang, Chairman of the CBRC to Jaime Caruana, Chairman of the Basel Committee on Banking Supervision: Comments and Suggestions on the New Basel Capital Accord]* 31 July (Beijing: CBRC).

China Banking Regulatory Commission (CBRC) (2005a)*中国银行业改革开放与监管的新进展 [The Reform and Opening of the Chinese Banking Industry and the Regulatory Outlook]* (Beijing: CBRC).

China Banking Regulatory Commission (CBRC) (2005b) *关于加大防范操作风险工作力度的通知 [Notice on Enhancing Work on Operational Risk Control]* (Beijing: CBRC).

China Banking Regulatory Commission (CBRC) (2006a) *刘明康在银监会 (2006) 年工作会议上强调以科学发展观统领监管工作全局 [Liu Mingkang Stresses at the CBRC (2006) Work Conference the Need for a Scientific Approach to Lead the Work of the CBRC]* (Beijing: CBRC).

China Banking Regulatory Commission (CBRC) (2006b) *农信社改革成效显著 [Effects of the RCCs' Reforms Start to Show]* (Beijing: CBRC).

China Banking Regulatory Commission (CBRC) (2006c) *2005年城市商业银行风险处置工作取得阶段性成果 [Risk Treatment Work at CCBs Has Realised Some Partial Results in 2005]* (Beijing: CBRC).

China Banking Regulatory Commission (CBRC) (2007) *Annual Report 2006* (Beijing: CBRC).

China Banking Regulatory Commission (CBRC) (2008) *Annual Report 2007* (Beijing: CBRC).

China Banking Regulatory Commission (CBRC) (2009a) 新型农村金融机构 2009-2011 年总体工作安排 [*General Work Schedule for the New Rural Financial Institutions 2009–2011*].

China Banking Regulatory Commission (CBRC) (2009b) 银监会对商业银行年底前 信贷审慎风险管理提出三点要求 [*CBRC Raises Three Points for Commercial Banks' Loan Risk Management Checks by Year End*], November.

China Banking Regulatory Commission (CBRC) (2009c) *Annual Report 2008* (Beijing: CBRC).

China Banking Regulatory Commission (CBRC) (2010) *Annual Report 2009* (Beijing: CBRC).

[China Business] 中国经营报 (2003a) 坏账指标期限紧逼基层 银行忙于粥锅掺水 [Running out of time for reducing NPLs, branches tend to dilute them], 28 July.

[China Business] 中国经营报 (2003b) 央行重庆报告:国有银行不良贷款下降玄机 [Report of the Central Bank in Chongqing: Secrets behind decreasing NPL levels at state-owned banks], 11 August.

[China Consumer Net] 中国消费网 (2005), 央行个人征信开始发威 信用有污点全国封杀 [PBOC's credit registry starts showing results, "credit" finger prints nationwide to push out bad ones], 16 December.

*[China Economic News Net]*中国经济信息网 (2005) 银监会拟明年出台IRB 指引 [CBRC plans a guidance on IRB for next year], 22 December.

China Economic Quarterly (CEQ) (2003) *China's Companies – A Special Issue*, 7(3) (London: Dragonomics Ltd).

China Economic Quarterly (CEQ) (2005) *Non-performing Loans – Voodoo Accounting*, 9(1) (London: Dragonomics Ltd).

*[China Industry and Economy Information Net]*中国产业经济信息网 (2005) 城市商业 银行 困境中寻机遇 [City Commercial Banks: Looking for opportunities in the middle of difficulties], 19 September.

*[China INFOBANK Limited]*中国资讯行-新闻频道 (2005a) 工行力争 07 年底达到巴 塞尔新资本协议初级法要求 [ICBC aims to reach foundation IRB approaches' requirements at the end of 2007], 29 August.

*[China INFOBANK Limited]*中国资讯行-新闻频道 (2005b) 安徽省内6家城市商行合并 步伐加快 [Six Anhui city commercial banks' merger gathers pace], 29 August.

[China National Audit Office (CNAO)] (2009) 中国农业银行股份有限公司 2008 年度资产负债损益审计结果 2009 [*Audit results of the balance sheet and P&L of the ABC at end-2008*]. Accessed on 21 July 2010 under http://www.audit.gov. cn/n1992130/n1992150/n1992500/2470535.html.

*[China Securities News]*中国证券报 (2006) 推进利率市场化央行将建再贴现率动态调 整机制 [To improve the marketisation of interest rates, the central bank will have to introduce a dynamic adjustment mechanism for setting the re-discounting interest rate], 9 February.

[CINDA Asset Management Company Research Center] 中国东方资产管理公司研 发中心 (2010) 中国金融不良资产市场 调查报告 [*China's NPA market: investigation report*], June.

Chu, C., Lin, K., Lin, L. and Marshall, D. (2006a) *China: Taking Stock of Banking System NPLs* (New York: FitchRatings).

Chu, C., Lin, K., Lin, L. and Marshall, D. (2006b) *The Chinese Banking System* (New York: FitchRatings).

Chu, C., Wen, C., Chen, F. (2009) *Chinese Banks: Soaring Credit Amid Weak Corporate Climate a Concern* (n.p.: Fitch Ratings).

Claessens, S., Demirgüc-Kunt, A. and Huizinga, H. (2001) How does foreign entry affect domestic banking markets? *Journal of Banking and Finance*, 25, pp. 891–911.

Clarke, D. C. (2003) *Corporate Governance in China: An Overview*. Working Paper. George Washington University Law School.

Clarke, G., Cull, R. and Martinez Peria, M. S. (2002) *Does Foreign Bank Penetration Reduce Access to Credit in Developing Countries? Evidence from Asking Borrowers* (Washington, DC: World Bank).

Clarke, G., Cull, R., Martinez Peria, M. S. and Sanchez, S. M. (2003) Foreign Bank Entry: Experience, implications for developing economies and agenda for further research. *World Bank Research Observer*, 18(1), pp. 25–59.

Cole, R. A. and Wu, Q. (2009) *Predicting Bank Failures Using a Simple Dynamic Hazard Model*, electronically accessible www.defaultrisk.com/pp_score_79.htm.

Crosby, D. C. (2007) Banking on China's WTO commitments: "same bed, different dreams" in China's financial services sector. *Journal of International Economic Law*, 11(1) pp. 75–105. Accessible online doi:10.1093/jiel/jgm041.

Cull, R. and Xu, L. C. (2000) Bureaucrats, State banks and the efficiency of credit allocation: The experience of Chinese state-owned enterprises. *Journal of Comparative Economics*, 28, pp. 1–31.

Dages, B. G., Kinney, D. and Goldberg, L. (2000) Foreign and domestic bank participation in emerging markets: Lessons from Mexico and Argentina. *Federal Reserve Bank of New York – Economic Policy Review*, 6(3) pp. 17–36.

Davydenko, S. and Franks, J. (2005) *Do Bankruptcy Codes Matter? A Study of Defaults in France, Germany and the UK* (London: London Business School).

Deloitte & Touche (2004) *Keeping Pace with the Times: Seeking Truth from the Facts* (London: Deloitte & Touche).

Deloitte & Touche (2005a) *From Framework to Execution: Effective Planning and Implementation of the Basel II Accord in Asia Pacific* (New York: Deloitte & Touche).

Deloitte & Touche (2005b) *Understanding the Framework: Adopting the Basel II Accord in Asia Pacific* (New York: Deloitte & Touche).

Demirgüc-Kunt, A. and Detragiache, E. (1998) *The Determinants of Banking Crises in Developing and Developed Countries* (Washington: IMF Staff papers, 45(1) March).

Demirgüc-Kunt, A. and Detragiache, E. (2000) *Does Deposit Insurance Increase Banking System Stability? An Empirical Investigation* (Washington: World Bank). Accessed online at http://info.worldbank.org/etools/docs/library/155468/finsecissues2003/pdf/demirguc_stability.pdf).

Demirgüc-Kunt, A. and Detragiache, E. (2005) *Cross-country Empirical Studies of Systemic Bank Distress: A Survey* (Washington: IMF working paper 05/96).

Demirgüc-Kunt, A. and Detragiache, E. (2009) *Basel Core Principles and Bank Soundness – Does Compliance Matter?* (Washington: World Bank Policy Research working paper 5129).

Demirgüc-Kunt, A. and Huizinga, H. (2010) *Are Banks Too Big to Fail or Too Big to Save? International Evidence from Equity Prices and CDS Spreads* (Washington: World Bank Policy Research working papers 5360).

Demirgüc-Kunt, A., Laeven, L. and Levine, R. (2003) *The Impact of Bank Regulations, Concentration and Institutions on Bank Margins* (Washington, DC: World Bank Policy Research working paper 3030).

Demirgüc-Kunt, A. and Levine, R. (1999) *Bank-based and Market-based Financial Systems: Cross-country Comparisons*, electronically accessible under papers.ssrn. com/sol3/papers.cfm?abstract_id=569255.

Demirgüc-Kunt, A. and Serven, L. (2009) *Are All Sacred Cows Dead? Implications of the Financial Crisis for Macro and Financial Policies*, World Bank Policy Research working paper 4807.

Denis, D. K. and McConnell, J. J. (2003) *International Corporate Governance*, European Corporate Governance Institute Working Paper No. 05/(2003).

Desombre, M. G. and Chen, W. (2004) New capital rules bring China's banking regulation up to global standards. *China Law and Practice*, 18(3) 28 April.

Dong, B. and Torgler, B. (2010) *The Causes of Corruption: Evidence from China* (Fondazione Eni Enrico Mattei working paper 72) available at papers.ssrn. com/sol3/papers.cfm?abstract_id=1628107.

Dong, F. and Featherstone, A. (2004) *Technical and Scale Efficiencies for Chinese Rural Credit Cooperatives: A Bootstrapping Approach in Data Development Analysis.* Working Paper WP 366, Iowa State University.

[Dong, Y.] 董欲晓 (2009) 汇丰迪拜风波 [HSBC Dubai distress]《财经》 *[Caijing Magazine]*, 7 December.

[Dong, Y.] 董欲晓 (2010a) 新资本协议适应症 [Making the new Basel accord fit] 《财经》 *[Caijing Magazine]*, 18 January.

[Dong, Y.] 董欲晓 (2010b) 银行业绩"被增长" [Banks' results were 'increased']《财经》 *[Caijing Magazine]*, 29 March.

Dougherty, S. and Herd, R. (2005) *Fast-Falling Barriers and Growing Concentration: The Emergence of a Private Economy in China.* OECD Economics Department Working Papers, No. 471 (Paris: OECD Publishing).

Dow Jones International News (2004) National individual credit database targeted '05. 16 Aug.

Du, J. and Girma, S. (2007) *Red Capitalists: Political Connections and the Growth and Survival of Start-up Companies in China* (Research paper series China and the World Economy 2007/40, University of Nottingham).

Du, J. and Girma, S. (2009) *Source of Finance, Growth and Firm Size – Evidence from China* (United Nations University, Research paper 2009/03).

Du, J., Lu, Y. and Tao, Z. (2008) *Bank Loans and Trade Credit Under China's Financial Repression.* Accessed under papers.ssrn.com/sol3/papers.cfm?abstract_id=1495600.

Du, X. (2005) *The Regulatory Environment for Microfinance in China.* Essays on regulation and supervisions, no. 11, University of Maryland.

[Du, Y.] 杜玉红 and [Xu, C.] 许传华 (2005) 城市商业银行公司治理结构问题探讨 [Discussing the issues in the corporate governance structure of CCBs].武汉金融 *[Wuhan Finance]*, 4(64) pp. 9–11.

[Duan, Q.] 段靖 (2010) China to standardize local government financing platform to ward off potential risk. *Xinhua's China Economic Information Service*, 12 March.

Economist Intelligence Unit (EIU) (2006a) Newfangled investments? *Business China*, 13 February.

Economist Intelligence Unit (EIU) (2006b) *China Hand – Finance (2006)* (London: EIU).

Economist Intelligence Unit (EIU) (2008) *China Hand – Finance (2007)* (London: EIU).

Economist Intelligence Unit (EIU) (2009a) Banking on the countryside. *Business China*, 16 March.

Economist Intelligence Unit (EIU) (2009b) Suddenly, money everywhere. *Business China*, 2 February.

Economist Intelligence Unit (EIU) (2009c) Lower expectations. *Business China*, 16 February.

Economist Intelligence Unit (EIU) (2009d), *China Hand – Finance (2008)* (London: EIU).

Economist Intelligence Unit (EIU) (2010a) *China Hand – Finance (2009)* (London: EIU).

Economist Intelligence Unit (EIU) (2010b) *China Hand – Taxation (2009)* (London: EIU).

Ernst & Young (E&Y) (2004) *Asia-Pacific Basel II Survey* (Hong Kong: Ernst & Young).

Ernst & Young (E&Y) (2006) *Global Non-performing Loan Report 2006* (n.p.: Ernst & Young).

European Union (EU) (2003) *Review of the Capital Requirements for Credit Institutions and Investment Firms: Third Quantitative Impact Study, EU Results*. Document prepared by the Applied Statistics Group of the Ispra Joint Research Centre, July.

Ewing, R. D. (2005) Chinese corporate governance and prospects for reform. *Journal of Contemporary China*, 14(43), pp. 317–38.

Fan, G. (2004) Créances douteuses et dette publique globale en Chine [NPLs and global public debt in China]. *Revue d'économie financière: Le devenir financier de la Chine*, 77.

Fan, S. (2003) Basel II: Its terms and its implications for Asian banks. *Asian Counsel*, November.

[Fang, H.] 方会磊 (2009) 银行次级债 "挤泡沫" [Banks' subordinated debt bubble] 《财经》 *[Caijing Magazine]*, 26 October.

[Feng, J.] 冯佳 and [Zhu, H.] 朱华彬 (2009) 商业银行房地产贷款压力测试分析 [Analysis of the stress tests of commercial banks for real estate loans], 五邑大学学报 *[Wuyi University Journal]* 2009 (23/4).

Ferri, G. (2008) *Banking in China: Are New Tigers Supplanting the Mammoths?* (Hong Kong Institute for Monetary Research: Working paper 05/2008) Mar 2008.

Ferri, G. and Liu, L. (2009) *Honor Thy Creditors Beforan Thy Shareholders: Are the Profits of Chinese State-owned Enterprises Real?* (Hong Kong Institute for Monetary Research: Working paper 16/2009) April.

[Financial News] 金融时报 (2005a) 诚实商业银行抽象调查的一些重要结论 [Some important insights from the sample survey of city commercial banks], 7 February.

[Financial News] 金融时报 (2005b) 十年树木 百年树人 寄语城市商业银行十周年 [Wood with 10 years of age and talent of 100 years, speech at the 10th-anniversary of the establishment of CCBs], 20 June.

[Financial News] 金融时报 (2005c) 资金联合投资显现活力 城商行: 夹缝中拓出生路 [Funds and Investments more lively – city commercial banks find a way through cracks], 29 July.

Financial Times (2010) Foreign banks in China, 18 June.

Findlay, C., Watson, A., Cheng, E. and Zhu, G. (eds) (2003) *Rural Financial Markets in China* (Canberra: Asia Pacific Press).

Firth, M., Lin, C., Liu, P. and Wong, S. M. L. (2009) Inside the black box: bank credit allocation in China's private sector. *Journal of Banking and Finance*, 33(6), pp. 1144–55.

FitchRatings (2004) *Demystifying Basel II: A Closer Look at the IRB Measures and Disclosure Framework* (New York: FitchRatings).

Flouzat, D. (2004) Les défis de la transition du système financier chinois [The challenges of the transition of the Chinese financial system]. *Revue d'économie financière: Le devenir financier de la Chine*, 77.

Foglia, A. (2008) *Stress Testing Credit Risk: A Survey of Authorities' Approaches.* (Rome: Banca d'Italia). Electronic copy available at: http://ssrn.com/abstract=1396243.

Gaenssmantel, F. (2003) China's debts: Mountain or molehill? *China Economic Quarterly*, 7(4) (London: Dragonomics Ltd).

García-Herrero, A. (2008) *Does the Chinese Banking System Benefit from Foreign Investors?* BOFIT dicussion papers (Helsinki: Bank of Finland).

García-Herrero, A., Gavilá, S. and Santabárbara, D. (2005) *China's Banking Reform: An Assessment of its Evolution and Possible Impact.* Documentos Ocasionales No. 0502 (Madrid: Banco de Espana).

Giles, T. and Milne, A. (2004) *Basel II and UK Banks – What are the Costs and Benefits of IRB Qualification?* Finance and Financial Products EU Practitioners Papers (London: Charles River Associates).

Girardin, E. (1997) *Banking Sector Reform and Credit Control in China.* Organisation for Economic Cooperation and Development (Paris: Development Centre Studies).

Goff, S. (2009) Bank of China offers mortgages to credit-starved UK borrowers. *Financial Times*, 25 July.

Goodhart, C. and Zeng, X. (2005) *China's Banking Reform: Problems and Potential Solutions.* Financial Markets Group Special Paper sp163.

Gottschalk, R. (ed.) (2010) *The Basel Capital Accords in Developing Countries – Challenges for Development Finance* (Basingstoke: Palgrave Macmillan).

Green, S. (2004) Privatisation: The great state sell-down. *China Economic Quarterly*, Q2.

Griffith-Jones, S., Segoviano, M. and Spratt, S. (2002) *Basel II and Developing Countries: Diversification and Portfolio Effects* (Brighton: Institute of Development Studies).

Griffith-Jones, S., Segoviano, M. and Spratt, S. (2003) *Submission to the Basel Committee on Banking Supervision: CP3 and the Developing World* (Brighton: Institute of Development Studies).

Griffiths, J. J. (2005) The use of CDO structuring for the disposal of non-performing loans in China. *Journal of Structured Finance*, 11(3), pp. 40–51.

Grimm, M. (2005) *Das Finanzsystem Chinas zwischen Markt und Politik [China's Financial System Between Market and Politics]* (Baden-Baden: Nomos Verlagsgesellschaft).

Gunasekarage, A., Hess, K. and Hu, A. (2007) The Influence of the Degree of State Ownership and the Ownership Concentration on the Performance of Listed Chinese Companies. *Research in International Business and Finance*, 21, pp. 379–95.

[Guo, L.] 郭立 (2005) 对当前民间融资的调查与思考 [Survey and thoughts on contemporary informal lending]. 金融理论与实践 [*Financial Theory and Practice*], 4(309), pp. 22–4.

[Guo, Q.], 郭琼 [Li, Z.] 历志钢 and [Yu, N.] 于宁 (2006a) 狙击信贷潮 [Snipe the loan tide].《财经》 *[Caijing Magazine]*, 1 May.

[Guo, Q.], 郭琼 [Li, Z.] 历志钢 and [Hu, J.] 胡蛟 (2006b) 博弈 "打捆贷款" [Game of "bundle loans"].《财经》 *[Caijing Magazine]*, 15 May.

Gup, B. E. (ed.) (2004b) *The New Basel Capital Accord* (New York: Thomson Corp).

Gutierrez de Rozas, L. (2007) *Testing for Competition in the Spanish Banking Industry: The Panzar–Rosse Approach Revisited*, Documentos de Trabajo No. 0726 (Madrid: Banco de Espana).

Halper, S. (2010) *The Beijing Consensus – How China's Authoritarian Model Will Dominate the Twenty-first Century* (New York: Basic Books).

Hansakul, S., Dyck, S. and Kern, S. (2009) *Chinas Finanzmärkte – neue globale Größe? [China's financial markets – a future global force?]* (Frankfurt/Main: Deutsche Bank Research).

Hansen, E. (2005) *Level of Preparedness of Asian Banks for Basel II* (Hong Kong: Ernst & Young).

Hansen, E. and Straley, P. (2004) *Asia-Pacific Basel II Survey* (Hong Kong: Ernst & Young).

Harner, S. M. (2004a) Bank reform: Earthquake! *China Economic Quarterly*, 8(3), pp. 42–8.

Harner, S. M. (2004b) China needs to stand by its new bank rules. *Financial Times*, 8 July.

Hasan, I., Wachtel, P. and Zhou, M. (2006) *Institutional Development, Financial Deepening and Economic Growth: Evidence from China* (BOFIT Research paper 12/2006, Bank of Finland). Accessed under http://www.bof.fi/NR/rdonlyres/D98B360E-38CC-4826-9976-15E45BD1F505/0/dp1206.pdf.

He, G., Du, X., Bai, C. and Li, Z. (2009) *China Microfinance Industry Assessment Report* (Beijing: China Association of Microfinance).

He, L., Sappideen, R. (2009) The payment system in China. *Journal of International Banking Law and Regulation*, 23(3) pp. 168–74.

He, Z. 何忠伟 (2004) 入世后农业信用合作社发展的制度分析 [System analysis of the RCCs' development after the WTO entry]. 调研世界 *[Survey World]*, pp. 19–21.

Heilmann, S. (2005a) Policy-making and political supervision in Shanghai's financial industry. *Journal of Contemporary China*, 14(45), pp. 643–68.

Heilmann, S. (2005b) Regulatory innovation by Leninist means: communist party supervision in China's finance industry. *China Quarterly*, 181, pp. 1–21.

Heilmann, S. (2008) Experimentation under hierarchy: policy experimentation in the reorganisation of China's state sector, 1978–2008, CID Working paper 172, Center for International Development at Harvard University.

Heilmann, S. (2009) Maximum tinkering under uncertainty: unorthodox lessons from China. *China Analysis* 73, May 2009 under www.chinapolitik.de.

Holland, T. (2009) Chinese banks may not be as solid as they look. *South China Morning Post*, 19 January.

Hong, S. (2009) *Restructuring and Insolvency in China*, Norton Rose, 3 March. Accessed through GT news.

Howson, N. C. (2009) China's restructured commercial banks: nomenklatura accountability serving corporate governance reform? In Zhu, M., Cai, J. and Avery, M. (eds) (2009) *China's Emerging Financial Markets – Challenges and Global Impact* (Singapore: John Wiley & Sons), pp. 123–64.

[Hu, C.] 胡采苹 (2010) 汇金换帅 [Huijin changes command]《财经》 *[Caijing Magazine]*, 12 April.

[Hu, C.] 胡采苹 and [Zhang, M.] 张曼 (2010) 潘功胜详解农行 IPO [Pan Gongsheng on ABC's IPO]《财经》 *[Caijing Magazine]*, 19 July.

Hu, F. (2002) *China Insight: Banking Reform in China* (Hong Kong: Goldman Sachs).

[Hu, J.] 胡敬艳 (2010) 央行人事新棋局 [PBOC's HR new game]《财经》 *[Caijing Magazine]*, 7 June.

[Hu, J.] 胡敬艳 and [Dong. Y.] 董欲晓 (2010) 银联困境 [CUP predicament]《财经》 *[Caijing Magazine]*, 21 June.

[Hu, Z.] 胡祖六 (2005) 银行改革需要国际战略投资吗 [Does the Chinese banks reform require international strategic investors?]《经济观察报》 *[Economic Observer]*, 12 December.

Huang, H. (2009) *Institutional Structure of Financial Regulation in China: Lessons from the Global Financial Crisis*. Electronic copy available at: http://ssrn.com/abstract=1512105.

Huang, R. H. and Orr, G. (2007) China's state-owned enterprises: Board governance and the Communist Party. *McKinsey Quarterly*, Issue 1.

Huang, Y. (2008) *Capitalism with Chinese Characteristics – Entrepreneurship and the State* (New York: Cambridge University Press).

Huang, Y., Saich, T. and Steinfeld, E. (eds) (2005) *Financial Sector Reform in China* (Cambridge, MA: Harvard University Press).

Huei, P. (2008) 740m farmers benefit from new policy. *Straits Times*, 20 October.

[Huo, K.] 霍侃, [Wang, J.] 王晶, [Yu, H.] 于海荣 and [Wang, L.] 王露 (2009) 货币宽松到何时? [When is it right to loosen monetary policy?]《财经》 *[Caijing Magazine]*, 20 July.

IMF & WB (2005) *Financial Sector Assessment – A Handbook* (Washington, DC: IMF & World Bank).

IMF & WB (2009) *Revised Approach to Financial Regulation and Supervision Standards Assessments in FSAP Updates* (Washington: IMF & World Bank).

IMF & WB (2009) *The Financial Sector Assessment Program after 10 Years – Background Material* (Washington: IMF & World Bank).

Institute of International Finance (IIF) (2006) *Corporate Governance in China: An Investor Perspective*. IIF Task Force Report.

International Association of Deposit Insurers (2008) *Core Principles for Effective Deposit Insurance Systems*. Accessed under http://www.iadi.org/docs/Core_Principles_final_29_Feb_08.pdf.

Intrater, M. (2004) Basel II for non-Basel II banks. *Bank and Accounting Finance*, October–November, pp. 3–9.

Intrater, M. and Garside, T. (2003a) *The New Rules of the Game – Strategic Implications of the Basel II Capital Accord* (New York: Mercer Oliver Wyman [MOW]).

Intrater, M. and Garside, T. (2003b) *The New Rules of the Game – Strategic Implications of the Basel II Capital Accord for the European Banking Industries* (New York: MOW).

Jain, S., Maheshwari, R. and Yoshizawa, R. (2009) *Credit Stress Testing Asia-Pacific Banks* (Standard & Poor's www.standardandpoors.com/ratingsdirect).

Jia, X. (2008) *Credit Rationing and Institutional Constraint – Evidence from Rural China* (Frankfurt am Main: Peter Lang Verlag).

[Jiang, J.] 姜建清 (2005)《国有商业银行改革实践》 *[Reform Practices in SOCBs]*. Speech at the Caijing Magazine Annual Conference: "(2006): Forecasts and Strategies", Beijing, 12 December.

[Jiang, X.] 姜旭朝 and [Ding, C.] 丁昌锋 (2004) 民间金融理论分析: 范畴、比较与制度变迁 [Analysis of the informal finance theory: Categories, comparison and system transition]. 金融研究 *[Finance Research (PBOC)]*, 08, pp. 100–11.

[Jing, X.] 景学成 (2005) 走向现代金融制度–兼论中国金融业『入世』 *[Towards a Modern Financial System – China's Finance Industry Entering the WTO]* (上海 [Shanghai]: 上海财经大学出版社 [Shanghai Finance and Economics University Press]).

Kaminsky, G. L. and Reinhart, C. M. (1999) The twin crises: the causes of banking and balance of payments problems. *The American Economic Review* June, pp. 473–500.

Kelleher, E. and Dyer, G. (2005) Experian eyes China car market. *Financial Times*, 8 September.

Koivu, T. (2008) *Has the Chinese Economy become more Sensitive to Interest Rates? – Studying Credit Demand in China* (Helsinki: Bank of Finland BOFIT).

KPMG (2005) *China's City Commercial Banks: Opportunity Knocks?* (Hong Kong: KPMG Financial Services).

KPMG (2009) *Card Payments in Asia-Pacific – The State of the Nations* (Switzerland: KPMG International).

Kudrna, Z. (2007) *Banking Reform in China: Driven by International Standards and Chinese Specifics* (TIGER Working paper series No. 109). Available at http://papers.ssrn.com/sol3/papers.cfm?abstract_id=1026854&rec=1&srcabs=854944.

Kuritzkes, A. and Schuermann, T. (2008) *What We Know, Don't Know and Can't Know About Bank Risk: A View From the Trenches*. Wharton Financial Institutions Center Working Paper No. 06-05. Available at SSRN: http://ssrn.com/abstract=887730.

Kwong, C. C. L. and Lee, P. K. (2005) Bad loans versus sluggish rural industrial growth: A policy dilemma of China's banking reform. *Journal of the Asia Pacific Economy*, 10(1), pp. 1–25.

Lau, A., Young, A. and Li, G. (2007) Rethinking corporate governance and law in China: the theories, rules and practices. *Compliance and Regulatory Journal* 2007 (Issue 2).

Lardy, N. R. (1999) The challenge of bank restructuring in China. *Strengthening the Banking System in China: Issues and Experience*, Joint BIS/PBOC Conference proceedings, Beijing, 1–2 March (Basel: BIS), pp. 17–39.

Leung, M. K. and Chan R. (2006) Are foreign banks sure winners in post-WTO China? *Business Horizons*, 49, pp. 221–34.

Leung, M. K., Rigby, D. and Young, T. (2003) Entry of foreign banks in the People's Republic of China: A survival analysis. *Applied Economics*, 35(1) pp. 21–31.

[Li, C.] 李昌宇 and [Jie, S.] 解淑青 (2004) 论农村信用社的产权制度改革 [About the reform of the ownership system in RCCs]. 边疆经济与文化 *[Frontier Economics and Culture]*, 1, pp. 83–5.

[Li, D.] 李德 (2006) 央行：中国资产管理公司运营状况分析 [PBOC: Analysis of the operational situation of Chinese AMCs]. 中国证券网–上海证券报 *[China Securities Net – Shanghai Securities Newspaper]*, 14 February.

Li, H., Meng, L. and Zhang, J. (2006) Why do entrepreneurs enter politics? Evidence from China. *Economic Enquiry*, doi:10,1093/ei/cbj031.

Li, J. and Hsu, S. (eds) (2009) *Informal Finance in China: American and Chinese Perspectives* (New York: Oxford University Press).

[Li, L.] 李莉莉 (2008) 新型农村金融机构发展进程与阶段性评价 [Development Course and Evaluation of New Rural Financial Institution], 金融理论与实践 [Financial Theory & Practice], 2008 (09).

[Li, P.] 李蒲秋 (2009) 地方商业银行信贷风险浅析 [Preliminary analysis into the credit risk of local commercial banks] 财政监督 *[Finance Supervision]*, 2009 (18).

Li, T. (2008) *China's Nonperforming Loans: A $540bn Problem Unsolved* Electronic copy available at: http://ssrn.com/abstract=1278235.

[Li, T.] 李涛, [Wen, X.] 温秀 and [Zhang, M.] 张曼 (2009a) 博弈信贷政策 [Playing the lending policy]《财经》*[Caijing Magazine]*, 14 September.

[Li, T.] 李涛, [Wen, X.] 温秀 and [Zhang, M.] 张曼 (2009b) 信贷接力棒 [Lending relay race]《财经》*[Caijing Magazine]*, 26 October.

Li, T. and Wen, X. (2009) Bank: Slowdown Tests Credit Control, *Caijing Magazine*, 4 February.

[Li, Z.] 历志钢 (2006) 必须加强合规风险管理 [It is necessary to strengthen rules-based risk management].《财经》*[Caijing Magazine]*, 1 May.

[Li, Z.] 李正华 (2004) 试论加入 WTO 我国商业银行的发展战略 [About the development strategy of Chinese commercial banks in the WTO entry]. 吉林省经济管理干部学院学报 *[Journal of Jilin Province Economic Management Cadre College]*, 18(6) pp. 8–10.

[Li, Z.] 李正华 (2005) 城市商业银行改革与发展的思考 [Reform of CCBs and thoughts about their development]. 吉林省经济管理干部学院学报 *[Journal of Jilin Province Economic Management Cadre College]*, 1(19), pp. 46–8.

Lin, H. (2008) *The Costs of Large Shareholders: Evidence from China.* Electronic copy available at: http://ssrn.com/abstract=1291527.

Lin, H., Tsao, C. and Yang, C. (2009) Bank reforms, competition and efficiency in China's banking system – are small city bank entrants more efficient? *China & World Economy*, 17(5), pp. 69–87.

Lin, J., Tao, R. and Liu, M. (2003) *Decentralization, Deregulation and Economic Transition in China*. London School of Economics Conference on Local governments, accessed electronically under: http://sticerd.lse.ac.uk/dps/decentralisation/China.pdf.

van der Linden, R. (2009) *China's Macro-policy and Regulatory Framework of the Financial Sector to be Tested by the Economic Slowdown* (Wolpertinger Conference of European Association of University Teachers of Banking and Finance in September 2009).

[Ling, H.] 凌华薇 (2005a) 周小川谈建行改革 [Zhou Xiaochuan talks about CCB's reform].《财经》*[Caijing Magazine]*, 28 November.

[Ling, H.] 凌华薇 (2005b) 农行重组尚无解 [Restructuring of ABC not yet decided]. 《财经》*[Caijing Magazine]*, 17 October.

[Ling, H.] 凌华薇 and [Guo, Q.] 郭琼 (2006) 银行:较之激励机 制的改革, 银行人事制度改革更为本质, 倘不能通过市场竞争选拔经理人,单方面的薪酬体制改革只 -能南辕北辙 [Banking: compared with the reform of the incentives system, the reform of human resources system is more crucial: if managers are not chosen competitively in the market, the unilateral reform of the remuneration system will drive nowhere]. 中国 (2006) 反思之年 *[Reflecting on China's year 2006]*.

[Ling, H.] 凌华薇 and [Zhang, X.] 张小彩 (2005) 工行改革难与易 [Hard and easy bits of the reform of ICBC].《财经》*[Caijing Magazine]*, 25 February.

Liu, G., Hui, O. and Zhang, J. (2010) *China Bond Market Overview* (Hong Kong: Nomura International).

[Liu, L.] 陆磊 (2004) 利率调整与商业银行状况 [Adjustment of interest rates and the situation at commercial banks].《财经》 *[Caijing Magazine]*, 29 November.

[Liu, L.] 陆磊 (2006a) 再看建行 [Look once more at CCB].《财经》 *[Caijing Magazine]*, 6 February.

[Liu, L.] 陆磊 (2006b) 金融业国际化、监管国际化和风险传递 [Internationalisation of the finance industry and of supervision and risk transmission].《财经》 *[Caijing Magazine]*, 9 January.

[Liu, M.] 刘明 (2004) 论农信社 "革命":难点与建议 [About the "Revolution" in RCCs: Difficulties and proposals]. 四川大学学报 *[Sichuan University Journal]*, 132(3) pp. 10–15.

[Liu, M.] 刘明康 (2005) 新资本协议助力银行业公司治理迈上新台阶 [The new capital accord helps corporate governance in the banking industry to move to the next step]. 中国金融家 *[China Financialyst]*, 01, pp. 19–21.

[Liu, M.] 刘明康 (2010) 回归稳健发展 刘明康主席在 "伦敦政治经济学院亚洲论坛"上的发言 [Returning to stable growth – Speech at the Asian Forum of the London School of Politics and Economics], 26 March.

[Liu, M.] 刘民权, [Xu, Z.] 徐忠, [Yu, J.] 俞建拖, [Zhou, S.] 周盛武 and [Zhao, Y.] 赵英涛 (2005) 农村信用社市场化改革探索 [Exploring the market reforms of RCCs]. 金融研究 *[Finance Research (PBOC)]*, 4, pp. 99–112.

Liu, S. (1999) China's experience in small and medium financial institution resolution. *Strengthening the Banking System in China: Issues and Experience*, Joint BIS/PBOC Conference proceedings, Beijing, 1–2 March (Basel: BIS), pp. 298–303.

Liu, Q. (2006) *Corporate Governance in China: Current Practices, Economic Effects and Institutional Determinants*. Working paper CESifo Economic Studies, doi:10,1093/cesifo/ifl001.

[Liu, Y.] 刘洋 (2006) 最差城商行: 退市还是扶持 [The Worst CCBs: Exit the market or get support]. 国际金融报 *[International Finance News]*, 16 Jan.

Longueville, G. and Ngo, N.-N. (2004) Le système bancaire chinois: un risque systémique [The Chinese Banking System: a systemic risk]. *Revue d'économie financière: Le devenir financier de la Chine*, 77.

Lou, J. (2000) China's Bank Non-performing Loan Problem: Seriousness and causes. *International Lawyer*, 34(4) pp. 1147–92.

Lu, D., Thangavelu, S. M. and Hu, Q. (2005) Biased lending and non-performing loans in China's banking sector. *The Journal of Development Studies*, 41(6), pp. 1071–91.

[Lu, M.] 陆岷峰 (2005) 城市商业银行个性风险特征和管理对策 [Characteristics and management response to specific risks of CCBs]. 青海金融 *[Qinghai Finance]*, 6.

[Lu, M.] 陆锦文 (2004) 论国有商业银行公司治理结构与道德风险防范 [About the structure of corporate governance in SOCBs and preventing moral hazard]. 中山大学学报论丛 *[Sun Yatsen University Forum]*, 124(16), pp. 219–24.

Lu, S. F. and Yao, Y. (2003) *The Effectiveness of the Law: Financial Development and Economic Growth in an Economy of Financial Depression: Evidence from China*. Center for Research on Economic Development and Policy Reform, 179.

Lu, T., Zhong, J. and Kong, J. (2009) How good is corporate governance in China? *China & World Economy*, 17(1), pp. 83–100.

[Lu, Y.] 卢彦铮 and [Long, X.] 龙雪晴 (2005) 广发行重组一波三折 [Restructuring of Guangdong Development Bank: one wave and three curves].《财经》 *[Caijing Magazine]*, 22 August.

[Lu, Y.] 卢彦铮 (2005) 建行 IPO: 阳光与阴影 [CCB's IPO sunshine and shadows]. 《财经》*[Caijing Magazine]*, 17 October.

Luo, D. and Yao, S. (2009) *World Financial Crisis and the Rise of Chinese Commercial Banks* (University of Nottingham Research paper series 2009/08).

[Luo, J.] 罗金生 (2002a) 何种银行产权安排更有利于经济转轨 [Which bank-property rights arrangement is more auspicious to the economic transition?]. 《财贸经济》*[Finance and Trade Economy]*, 4, pp. 20–4.

[Luo, J.] 罗金生 (2002b) 利益博弈与不良债权的形成 [Interest games and the apparition of non-performing debts]. 《经济理论与经济管理》*[Economic Theory and Economic Management]*, 1, pp. 22–5.

Luo, P. (2003) *Challenges for China's Banking Sector and Policy Responses.* Speech at the Conference: "A Tale of Two Giants: India's and China's Experience with Reform and Growth", New Delhi, 14–16 November. Accessed online under www.imf.org/external/np/apd/seminars/2003/newdelhi/ping.pdf [15 Nov. 2005].

Luo, P. (2008) China's convergence to IFRS with particular respect to its banking industry. *Financial Markets, Institutions & Instruments*, 17(1), pp. 43–9.

Ma, D. (2010) *Urban and Rural Integration in China* (Beijing: Speech at the 2010 Capital Financial Forum), 16 April.

Ma, G. and Fung, B. (2002) *China's Asset Management Corporations.* BIS Working papers (Basel: BIS).

Ma, G. and Wang, Y. (2010) *China's High Saving Rate: Myth and Reality.* BIS Working papers (Basel: BIS).

[Ma, S.] 马述昆, [Zou, H.] 邹惠琳 and [Xiong, C.] 熊聪茹 (2009) China Focus: China's rural market draws new interest from foreign, domestic bank, *Xinhua's China Economic Information Service*, 24 April.

Mallet, V., Anderlini, J. (2010) Santander steps cautiously into China, *Financial Times*, 13 January.

Mandanis Schooner, H. and Taylor, M. W. (2009) *Regulation of Global Banking: Principles and Policies* (Burlington, VT: Academic Press).

Marshall, D., Lin, K. and Lin, L. (2004a) *China Bank Prudential Regulations* (New York: FitchRatings).

Marshall, D., Lin, K. and Lin, L. (2004b) *Chinese Banks' Asset Quality and Capital Adequacy: Data and Trends* (New York: FitchResearch).

Marshall, D., Lin, K., Lin, L. and Tebbutt, P. (2005a) *Chinese Banks: 2004 Review and 2005 Outlook* (New York: FitchResearch).

Marshall, D., Tebbutt, P., Toritani, R. and Srivastava, A. (2005b) *Asian Banks and Basel II* (New York: FitchResearch).

Mattlin, M. (2007) *The Chinese Government's New Approach to Ownership and Financial Control of Strategic State-owned Enterprises* (BOFIT Discussion papers 10/2007, Bank of Finland).

McGregor, R. (2009) The party organiser. *Financial Times*, 30 September.

McGregor, R. (2010) *The Party – The Secret World of China's Communist Rulers* (New York: HarperCollins Publishers).

McKinsey Global Institute (MGI) (2006) *Putting China's Capital to Work: The Value of Financial System Reform* (Sydney: McKinsey & Co).

McMahon, D. (2010a) China tries to wean banks off loans – Regulators shift gears to control credit expansion, but banks rely on robust loans; tension has jolted markets. *The Wall Street Journal Asia*, 28 January.

McMahon, D. (2010b) China scrutinizes loans to local governments, *The Wall Street Journal*. 28 July.

Melka, J. and Xu, W. (2004) Le poids des créances douteuses dans l'économie chinoise: existe-t-il un risque systémique? [The weight of NPLs on the Chinese Economy: Is there a systemic risk?]. *Revue d'économie financière: Le devenir financier de la Chine, 77.*

Metcalfe, B. (2005) *Foreign Banks in China* (Hong Kong: PwC).

Miao, J., Tian, G. and Bhati, S. (2009) *The Impact of Loan Characteristics on Credit Risk of Chinese Listed Firms Under New Banking Regulatory System*. Electronic copy available at: http://ssrn.com/abstract=1460445.

Miller, A. (2008) The CCP Central Committee's Leading Small Groups. *China Leadership Monitor*, No. 26, accessed under http://www.hoover.org/publications/china-leadership-monitor/article/5689.

Mitchell, T. and Lau, J. (2006) A Piece of the Action: Why investors are fired up by Chinese IPOs. *Financial Times*, 1 June.

Mo, Y. K. (1999) A review of recent banking reforms in China, *Strengthening the Banking System in China: Issues and Experience*, Joint BIS/PBOC Conference proceedings, Beijing, 1–2 March (Basel: BIS), pp. 90–109.

Mohanty, M. S. and Turner, P. (2010) *Banks and Financial Intermediation in Emerging Asia: Reforms and New Risks*. BIS Working papers (Basel: BIS).

Montes-Negret, F. (1995) China's Credit Plan: An overview. *Oxford Review of Economic Policy*, 11(4), pp. 18–25.

Moshirian, F. and Wu, O. (2008) *Banking Industry Volatility and Banking Crises*. Available at SSRN: http://ssrn.com/abstract=1104891.

Mrak, M. (2003) *Implementation of the New Basel Capital Accord in Emerging Market Economies: Problems and Alternatives* (Warwick: University of Warwick).

Naughton, B. (2007) Strengthening the Center, and Premier Wen Jiabao (Hoover: *China Leadership Monitor*, No. 21). Accessed under http://media.hoover.org/sites/default/files/documents/CLM21BN.pdf.

[Niu, M.] 钮明, [Zhang, X.] 张欣 and [Lin, H.] 邻淮 (2004) 民间借贷: 现状与抉择 [Informal lending: Current situation and choices]. 金融理论与实践 *[Financial Theory and Practice]*, 6(299) pp. 15–18.

Ong, M. K. (ed.) (2004) *The Basel Handbook: A Guide for Financial Practitioners* (London: Risk Books).

Organisation for Economic Cooperation and Development (OECD) (2004) *Principles of Corporate Governance* (Paris: OECD Publishing).

Organisation for Economic Cooperation and Development (OECD) (2005) *China OECD Economic Survey* (2005)/13, Sept. (Paris: OECD Publishing).

Park, A., Ren, C. and Wang, S. (2003) *Microfinance, Poverty Alleviation and Financial Reform in China*. Workshop on Rural Finance and Credit Infrastructure in China, 13–14 October, Paris, France.

Park, A. and Sehrt, K. (2001) Tests of financial intermediation and banking reform in China. *Journal of Comparative Economics*, 29, pp. 608–44.

PBOC net (2009) 巴塞尔银行监管委员会发布新规征求各方意见 *[BCBS has issued a new rule open for comments]*, 18 December.

Pearson, M. M. (2010) The impact of the PRC's economic crisis response on regulatory institutions: preliminary thoughts. *China Analysis*. Accessed February 2010 under www.chinapolitik.de.

Pei, M. (2006) *China's Trapped Transition – The Limits of Developmental Autocracy* (Cambridge, MA: Harvard University Press).

Pei, M. (2006a) China is stagnating in its "trapped transition". *Financial Times*, 24 February.

Pei, M. (2006b) How rotten politics feeds a bad loan crunch in China. *Financial Times*, 8 May.

Peng, Y. (2007) *The Chinese Banking Industry – Lessons from History for Today's Challenges* (London: Routledge).

People's Bank of China (PBOC) (2003) *Almanac of Banking and Finance* (Beijing: PBOC).

People's Bank of China (PBOC) (2004) 中国中小企业金融制度调查 [*Survey on SME Financing Structure in China*], Internal report (unpublished).

People's Bank of China (PBOC) (2005a) *Monetary Policy Report 1st Quarter* (Beijing: PBOC).

People's Bank of China (PBOC) (2005b) *Monetary Policy Report 2nd Quarter* (Beijing: PBOC).

People's Bank of China (PBOC) (2005c) *Monetary Policy Report 4th Quarter* (Beijing: PBOC).

People's Bank of China (PBOC) (2005d) 中国金融稳定报告 *(2005) [China Financial Stability Report 2005]* (Beijing: PBOC).

People's Bank of China (PBOC) (2006) *Monetary Policy Report 4th Quarter* (Beijing: PBOC).

People's Bank of China (PBOC) (2007) *Monetary Policy Report 4th Quarter* (Beijing: PBOC).

[People's Bank of China (PBOC)] 中国人民银行 (2008a) 加快推进农村金融产品和服务方式创新 PBOC 支持和促进社会主义新农村建设 [*To accelerate the innovation of rural financial products and services, PBOC supports and spurs the establishment of new rural financial institutions*].

People's Bank of China (PBOC) (2008b) *Monetary Policy Report 4th Quarter* (Beijing: PBOC).

[People's Bank of China (PBOC)] (2009a) 全面做好汽车金融服务 支持汽车产业调整振兴 [*Doing a good service on car finance – supporting the revitalisation and adjustment of the car industry*], PBOC website, 16 January.

[People's Bank of China (PBOC)] 中国人民银行 (2009b) 中小企业人民币贷款比年初增长 28% [*SME loans surge 28% compared to year begin*]. Accessed under www.gov.cn, 23 October.

[People's Bank of China (PBOC)] 中国人民银行 (2009c) 公安部联合整治银行卡违法犯罪工作取得阶段性成果 [*Public security bureau achieves first success in tackling credit card fraud*], PBOC website, 18 November.

People's Bank of China (PBOC) (2009d) *Monetary Policy Report 4th Quarter* (Beijing: PBOC).

[People's Bank of China (PBOC)] 中国人民银行 (2010a) 中国人民银行 银监会 证监会 保监会关于进一步做好中小企业金融服务工作的若干意见 [*Opinion on the SME lending services work by PBOC, SBRC, CSRC and CIRC*], July.

[People's Bank of China (PBOC)] 中国人民银行 (2010b) 中国支付体系发展报告 2009 [*China payment system development report 2009*] (Beijing: 中国金融出版社 [China Finance Press]).

[PBOC Rural finance research group] 中国人民银行农村金融服务研究小组 (2008) 中国农村金融服务报告 [*China rural finance services report*] (Beijing: PBOC) September.

[*People's Net – Jiangnan Times*] 人民网 江南时报 (2005) 国家不再为银行经营亏损埋单 [The state will not foot the bill again for banks' operational losses].

Pitsilis, E. V., Woetzel, J. R. and Wong, J. (2004) Checking China's vital signs. *McKinsey Quarterly*, Special Edition.

Podpiera, R. (2006) *Progress in China's Banking Sector Reform: Has Bank Behavior Changed?* IMF Working Paper (WP/06/71, March) (Washington, DC: IMF).

Pomerleano, M. (1999) The Framework for Financial Supervision in China: Offsite supervision and credit information. In *Strengthening the Banking System in China: Issues and Experience*, Joint BIS/PBOC Conference proceedings, Beijing, 1–2 March (Basel: BIS), pp. 189–210.

Poncet, S., Steingress, W. and Vandenbussche, H. (2009) *Financial Constraints in China: Firm-level Evidence*, Discussion paper 2009-35, Institut de Recherches Economiques et Sociales de l'Université Catholique de Louvain.

Powell, A. (2002) *A Capital Accord for Emerging Economies?* (Washington, DC: World Bank).

Powell, A. (2004) *Basel II and Developing Countries: Sailing Through the Sea of Standards*. Policy Research Working Paper 3387 (Washington, DC: World Bank).

PriceWaterhouseCoopers (PwC) (2004a) *Basel II Navigator Tool* (n.p.: PwC).

PriceWaterhouseCoopers (PwC) (2004b) *Study on the Financial and Macroeconomic Consequences of the Draft Proposed New Capital Requirements for Banks and Investment Firms in the EU* (Brussels: European Commission).

PriceWaterhouseCoopers (PwC) (2004c) *China NPL Investor Survey 2004* (n.p.: PwC).

PriceWaterhouseCoopers (PwC) (2004d) *China's Proposed New Bankruptcy Law – the Practical Implications* (HongKong: PwC).

PriceWaterhouseCoopers (PwC) (2005) *NPL Asia* (n.p.: PwC).

PriceWaterhouseCoopers (PwC) (2006) *NPL Asia* (n.p.: PwC).

PriceWaterhouseCoopers (PwC) (2007a) *China's New Enterprise Bankruptcy Law* (n.p.: PwC).

PriceWaterhouseCoopers (PwC) (2007b) *NPL Asia Newsletter* (n.p.: PwC).

PriceWaterhouseCoopers (PwC) (2008) *NPL Asia Newsletter* (n.p.: PwC).

PriceWaterhouseCoopers (PwC) (2009a) *China's Enterprise Bankruptcy Law: Can It Help Foreign Financiers Recover Their Debts?* Accessed under http://www.pwc.com/gx/en/banking-capital-markets/journal/journal-0709-chinas-enterprise.html.

PriceWaterhouseCoopers (PwC) (2009b) *NPL Asia Newsletter* (n.p.: PwC).

PriceWaterhouseCoopers (PwC) (2009c) *Chinese Bankers Survey 2009 – Executive Summary*, accessed in Oct. 2009 under http://www.pwchk.com/webmedia/doc/633922589297244455_bcm_cn_bankers_survey_sep2009.pdf.

PriceWaterhouseCoopers (PwC) (2010a) *Analysis of Major Banks' Results for 2009*, Banking newsletter, Jun 2010. Accessed on pwccn.com.

PriceWaterhouseCoopers (PwC) (2010b) *Foreign Banks in China*. Accessed on pwccn.com.

[Qian, X.] 钱小安 (2004) 市场化改革中的资金配置机制、结构及其影响 [The funds allocation mechanism, structure and its influence in the market-driven reforms]. 金融研究 [*Finance Research* (PBOC)] 03, pp. 16–27.

[Qiao, X.] 乔晓会, [Dong, Y.] 董欲晓 and [Yuan, M.] 袁满 (2010) 金监"三会"新政 [New finance regulatory policies from the three regulatory commission]《财经》 [*Caijing Magazine*] 18 January.

[Qin, X.] 秦晓 (2010) 是制度缺陷, 还是制度创新 [Is it system failure or system innovation?]《财经》 [*Caijing Magazine*], 18 May.

[Qiu, L.] 仇琳 (2009) China Focus: Rural cooperatives let Chinese farmers thrive together, *Xinhua's China Economic Information Service*, 16 December.

Quagliariello, M. (ed.) (2009) *Stress-testing the Banking System* (New York: Cambridge University Press).

Rahman, M. W. and Luo, J. (2010) *The Development Perspective of Finance and Microfinance Industry in China: How Far is MFIs Regulations?* Accessed under papers.ssrn.com/sol3/papers.cfm?abstract_id=1587950.

Ramos, R., Ma, N., Meng, J. and Inamdar, T. (2005) *China Banks – The USD 10 bln Question: Where to for Bank Reform?* (New York: Goldman Sachs).

Ren, D. (2009) Mainland credit card debt surges Unpaid bills jump 126pc. *South China Morning Post*, 1 December.

Ren, D. (2010) Bank card use boosts retail sales. *South China Morning Post*, 9 February.

[Ren, Y.] 任宇航, [Li, X.] 孙孝坤, [Cheng, G.] 程功 and [Xia, E.] 夏恩君 (2007) 信用风险压力测试方法与应用研究 (Empirical research and stress testing methods) *财经论坛 [Finance Forum]*.

Reuters News (2009a) Bad loans to stay manageable – Bank of China exec, 28 January.

Reuters News (2009b) China may differentiate capital rules for banks – paper, 9 April.

Reuters News (2009c) China to give some rural lenders 2 pct subsidy, 20 May.

Reuters News (2009d) China tells banks to improve capital info disclosure, 16 December.

Reuters News (2010a) China local govt debt may top 8 trn yuan, 3 March.

Reuters News (2010b) China banks can withstand 30 pct housing price fall – report, 8 June.

Rösch, D., Scheule, H. (ed.) (2008) *Stress Testing for Financial Institutions – Applications, Regulations and Techniques* (London: Incisive Media).

Sapienza, P. (2004) The effects of government ownership on bank lending. *Journal of Financial Economics*, 72, pp. 357–84.

Schlotthauer, N. (2003) *Unternehmens- und Bankenreform in China [Enterprise and Banking Reform in China]* (Frankfurt am Main: Peter Lang).

Schmitz, E. (2004) *Bankenreform und geldpolitische Steuerung in der Volksrepublik China: Entwicklung, Stand und Perspektiven [Banking Reform and Monetary Policies in the PRC: Development, Situation and Perspectives]* (Düsseldorf: s.n.).

Segoviano, M. A. and Lowe, P. (2002) *Internal Ratings, the Business Cycle and Capital Requirements: Some Evidence from an Emerging Market Economy*. BIS Working Papers 117 (Basel: BIS).

Shang, B. (2010) New law allows public posting of citizen's credit records, *China Daily*, 30 March.

[Shanghai Securities Times] 上海证券报 (2004) 央行加快中央基础信用信息系统建设 [PBOC accelerates the establishment of a central basic credit information system], 21 October.

Shen, C., Lu, C. and Wu, M. (2009) Impact of foreign bank entry on the performance of Chinese banks. *China & World Economy*, 17(3), pp. 102–21.

[Shen, L.] 沈理明 and [Hua, J.] 华金辉 (2005) 加入 WTO 后外资银行地位及竞争策略 [The position and competitive strategy of foreign banks after the WTO entry]. 黑龙江对外经贸 *[Heilongjiang Foreign Economic Relations and Trade]*, 5(131), pp. 37–9.

[Shen, M.] 沈明高 (2009) 警惕 "信贷财政化" [Warning about the politicization of lending] 《财经》 *[Caijing Magazine]*, 8 June.

Shen, M. and Cheng, E. (2004) *Restructuring China's Rural Financial System: Existing Approaches, Challenges and the Future of Microfinance.* Background Paper for the German Agency for Technical Cooperation (GTZ).

Sheng, A., Xiao, G. and Wang, Y. (2005) Property rights and "original sin" in China. *Perspectives*, 6(1), pp. 6–17.

Shih, V. (2004) Factions Matter: Personal networks and the distribution of bank loans in China. *Journal of Contemporary China*, 13(38), pp. 3–19.

Shih, V. (2005) China's uphill battle for stronger banks. *Far Eastern Economic Review*, 168(10) November.

Shih, V. (2009) *Factions and Finance in China – Elite Conflict and Inflation* (New York: Cambridge University Press).

Shih, V., Huang, L. and Lee, J. (2005a) Stuck in the quicksand. *China Economic Quarterly*, Q4, pp. 48–51.

Shih, V., Zhang, Q. and Liu, M. (2005b) *Comparing the Performance of Chinese Banks: A Principal Component Approach* (Chicago: Northwestern University Press), pp. 15–34.

SinoCast Banking Beat (2009a) China to Offer Subsidy to Rural Financial Institutions, www.cnstock.com, 21 May.

SinoCast Banking Beat (2009b) HSBC, WWB Attempt Microfinance in China, 14 October.

SinoCast Banking Beat (2009c) UCB for Minsheng CMBC Suffers Loss from Investment in United Commercial Bank, 11 November.

SinoCast Banking Beat (2009d) Smaller Lenders Tightened Loan Expansion in Oct, www.nanfangdaily.com.cn, 12 November.

SinoCast Banking Beat (2009e) Government, Big 4 Lenders Help SMEs with Financing, 2 December.

SinoCast Banking Beat (2009f) 10% of Zhuzhou City Commercial Bank Is Auctioned, 21 December.

SinoCast Banking Beat (2010a) CDB 7 Village Banks Profitable in 2009, 24 February.

SinoCast Banking Beat (2010b) China Small-amount Loan Firms Emerging, 26 March.

SinoCast Banking Beat (2010c) Large Banks Top Executives not See Annual Salary Reduction 30 March.

SinoCast Banking Beat (2010d) Rural Credit Community Concept Debuts, 28 April.

SinoCast China Business Daily News (2005) PBC to establish state credit bureau, 16 June.

SinoCast Investment & Securities Beat (2009) Chinese MOC Compiling Overseas Investment Manuals, 29 June.

Situ, P. (2003) *Microfinance in China and Development Opportunities* (Frankfurt am Main: GTZ).

[Song, J.] 宋继水 (2009) 法人金融机构信用风险压力测试的实证分析 ———以淄博某农信社为例 [Empirical analysis of the credit risk stress testing at financial institutions – based on the example of one Zibo RCC] 金融发展研究 [*Research in Finance Development*], 2009 (12).

South China Morning Post (2005a) ICBC heeds Call to Boost SME Lending – Mainland's biggest commercial bank has increased funds to small firms by 31.8 bln yuan since the beginning of the year, 29 December.

South China Morning Post (2005b) Mainland marks first with hybrid lender, 29 December.

South China Morning Post (2010) Money is no object – as long as ABC gets listed, 10 July.

State Council Development Research Centre (SCDRC) (2005) 城市商业银行调查 [Survey of city commercial banks].*发展 [Development]*, 07.

Steinfeld, E. (2005) China's Program of Debt–Equity Swaps: Government failure or market failure? In Huang, Y., Saich, T. and Steinfeld, E. (eds), *Financial Sector Reform in China* (Cambridge, MA: Harvard University Press).

Stephanou, C. and Mendoza, J. C. (2005) *Credit Risk Measurement under Basel II: An Overview and Implementation Issues for Developing Countries*, World Bank Policy Research Paper 3556 (Washington, DC: World Bank).

Studwell, J. (2002) *The China Dream – The Elusive Quest for the Greatest Untapped Market on Earth* (London: Profile Books).

[Sun, M.] 孙铭 (2005) 独立董事与党委是什么关系？ [What is the relation between the directors and the Party Committee?]. *发展月刊 [Development Monthly]*, 1(171), pp. 14–15.

[Sun, M.] 孙铭 (2006) 五部委紧急叫停打捆贷款进一步加强宏观调控 [To increase macro-economic adjustments, five ministries and agencies urge to end the provision of bundle loans]. *21 世纪经济报道 [21st Century Business Herald]*. 12 May.

Suzuki, Y., Miah, M. D. and Yuan, J. (2008) China's non-performing bank loan crisis: the role of economic rents. *Asian-Pacific Economic Literature*, 22(1), pp. 57–70.

Taleb, N. N. (2008) *The Black Swan: The Impact of the Highly Improbable*. (New York: Penguin).

Tan, J., Li, S. and Xia, J. (2007) When iron fist visible hand and invisible hand meet – firm-level effects of varying institutional environments in china, *Journal of Business Research*, doi:10.1016/j.jbusres.2007.03.003.

Tan, K. (2010) *Is China Ready to Become the Next Economic Superpower?* (Standard & Poor's www.standardandpoors.com/ratingsdirect).

Tan, K. and Hess, W. (2010) *How Big a Worry are Chinese Local Government Debts* (Standard & Poor's www.standardandpoors.com/ratingsdirect).

[Tang, H.] 唐宏飞 (2004) 加入 WTO 中国银行法制面临的挑战及对策 [Challenges faced by Chinese banks' legal system through the WTO entry and their responses].*甘肃农业 [Gansu Rural Industry]*, 12(221) pp. 89–90.

The Asian Banker (2004b) China: CBRC introduces risk assessment system for joint-stock commercial banks, 15 March.

The Asian Banker (2005a) Fitch: Long-run benefits for Asian banks from Basel II, 31 January.

The Asian Banker (2005b) City banks band together, 15 February.

The Banker (2004) Reality check on Basel II. Special supplement, Published in association with Accenture, Mercer Oliver Wyman and SAP, 1 July.

The Economist (2006) Atomised, 1 June.

The Economist (2008) Silent busts, 9 October.

The Economist (2009) Deliver us from competition, 25 June.

The Economist (2010a) China's financial system Red mist, 4 February.

The Economist (2010b) Shell game Beijing signals a crackdown on borrowing by local governments, 11 March.

The Economist (2010c) Home truths China's economic boom can survive a property bust, 27 May.

The Wall Street Journal (2010a) International Finance: CCB Dials Back Loan Amounts – Under Guidance From China, Lending Quota Is Cut by 20%, 9 February.

The Wall Street Journal (2010b) China Cracks Down on Loan Repackaging, 6 July.

The Wall Street Journal Asia (2010a) Beijing seeds rural lenders – Tax breaks could improve prospects for an initial stock offer by Agricultural Bank of China, 28 May.

The Wall Street Journal Asia (2010b) AgBank adds more cornerstone investors – As giant IPO nears, Standard Chartered, China Life Insurance and Rabobank are expected to be on the list, 18 June.

Thompson, J. (2005) Governance of banks in China. *Financial Market Trends*. OECD, November (2)89, pp. 67–105.

Tomasic, R. A. (2010) *The Conceptual Structure of China's New Corporate Bankruptcy Law.* Available at SSRN: http://ssrn.com/abstract=1546556.

Tsai, K. S. (2001) *Beyond Banks: The Local Logic of Informal Finance and Private Sector Development in China.* Paper prepared for the conference on Financial Sector Reform in China, China Public Policy Program at the Kennedy School of Government, Harvard Business School and Massachusetts Institute of Technology, Cambridge, MA, 11–13 September.

Tsang, R. (2010) *Are Chinese Banks Strong Enough to Withstand a Likely Spike in Bad Loans?* (Standard & Poor's www.standardandpoors.com/ratingsdirect).

Tucker, S. and Anderlini, J. (2010) ICBC steps up recruiting drive, *Financial Times*, 20 April.

von Emloh, D. A. and Wang, Y. (2004) Retail banking in China. *McKinsey Quarterly*, Special Edition.

Walter, C. E. and Howie, F. J. T. (2006) *Privatizing China – Inside China's Stock Markets* (Singapore: JohnWiley & Sons).

[Wang, C.] 王聪 (2005) 加快建立存款保险制度势在必行 [Speeding up the establishment of a deposit insurance scheme is a must].《中国金融》 [China Finance], 27 October.

[Wang, C.] 王聪 (2009) China busts 40 illegal banks in five months, Xinhua News Agency, 9 January.

Wang, J. (2009) Commercial banking reform. In Zhu, M., Cai, J. and Avery, M. (eds) (2009) *China's Emerging Financial Markets – Challenges and Global Impact* (Singapore: John Wiley & Sons), pp. 107–22.

[Wang, P.] 王培成 (2010) 征信立规难产 [Difficulties for the credit registry]《财经》 [Caijing Magazine], 7 June.

[Wang, X.] 王晓青 and [Huang, Y.] 黄友萍 (2004) 中国的商业银行改革：产权结构、公司治理与市场竞争 [Reform of Chinese Commercial Banks: ownership structure, corporate governance and market competition].济南金融 [Ji'nan Finance], 7, pp. 10–13.

Wang, Z. (2009) China's banking industry: moving towards in accord with reform and opening. In Zhu, M., Cai, J. and Avery, M. (eds) (2009) *China's Emerging Financial Markets – Challenges and Global Impact* (Singapore: John Wiley & Sons), pp. 73–90.

Ward, J. (2002) *The New Basel Accord and Developing Countries: Problems and Alternatives.* ESRC Centre for Business Research Working Paper 4 (Cambridge: Cambridge University).

Watson, A. (2003) Financing farmers. In Findlay, C., Watson, A. and Cheng, E. (eds), *Rural Financial Markets in China* (Canberra: Asia Pacific Press), pp. 63–88.

Weder di Mauro, B. (2009) The dog that didn't bark, *The Economist*, 1 October.

Wei, G. (2007) Ownership structure, corporate governance and company performance in China. *Asia Pacific Business Review*, 13(4), pp. 519–45. Accessible online under http://dx.doi.org/10.1080/13602380701300130.

Wei, W. (2005) *The Banking Law System in Transitional China – A Comparative Review in the Light of EU Banking Rules* (Zürich: Schulthess Juristische Medien).

Weigelin-Schwiedrzik, S. (2004) Zentrum und Peripherie in China und Ostasien. In Weigelin-Schwiedrzik, S. and Linhart, S. *Ostasien 1600–1900* (Wien: Promedia) pp. 88–92.

[Wen, J.] 文军 (2010) 张红力率先履新 [Zhang Hongli takes the initiative]《财经》 *[Caijing Magazine]*, 26 April.

[Wen, X.] 温秀 and [Lan, F.] 兰方 (2009) 求解央企"薪病" [Understanding the compensation ills at central SOEs]《财经》 *[Caijing Magazine]*, 28 September.

[Wen, X.] 温秀, [Zhang, M.] 张曼 and 方会磊 [Fang, H.] (2009) 信贷: 7万亿怎样炼成？ [Lending: what about the 7trn?]《财经》 *[Caijing Magazine]*, 20 July.

Wen, Y. (2005) 银行业反腐三题 [Three topics on corruption in the banking industry].《财经》*[Caijing Magazine]*, 26 December.

World Bank (WB) (2003)贷款分类和准备计提的现行做法的调查报告 *[Results of the Review of the Current Treatment of Loan Classification and Provisioning]* 巴塞尔核心原则联络小组成员国 [Liaison group for Basel core principles] (Beijing: World Bank).

World Bank (WB) (2005) *Doing Business Report 2005: Removing Obstacles to Growth* (Washington, DC: World Bank).

World Bank (WB) (2006) *China – Governance, Investment Climate, and Harmonious Society: Competitiveness Enhancements for 120 Cities in China* (Washington, DC: World Bank).

World Bank (WB) (2010) *Doing Business Report 2009* (Washington, DC: World Bank).

World Trade Organisation (WTO) (2001a) *Report of the Working Party on the Accession of China*. Ministerial conference 4 session, Doha, 9–13 November, WT/MIN(01)/3, 10 November.

World Trade Organisation (WTO) (2001b) *Report of the Working Party on the Accession of China – Addendum 1*. Ministerial conference 4th session, Doha, 9–13 November, WT/MIN(01)/3/Add1, 10 November.

World Trade Organisation (WTO) (2001c) *Report of the Working Party on the Accession of China – Addendum 2*. Ministerial conference 4th session, Doha, 9–13 November, WT/MIN(01)/3/Add2, 10 November.

World Trade Organisation (WTO) (2001d) *Accession of the People's Republic of China*. Ministerial conference 4th session, Decision, Doha, 9–13 November, WT/L/432, 23 November.

Wormuth, M. (2004) *Das Konkursrecht der VR China – Kontinuität und Wandel [The Bankruptcy Law of the PRC – Continuity and Change]* (Hamburg: Institut für Asienkunde).

Worthington, S. (2003) The Chinese Payment Card Market: An explanatory study. *International Journal of Bank Marketing*, 21(6/7) pp. 324–34.

Worthington, S. (2005) Entering the Market for Financial Services in Transitional Economies – a case study of credit cards in China. *International Journal of Bank Marketing*, 23(5) pp. 381–96.

Wu, M. and Wang, X. (2009) *The Quality of Financial Reporting in China*, electronically available under papers.ssrn.com/sol3/papers.cfm?abstract_id=1283343.

[Wu, W.] 吴文森 (2009) 农村信用社信贷风险防范措施探讨 [Investigation into the measures to mitigate credit risks at RCCs], 全国商情 *[China Business]* 2009, 14.

Wu, X. (2005) *Conditions and Environment for Improving Corporate Governance Structure of China's Financial Enterprises.* Speech by Ms Wu Xiaoling, Deputy Governor of the PBOC, at the 2005 China International Finance Development Forum, 23 April.

[Xiao, Z.] 萧灼基 (ed.) (2005) *中国金融市场分析与预测 – 2005 年金融金皮书 [Analysis and Forecast of the Chinese Financial Markets – 2005 Finance Gold Book]* (北京 [Beijing]: 经济科学出版社 [Economic Sciences Publishing House]).

[Xiao, Z.] 萧灼基 (ed.) (2006) *中国金融市场分析与预测 – 2006 年金融金皮书 [Analysis and Forecast of the Chinese Financial Markets – 2006 Finance Gold Book]* (北京 [Beijing]: 经济科学出版社 [Economic Sciences Publishing House]).

Xie, D. 谢登科 (2005) 近 30 家高风险城市商业银行初步摆脱困难局面 [Almost 30 high-risk CCBs start freeing themselves from their difficulties]. 新华网 *[Xinhua Net]*, 6 July.

Xie, P. 谢平 (2006) 与不良资产有关的十大串谋 [Ten collusions related to non-performing assets].《财经》*[Caijing Magazine]*, 20 March.

[Xie, P.] 谢平 and [Lei, L.] 陆磊 (2005) 金融腐败求解 [Financial corruption report].《财经》*[Caijing Magazine]*, 24 January.

Xie, P., Xu, Z., Cheng, E. and Shen, M. (2005) *Establishing a Framework for Sustainable Rural Finance: Demand and Supply Analysis in Guizhou Province of the PRC* (Manila: Asian Development Bank).

[Xie, P.] 谢平, [Xu, Z.] 徐忠 and [Shen, M.] 沈明高 (2005a) 农信社改革得失调查 [Investigation into success and failure of the reform of RCCs].《财经》*[Caijing Magazine]*, 12 December.

[Xie, P.] 谢平, [Xu, Z.] 徐忠 and [Shen, M.] 沈明高 (2005b) 农信社改革下一步 [Next step in the reform of RCCs].《财经》*[Caijing Magazine]*, 12 December.

[Xie, P.] 谢平, [Xu, Z.] 徐忠 and [Shen, M.] 沈明高 (2005c) *农村信用社改革: 我们做了什么? 我们还需要做什么? [Reform of RCCs: What Have We Done? What Do We Still Need to Do?]* (Beijing: Development Research Center).

Xinhua China Facts and Figures (2010) Banks ceases revolving loans to prevent funds rush into stock market, *Xinhua News Agency* 4 May.

Xinhua China Money (2009) China's three leading banks: no holding of Dubai World bonds, 8 December.

[Xinhua Chinese News] 新华社中文新闻 (2010) 2 0 0 9 年中国房地产贷款增长迅猛 [Real estate loans surge in 2009], 11 February.

[Xinhua Economic Focus] 新华经 济热点 (2010) 银行业资本充足率全达标 - 银监会五年规划见成效 [All banks comply with CAR – CBRC standards take hold], 29 June.

[Xinhua Economic Focus] 新华经济 热点 (2010) 中国城市商业银行格局发生重大变化 [Big changes are taking place at CCBs], 7 May.

Xinhua Economic Information Service (2005a) China's banking industry, 17 January.

Xinhua Economic Information Service (2005b) Local governments bailout city commercial banks, 6 June.

[Xinhua Economic News] 新华社经济信息 (2005) 中国个人信用数据库继 2004 年 12 月七城市试运行后, 目前已基本实现 [Since the first trial of the individual borrower database in seven cities at the end of 2004, it is now becoming reality], 31 August.

[Xinhua Net] 新华网 (2003) 人民银行: 银行信贷登记咨询系统实现全国联网 [PBOC: Banks loan registration system goes online nationwide], 9 June.

[Xinhua Net Comprehensive] 新华网综合 (2009) 银行季末放贷冲动强烈 银监会紧急 "窗口指导" [Strong compulsion to lend by banks: CBRC issues 'window guidance'] 24 June.

[Xu, D.] 徐德芳 and [Feng, Q.] 冯析善 (2008) 外资银行进入对我国商业银行效率影响的实证研究 [Empirical research into the impact of foreign banks entry on Chinese banks' efficiency],《新西部》 *[New Western]*, 2008 (18).

Xu, L. C., Zhu, T. and Lin, Y. (2002) *Politician Control, Agency Problems and Ownership Reform: Evidence from China.* SSRN Working paper.

[Xu, Y.] 徐樱 (2006) 调整银行信贷结构势在必行 [The imperative of adjusting banks' loan structures].《现代商业银行》 *[Modern Commercial Bank]*, 1.

Yan, H. and Huang, Y. (2008) Deposit insurance and banking supervision in China: the agenda ahead. *The Geneva Papers*, 2008 (33), pp. 547–65.

Yan, M. (2005) *China – Reforms on Track, But More Needed: Banking System Outlook* (New York: Moody's).

Yan, M. (2006) *China City Commercial Banks: Uncovering the Myths* (New York: Moody's).

[Yan, Q.] 阎庆民 (2010) 金融调控促经济转型 [finance regulation to promote economic transformation]《财经》 *[Caijing Magazine]*, 2 August.

[Yang, C.] 杨成军 (2009) China Focus: Banking on forbidden land, *Xinhua's China Economic Information Service*, 31 December.

[Yang, J.] 杨家才 (2005) 新理念下的银行监管 [Banking supervision under the new concepts] (北京 [Beijing]: 中国金融出版社 [China Finance Publishing House]).

[Yang, Q.] 杨青丽 (2009) 银行仍应慎贷 [Banks should still lend carefully]《财经》 *[Caijing Magazine]*, 16 February.

[Yang, X.] 杨小苹 and [Shen, S.] 沈松庆 (2004) 改革农信社产权制度, 完善法人治理结构 [Reform the ownership system of RCCs, perfect the corporate governance structure]. 浙江金融 *[Zhejiang Finance]*, 6, pp. 10–13.

Yao, K. (2006) China's trapped entrepreneurs fuel pawn broking boom. *Reuters*, 27 February.

[Ye, W.] 叶伟强 and [Hu, J.] 胡蛟 (2006) 吴晓灵谈金融改革 [Wu Xiaoling discusses financial reforms].《财经》 *[Caijing Magazine]*, 20 February.

[Yu, F.] 余丰慧 (2005) 金融股权外卖盲目跟风不好 [Blind selling of financial shares is a negative fashion]. 证券时报 *[Securities Times]*, 7 November.

[Yu, L.] 羽良 (2006) 地下信贷转正是否能成为创造性破坏 [Can the formalisation of underground finance wreak creativity?].《董事会》 *[Board of Directors]*, 7 March.

[Yu, N.] 于宁, [Wen, X.] 温秀, [Fang, H.] 方会磊 and [Zhang, Y.] 张宇哲 (2009) 金融限薪令争议 [Row over finance sector compensation limits]《财经》 *[Caijing Magazine]*, 30 March.

[Yu, N.] 于宁 (2005), 细解央行再贷款 [Explaining central on-lending].《财经》 *[Caijing Magazine]*, 25 July.

[Yu, N.] 于宁 (2006) 中行工行上市渐行渐难 [One step forward, one step backward in BoC's and ICBC's market listings].《财经》 *[Caijing Magazine]*, 20 February.

[Yu, N.] 于宁 and [Li, Z.] 历志钢 (2006) 银监会特急警示票据风险 [CBRC urgently calls attention on bills' riskiness].《财经》 *[Caijing Magazine]*, 1 May.

[Yu, N.] 于宁, [Li, Z.] 历志钢 and [Zhang, J.] 张洁 (2006) 房贷之危 [the risks in real estate lending].《财经》 *[Caijing Magazine]*, 29 May.

[Yu, Y.] 余云辉 and [Luo, D.] 骆德明 (2005a) 谁将掌控中国的金融? [Who wants to control the Chinese finance industry?].《上海证券报》 *[Shanghai Securities Newspaper]*, 25 October.

[Yu, Y.] 余云辉 and [Luo, D.] 骆德明 (2005b) 全球化背景下的中国金融版图告急 [The Chinese finance domain is in a state of emergency in the context of globalisation]. 《董事会》 *[Board of Directors]*, 26 October.

[Yuan, J.] 袁剑 (2005) 金融改革的困局与赌注 [Predicament and stakes of the financial sector reform]. 新浪财经 *[Sina Finance News]*, 22 November.

[Yue, G.] 岳刚 (2005) 设副部级理事会 年内有望推出 – 存款保险运作路径解析 [A vice-ministerial council set up, their propositions expected for deposit insurance expected within this year, analysis of the operations]. 经济观察报 *[Economic Observer]*, 17 January.

[Zeng, J.] 曾建中 and [Liang, H.] 梁煌 (2008) 中国农业银行娄底市分行信贷管理的 SWOT 分析及对策 [SWOT Analysis and Countermeasures about the Credits Management of Loudi Branch of Agricultural Bank of China] 湖南人文科技学院学报 *[Journal of Hunan Institute of Humanities, Science and Technology]*, 2008(06).

[Zhang, H.] 张宏 and [Cheng, M.] 程明霞 (2003) 财政为四大行买单千亿 "输血" 金融能持续多久 [100 billion for paying the bills of the SOCBs, how long can we sustain the transfusion?]. 经济观察报 *[Economic Observer]*, 6 December.

[Zhang, J.] 张炯伟, [Zhang, L.] 张利民 and [Zheng, H.] 郑红霞 (2008) 银行信贷风险问题研究 [Research into the problem of bank credit risk], 华北金融 *[Huabei Finance]* S1.

[Zhang, J.] 张吉光 (2005) 中国城市商业银行十大发展特征 [Ten main development characteristics of CCBs]. 数字财富 *[Digital fortune]*, 10 January, pp. 65–71.

[Zhang, J.] 张继伟, [Yu, N.] 于宁 and [Guo, Q.] 郭琼 (2006) 杨凯生:工行自有路 [Yang Kaisheng: ICBC's own way]. 《财经》 *[Caijing Magazine]*, 15 May.

Zhang, L. (2005) The impact of China's post-1993 financial reforms on SOEs – the case of Shanghai. In Huang, Y., Saich, T. and Steinfeld, E. (eds), *Financial Sector Reform in China* (Cambridge, MA: Harvard University Press), pp. 29–49.

[Zhang, M.] 张曼 and [Dong, Y.] 董欲晓 (2010) 信贷慢转弯 [Lending changing tides] 《财经》 *[Caijing Magazine]* 7 June.

[Zhang, M.] 张曼 and [Wang, P.] 王培成 (2010) 小额贷款公司跃进 [Leap forward for small loan companies] 《财经》 *[Caijing Magazine]*, 12 April.

Zhang, M. (2009) Central Bank Imposes One-year Bills on Some Banks, *Caijing Magazine*, 15 September.

[Zhang, M.] 张曼 (2010a) 博弈信用债定价 [Playing credit risk pricing] 《财经》 *[Caijing Magazine]*, 15 February.

[Zhang, M.] 张曼 (2010b) 地方融资平台规范破题 [Local government financing platforms' problematic standardisation] 《财经》 *[Caijing Magazine]*, 15 March.

[Zhang, M.] 张曼 (2010c) 融资平台：探路市场化 [Finance platforms: marketisation] 《财经》 *[Caijing Magazine]*, 21 June.

[Zhang, M.] 张曼 (2010d) 刘明康谈农行 [Liu Mingkang on ABC] 《财经》 *[Caijing Magazine]*, 19 July.

[Zhang, R.] 张燃 and [Hou, G.] 侯光明 (2005) 内部评级法与我国商业银行信用风险管理 [IRB approach and credit risk management in China's commercial banks]. 北京理工大学学报 *[Journal of Beijing University of Technology]*, April, 7(2).

Zhang, R. (2010) Santander, CCB plan joint venture. *China Daily*, 13 January.

[Zhang, X.] 张小彩 (2004a) 利率市场化 "行路难" [The difficult way to marketisation of interest rates]. 《财经》 *[Caijing Magazine]*, 29 November.

[Zhang, X.] 张小彩 (2004b) 专访中央汇金公司总经理谢平 [Interview with Xie Ping, General Manager of Central Huijin Co,].《财经》*[Caijing Magazine]*, 2 November.

[Zhang, Y.] 张宇哲 (2009a) 农信社难尝第二次 "免费的午餐" [RCCs try out a second 'free lunch']《财经网》*[Caijing Net]*, 13 April.

Zhang, Y. (2009b) Strategic Investors May Help Restructure Rural Credit Cooperatives, *Caijing Magazine*, 15 April.

[Zhang, Y.] 张宇哲 (2009c) 农村金融 "集结号" [Rural finance "accumulation number"]《财经》*[Caijing Magazine]*, 27 April.

[Zhang, Y.] 张宇哲 (2009d) 农信社改革新关口 [RCCs' new pass]《财经》*[Caijing Magazine]* 11 May.

[Zhang, Y.] 张宇哲 and [Fang, H.] 方会磊 (2009) 农信社 "测温" [Loan Surge Sows Risk at Rural Credit Co-ops],《财经》*[Caijing Magazine]*, 12 October.

[Zhang, Y.] 张宇哲 and [Li, Z.] 历志钢 (2006) "渝富": 一场没有完成的演化 [Yufu Company: an unfinished evolution].《财经》*[Caijing Magazine]*, 3 April.

Zhao, R. (2005) Banks value Basel II requirements. *China Daily*, 21 February.

[Zhao, S.] 赵霜茁 (ed.) (2004) 现代金融监管 *[Modern financial supervision]* (北京 [Beijing]: 对外经济贸易大学出版社 [Foreign Economic Trade University Press]).

[Zheng, L.] 郑录军 and [Cao, Y.] 曹延求 (2005) 我国商业银行效率及其影响因素的实证分析 [Analysis of the efficiency of Chinese commercial banks and its influencing factors]. 金融研究 *[Finance Research (PBOC)]*, 1, pp. 91–101.

Zheng, Y. (2003) Financial systems, credit policies and development in rural areas. In Findlay, C., Watson, A. and Cheng, E. (eds), *Rural Financial Markets in China* (Canberra: Asia Pacific Press), pp. 1–12.

[Zhong, J.] 钟加勇 (2004) "整编" 城市商业银行 [Reorganising CCBs]. 商务周刊 *[Business watch]*. 20 October.

[Zhou, S.] 周韶扬 (2004) 试析入世后外资银行入股中资银行的可行性 [On the-feasibility of foreign banks becoming shareholders in Chinese banks after the WTO entry]. 安康师专学报 *[Journal of Ankang Teachers College]*, 16, pp. 22–4, 27.

Zhou, W. 周伟 (2005) 城市商业银行的引资之惑 [The temptation of attracting new capital for CCBs]. 中国信贷风险信息库 *[News database for China's credit risk]*, 24 November.

Zhou, X. (2004a) *Capital Accord II and Regional Disparities in Financial Risks*. Speech of Governor Zhou Xiaochuan at the Seminar on risk management and internal control of the commercial banks, 8 January.

Zhou, X. (2004b) *Improve Corporate Governance and Develop Capital Market*. Speech by Mr Zhou Xiaochuan, Governor of the PBOC at the "China Forum: Capital Market and Corporate Governance", 1 December.

Zhou, X. (2004c) *Improve Legal System and Financial Ecology*. Speech by Mr Zhou Xiaochuan, Governor of the PBOC at the "Forum of 50 Chinese Economists", 2 December.

Zhou, X. (2005) 周小川: 国有商业银行如何充实资本 [Zhou Xiaochuan: How SOCBs should replenish their capital].《财经》*[Caijing Magazine]*, 28 November.

Zhou, X. (2009) Introduction, in: Zhu, M., Cai, J. and Avery, M. (eds) (2009) *China's Emerging Financial Markets – Challenges and Global Impact* (Singapore: John Wiley & Sons), pp. xiii–xxii.

Zhu, Y., Li, P., Zeng, Y. and He, J. (2009) *Foreign Ownership and the Risk Behavior of Chinese Banks: Do Foreign Strategic Investors Matter?* Eletronic copy available at: http://ssrn.com/abstract=1460541.

References for laws and regulations

1. 中华人民共和国商业银行法 (修正) [Commercial banking law], first issue 1995, revision 2003.
2. 中华人民共和国银行业监督管理法 [Law of banking supervision and administration], 2003.
3. 中华人民共和国中国人民银行法 (修正) [Law of the People's Bank of China], first issue 1995, revision 2003.
4. 金融企业会计制度 [Accounting system for financial companies], 2001.
5. 商业银行风险监管核心指标 (试行) [Core indicators for the risk supervision of commercial banks], 2006.
6. 商业银行市场风险管理指引 [Directive for the risk management of market risks in commercial banks], 2004.
7. 股份制商业银行董事会尽职指引 (试行) [Directive on the duty of directors in JSCBs], 2005.
8. 商业银行集团客户授信业务风险管理指引 [Directive regarding the risk management and approval authorities for group exposures], 2003.
9. 商业银行授信工作尽职指引 [Directive regarding authorities and approval limits at commercial banks], 2004.
10. 贷款风险分类指导原则 (试行) [Directive principles for the categorisation of loan risks (trial)], 2001 and updated in 2007 贷款风险分类指引 [Directive for the categorisation of loan risks].
11. [Guidelines on rural household micro-credit by RCCs], 2001.
12. 中国银行、中国建设银行公司治理改革与监管指引 [Guidelines on corporate governance reforms and supervision of BoC and CCB], 2004.
13. 中华人民共和国外资金融机构管理条例实施细则 [Implementation details of the management rule regarding foreign-invested institutions], 2004.
14. 合作金融机构行政许可事项实施办法，外资金融机构行政许可事项实施办法, 中资商业银行行政许可事项实施办法,行政许可实施程序规定 [Implementation rule for licensing of cooperative financial institutions, of foreign invested financial institutions, for Chinese-invested commercial banks, and for the licensing procedures], 2006.
15. 贷款通则 [Loan principles], 1995 (a new version is being prepared).
16. 金融企业呆账核销管理办法 [Management rule on recognising bad debts in finance companies] 2008 and previously 金融企业呆账准备提取及呆账核销管理办法 [Management rule on recognising bad debts and raising bad debt provisions for finance companies], 2005.
17. 商业银行与内部人和股东关联交易管理办法 [Management rule regarding commercial banks and transactions with insiders and shareholders], 2004.
18. 外资金融机构驻华代表机构管理办法 [Management rule regarding representative offices of foreign-invested financial institutions in China], 2002.
19. 境外金融机构投资入股中资金融机构管理办法 [Management rule regarding the entry of foreign financial institutions into Chinese financial institutions], 2003.
20. 个人债权及客户证券交易结算资金收购意见 [Opinion on purchasing personal creditor's rights and client securities transaction liquidation funds], 2004.
21. 商业银行服务价格管理暂行办法 [Provisional management rule regarding the service prices of commercial banks], 2003.
22. 商业银行内部控制评价试行办法 [Provisional rule for assessing internal controls at commercial banks], 2004.

23. 农村信用社省 (自治区、直辖市) 联合社管理暂行规定 [Provisional regulation for the management of RCCs' unions], 2003.
24. 农村商业银行管理暂行规定 [Provisional regulation for the management of rural commercial banks], 2003.
25. 农村合作银行管理暂行规定 [Provisional regulation for the management of rural cooperative banks], 2003.
26. 商业银行不良资产监测和考核暂行办法 [Provisional rule regarding the supervision and assessment of NPLs at commercial banks], 2004.
27. 商业银行信息披露暂行办法 [Provisional rule for the information disclosure at commercial banks], 2002.
28. 商业银行资本充足率管理办法 [Regulation governing the capital adequacy of commercial banks], 2004.
29. 股份制商业银行风险评级体系(暂行) [Risk grading system for JSCBs (provisional)], 2004, amended through 商业银行风险监管核心指标（试行）的通知 [Notice on commercial banks' risk supervision core indicators (provisional)] in 2005.
30. 外资银行并表监管管理办法 [Rule governing the consolidated supervision of foreign banks], 2004.
31. 金融机构摊消条例 [Rule on dissolution of banks], 2001.
32. 商业银行次级债券发行管理办法 [Rules on the issuance of subordinated bonds by commercial banks], 2004.
33. 金融机构信贷资产证券化试点监督管理办法 [Trial supervisory management rule regarding the asset securitisation at financial institutions], 2005.
34. 国有商业银行公司治理及相关监管指引 [Directive regarding the corporate governance in state-owned commercial banks and related supervision], 2006.
35. 关于加强宏观调控整顿和规范各类打捆贷款的通知 [Notice concerning the strengthening of macro-economic adjustments to clean and normalise bundle loans], 2006.
36. 中华人民共和国外资金融机构管理条例 [Management rule regarding foreign-invested institutions], 2002.
37. 银行并表监管指引 (试行) [Directive on banks consolidated supervision], 2008.
38. 关于进一步做好金融服务支持重点产业调整振兴和抑制部分行业产能过剩的指导意见 [Opinion on supporting industrial adjustment and keeping down energy consuming industries], 2009.
39. 银行业金融机构国别风险管理指引 [Management directive on financial institutions' sovereign risk management], 2010.
40. 中华人民共和国物权法 [PRC Property law] 2007.
41. 中华人民共和国企业破产法 [PRC Enterprise bankruptcy law] 2006.
42. 中华人民共和国公司法 [PRC Company Law] 2005.
43. 商业银行稳健薪酬监管指引 [Supervisory guidelines on compensation practices of commercial banks], 2010.
44. 中华人民共和国反洗钱法 [PRC money laundering law] 2006.
45. 关于调整放宽农村地区银行业金融机构准入政策更好支持社会主义新农村建设的若干意见 [Opinions on adjusting the entry policies for financial institutions into rural areas to better support the establishment of new countryside], 2006.
46. 关于银行业金融机构大力发展农村小额贷款业务的指导意见 [Guiding opinions on financial institutions developing small rural loans business], 2007.
47. 个人贷款管理暂行办法 [Provisional rule for managing personal loans], 2010.
48. 关于小额贷款公司试点的指导意见 [Guiding opinions on the trial of small loan companies], 2008.

49. 股份制商业银行公司治理指引 [Directive on the corporate governance of joint-stock commercial banks], 2002.
50. 农村信用社不良资产监测和考核办法 [Rule for examination and monitoring of RCCs' non-performing loans], 2007.
51. 银行贷款损失准备计提指引 [Directive on loan loss provisions for bank loans], 2002.
52. 中国银行业实施新资本协议指导意见 [Guiding opinion on Chinese bank industry implementing the new capital accord], 2007.
53. 第一批新资本协议实施监管指引的通知 [Notice on supervisory directive concerning the first batch of new capital accord implementation], 2008 with 商业银行银行账户信用风险暴露分类指引 [Directive on commercial banks' banking book credit risk exposures categories], 商业银行信用风险内部评级体系监管指引 [Supervisory directive on commercial banks' credit risk internal rating system], 商业银行专业贷款监管资本计量指引 [Directive on measuring supervisory capital for commercial banks' special lending], 商业银行信用风险缓释监管资本计量指引 [Directive on measuring supervisory capital for commercial banks' credit risk mitigation], 商业银行操作风险监管资本计量指引 [Directive on measuring supervisory capital for commercial banks' operational risk].
54. 商业银行资本充足率监管检查指引 [Supervisory directive on commercial banks' capital adequacy], 商业银行流动性风险管理指引 [Directive on commercial banks' liquidity risk management], 商业银行资本计量高级方法验证指引 [Directive on validation of the advanced approach for capital calculation of commercial banks], 商业银行资产证券化风险暴露监管资本计量指引 [Directive on supervisory capital calculation for commercial banks' asset securitisation exposures], 资本充足率信息披露指引 [Directive on information disclosure of capital adequacy], 商业银行资本充足率计算指引 [Directive on calculation of capital adequacy of commercial banks], 商业银行银行账户利率风险管理指引 [Directive on banking book interest risk management for commercial banks], 市场风险资本计量内部模型法监管指引 [Supervisory directive on calculation of market risk with internal models], 2008.
55. 关于完善商业银行资本补充机制的通知 [Notice on mechanisms to perfect commercial banks' capital buffer], 2009.
56. 关于加强地方政府融资平台公司管理有关问题的通知 [Notice on issues relevant to the strengthening of the management of local government financing platforms], 2010.
57. 汽车金融公司管理办法 [Administrative rules for auto financing companies], 2008.
58. 汽车贷款管理办法 [Administrative rules for auto loans] 2004.
59. 消费金融公司试点管理办法 [Management rule for consumer loans companies], 2009.
60. 中华人民共和国外资银行管理条例 [PRC Management ordinance on foreign banks], 2006 as well as 中华人民共和国外资银行管理条例实施细则 [Implementation guidelines on PRC Management ordinance on foreign banks], 2006.
61. 银行控股股东监管办法 (征求意见稿) [Management rule on bank controlling shareholders (for comments)], 2008.
62. 中国人民银行关于取缔地下钱庄及打击高利贷行为的通知 [PBOC notice on underground finance and usurious interest rates], 2002.

63. 关于进一步改进外商投资审批工作的通知 [Notice on improving approvals of foreign investors], 2009 and 境外投资管理办法 [Management rule on foreign investors], 2009.
64. 关于进一步规范银信合作有关事项的通知 [Notice on matters relevant to standardising cooperation between banks and trusts], 2009.
65. 商业银行压力测试指引 [Directive on commercial banks' stress testing], 2007.
66. 小额贷款公司改制设立村镇银行暂行规定 [Provisional rule on small companies upgrading into village and township banks], 2009.
67. 农村资金互助社、贷款公司、村镇银行组建审批工作指引 [Approval work guidance for establishing rural mutual funding groups, loan companies and village and township banks] 2007.
68. 农村信用社监管内部评级指引 (试行) [Directive on internal ratings supervision for RCCs (provisional)] 2007.

The above lists only those regulations which were cited in the text, it is not an exhaustive list of banking relevant laws and regulations.

Major websites

Bank for International Settlements (BIS)	www.bis.org
China Banking Regulatory Commission (CBRC)	www.cbrc.gov.cn
China Insurance Regulatory Commission (CIRC)	www.circ.gov.cn
China Securities Regulatory Commission (CSRC)	www.csrc.gov.cn
International Institute of Economics	www.iie.com
International Institute of Finance	www.iif.com
International Monetary Fund (IMF)	www.imf.org
World Bank	www.worldbank.org
Organisation for Economic and Cooperation Development (OECD)	www.oecd.org
People's Bank of China (PBOC)	www.pbc.gov.cn
State Administration for Foreign Exchange (SAFE)	www.safe.gov.cn
China National Audit Office (CNAO)	www.cnao.gov.cn
Governance matters (World Bank)	info.worldbank.org/ governance/wgi
Transparency International	www.transparency.org
MIX Market	www.mixmarket.org

Banks' and institutions' annual reports

All are audited, unqualified, according to the new PRC-GAAP. All of the annual reports of SOCBs and JSCBs can be found on their websites for 2009 and September 2008. Some smaller local banks also provide them on their websites. ABC's listing memorandum from 2010 is accessible on its website as is CIC's annual report for 2008 and 2009. Quarterly reports for monetary policy are published regularly by the PBOC on its website – at least in the Chinese version. The CBRC publishes a yearly Chinese- and English-language annual report.

Sources of news and information

All news and articles from newspapers and newsfeeds were accessed through Factiva.

Factiva	www.factiva.com
Sina News	www.sina.com.cn
Economic Observer	www.eeo.com.cn
Caijing Magazine	www.caijing.hexun.com
Southern Weekend	www.nanfangdaily.com.cn

Index

Lightning Source UK Ltd.
Milton Keynes UK
UKHW020903240520
363729UK00007B/485